JDW · 15·4·01

Rathcormick

A Childhood Recalled

Rathcormick

A Childhood Recalled

Homan Potterton

With drawings by Jeremy Williams

**NEW
ISLAND**

RATHCORMICK

A CHILDHOOD RECALLED

First published 2001
by New Island Books
2 Brookside
Dundrum Road
Dublin 14
First published in paperback 2002 by New Island

ISBN 1 902602 97 8

New Island receives financial assistance from The Arts Council
(An Chomhairle Ealaíon), Dublin, Ireland.

Jacket design: Slick Fish Design
Jacket illustration: Homan Potterton
Interior illustrations: Jeremy Williams
Printed in Scotland by Omnia Books Ltd.

In Fond Remembrance of my Parents
Thomas Edward Potterton (1896-1960)
and
Eileen Catherine, née Tong (1903-1990)

Contents

Prologue

I suppose I was about six or seven when I discovered my mother had a secret.

She used to disappear.

Every day, at the same time after dinner: gone. She always came back again about half-an-hour later but the puzzling part of it was that she went missing in the first instance.

Her vanishings frightened me to a point of terror and, even though I would try to shadow her at the times when I knew they were likely to occur, she always managed to elude me.

'You'll have to go and get Rusty a bowl of water, Homan,' she might say. 'He'll be thirsty when he finishes his dinner. Those scraps of ham are very salty.'

But when I would come back from the scullery with the water — inching carefully through the breakfast room and out to the garden where Rusty, without having eaten a morsel much less being thirsty as a result, would be antagonising the cats by standing guard over a tasty dish of ham, boiled potatoes, and parsley sauce — Mamma would be gone.

Molly, who would be clearing the table, was never able to shed any light on the phenomenon.

'She was here a minute ago', was all she would ever say.

At that, I would run upstairs, even as far as the boys' room and the nursery on the top floor, and then down again — flight by flight, two, even three, steps at a time — darting into several of the rooms and down the passage to Rosina's room. I would look out, first one window towards the greenhouse and behind it to the farmyard and then, climbing up on a chair, through the other which opened unto a view of the garden. I could see she was not at work in any of the flowerbeds and I could see the box-hedges and knew she was unlikely to have gone in there. That left the tennis court and beyond it the shrubbery and beyond that again the laurels. But none of that part of the garden was visible from Rosina's window and besides, by this stage I would have resigned myself to the fact that she was gone.

I would mope downstairs again. Alan and Raymond would, by now, have returned to playing up the yard; Papa, if he had been in for dinner that day, would be back in the office dictating letters to Miss Shannon; Rosina would be tidying the cutlery drawer or putting away the condiments; and Elliott would have departed in the car. Only Rusty would remain where I had last seen him, his attention still focused exclusively on the cats, and he would make it clear — with an impatient scowl in my direction — that he regarded my reappearance only as an intrusion.

I would be alone.

The sensation of being on my own in the empty house with all the afternoon ahead and no Mamma there to share it was made all the more acute as I was often lonely as a child. By some quirk or other, I was different in temperament to my brothers so that despite being the youngest of a very large and happy family, I frequently felt that I was an oddity and an outsider.

When Mamma disappeared I would remember the times when I had heard her announce: 'I am not sure how much more of this barging I can stand.' She might have emerged from the bathroom where Papa was shaving, before closing the door firmly after her and making her way down the stairs.

'It'll be the death of me and that's all that's to it,' I would hear her mutter.

On other occasions, she would be more specific.

'You don't mean to tell me that the Master has gone back out to the yard in his suit when I have just sponged and pressed the trousers,' she would say to Molly.

And when Molly replied that she thought he had, Mamma would say, 'That man will be the death of me.'

It was a statement like this — and a statement of fact is what I interpreted it to be — that led me to believe that Mamma might really want to leave us; and, even though such outbursts were not all that common, when I gave the matter any thought at all it appeared to me that she might well be intent on doing so as her certain death and Papa seemed — for reasons which I did not fully understand — so intricately intertwined. As a result, the anxiety I felt in relation to her daily disappearances became all the more urgent, and I devoted hours to contemplating the life that lay ahead of us when she would no longer be around.

In time, I discovered that she always reappeared on the far side of the tennis court: not from the end, where there was netting in front of a plantation of spindly Douglas fir, but from the far side where the lilacs were. Some of them, the common purples, were almost trees but the whites — fewer in number — still retained the semblance of a bush and, dotted between them, one or two specimen varieties, their flowers so mauve that they were virtually black. I became frightened, too frightened, ever to go anywhere near that corner of the garden and never wandered beyond the lilacs to penetrate the banks of laurel that were planted behind them, dividing the grounds at this point from the front avenue beyond.

Then one day when Alan and I were looking for birds' nests we came through to the woods from the other side and, when I found myself in a clearing, I did not immediately realise where I was. The laurels were very high and dense there, so dense that it was impossible to see the sky, while even the lower branches, in clambering up to the light, were so far off the ground that there was no difficulty in standing up within the bushes and even walking around. The ground underneath was completely clear of any twigs or leaves and then I noticed that it had been cleared, brushed clean in fact, and in a corner, like a throne from some forgotten dynasty, was a green garden chair. I recognised it as the chair which had stood in a sunny spot on the path outside the kitchen window for as long as I could recall

Like a throne from some forgotten dynasty …

but it was only on seeing it again now that I realised it had been missing for some time.

It was cold in there and I sensed the goose-pimples forming on my thighs and, when the chill began to trickle up my spine, I shot out in the direction of the garden. A thrush, disturbed by the noise I made, shuffled the leaves above my head as she too fought her way through the bushes and out into the open.

'Come back,' Alan called after me. 'There's a thrush's nest here and it has eggs in it. Give me a leg up and I'll be able to get them.'

But, in realising that this was where Mamma spent her time and in the belief that, one day, she might stay here permanently, I thought I had discovered her secret. Even the promise of a nest of thrush's eggs, any number of nests in fact, could not induce me ever to return to the place again.

1. Out of the Blue

When my mother was seventeen, my father, who was then twenty-four and living nearby, wrote in her autograph book: 'Thou shalt not covet thy neighbour's wife, his ox thou shalt not slaughter, but thank the Lord it is no sin, to covet thy neighbour's daughter.' He married her six-and-a-half years later.

Before the wedding, he went to see his prospective father-in-law to discuss the matter of a dowry but Grandpa Tong was fairly wily and Papa came away empty-handed, dismissed in fact. The incident was to sour his relations with his in-laws forever after. He wrote to Mamma afterwards: 'My own Beloved Girl, My conversation with your Pappy was not pleasant or satisfactory from my point of view and we seem to look at things in a different light. So I write these few lines to say that my heart is, <u>and still shall be ever yours</u> and I look forward to having you on the 3rd of August as my very own. With regard to anything I have said, I am prepared to forget, and I shall always honour your parents. I really do believe you know I am <u>not</u> or <u>never</u> thought of marrying you for what you had. With ever my unchanging and everlasting love, Eddie.'

When they were on their way home from their honeymoon they called on a cousin, Old Elliott Potterton, who lived at Rathcormick, near Athboy in County Meath. In actual fact, Old Elliott, a first cousin of Papa's father, was never old at all: he was only seventy-three when he died, and that was before most of us were born, but we always referred to him as Old Elliott.

He had given Mamma and Papa a japanned mantel-clock as a wedding-present and in sending it had asked that they would call. Papa's younger brother, Arthur, who was living at Rathcormick at the time and working as Old Elliott's secretary, collected them when they arrived by the Mail Boat at Kingstown and drove them down in Old Elliott's Rover.

Mamma always remembered the visit vividly.

'I was a bit in awe going there I can tell you,' she would say. 'I was only just twenty-four and I knew well that Old Elliott only wanted to take a look at me and see what Papa had taken on.'

She remembered Nancy, Old Elliott's wife, showing her all over the house and eventually up to the bedrooms on the top floor. As they looked out the windows, Nancy said: 'Do you see that thing glinting, way off in the distance, over there, to the left of those trees?'

'Yes,' said Mamma. 'I do. What is it?'

'It's the roof of the greenhouse at Moyrath. It always catches the sun at this time of the afternoon and we see it — almost like a mirror — from here.'

'How far away would it be?'

'About three miles. The lands of Moyrath adjoin Rathcormick at the end of the Bottoms. Pottertons used to live there too, for generations in fact, but then the family has been in these parts for a very long time, you know.'

'Yes,' said Mamma.

'There's a big map hanging in the hall — I'll point it out to you when we go down — which shows all the different farms they had. That was in centuries gone by when they were tenants of Lord Darnley.'

They moved back out to the landing and Nancy closed the doors.

'But the house is far too big ...' she said.

She started down the stairs.

'... all empty rooms, it has to be over fifty years since anyone slept in them.'

She stood for a moment in the sun from the landing window and then she turned again to Mamma.

'It's a help having Arthur here,' she said, 'but it's so long since there were ever any children in the house. Dora, Jane, and Lily — my husband's sisters — were the last and, of course, Little Jim. But they are all over sixty now.'

There was a listlessness, a languor, in her movements. She ran her hand along the lid of the rug-box as she passed and then made a gesture of straightening one of the pictures on the wall.

'It's a house that needs children,' she said.

Rathcormick was so very different to the Wood-of-O, where Mamma's own childhood alone with her uncles and aunt had been so happy, that she had difficulty in imagining the house as a home to children at all.

'Impossible to fill', was what she thought. 'No gaiety about the place, it's like a barracks.'

It seemed to her to be one room after another. The wallpapers had not been changed in years and many of the rooms had none at all: only pink distemper. The staircase was lined with a heavy canvas — also painted pink — which hung loose and bulged here and there; it had become detached in places from the batons which held it to the wall and, as a result, it trembled — wobbled from top to bottom — at even the merest touch. The woodwork everywhere, including all the doors, was grained and stained and on the stairs it had darkened almost to mahogany from the sun. The general atmosphere of loneliness was made all the more acute by the fact that all the beds were made up, their eiderdowns and quilts of colourful knitted-squares all in place, as though a house-party was expected that very afternoon.

Nancy was Old Elliott's second wife. He had only married her six years previously — exactly two years after the death of his first wife — and so far, and at this time she was thirty-eight, they had no children. Nor had Old Elliott any children by his first wife. That was the point: Old Elliott had no immediate heir. He made his will just seven months after Mamma and Papa's visit and when he died less than a year after that — "suddenly" the announcement in *The Irish Times* read — he left Rathcormick to them.

'It was completely out of the blue,' Mamma said. 'No one expected it, least of all ourselves.'

Then her eyes would twinkle.

'But Papa always gave the credit to me. He said that if Old Elliott had not approved of me that afternoon, such a thing would have been out of the question.'

In point of fact, apart from his own brother (whom we called Uncle Jim), Papa was the eldest of Old Elliott's closest male relatives. Even still — and notwithstanding his supposed endorsement of Mamma — he took no chances when it came to making his will. Instead of leaving Rathcormick to Papa outright, he left it to him only "for his life in trust for his eldest legal male issue", but, as Mamma and Papa had no children when he made the will, he covered the eventuality of their never having a son by adding the provision that, should that circumstance arise, the place would revert to his executor (who was Uncle Hubert) to be assigned by him "to any male Potterton to carry on the name where our forefathers have lived and died for over three hundred years".

When Old Elliott died, my sister Alice, the eldest of our

family, was just eight months old and that was that. Papa had no son — no "legal male issue" — so that, on the day of the funeral, a Sunday in early January when every Potterton, no matter how distantly related, was assembled at Rathcormick and the conditional nature of the will became known, a wave of speculation rippled through the company.

'No one could have known then that we would eventually have six sons,' Mamma often said. 'Had they done so, that would have put paid to all their surmising.'

In his will, Old Elliott provided for his widow with a capital sum and an income for life and he directed his executors to allow her "to reside in Rathcormick with use of garden and such portion of the out offices that may be in their discretion reasonable for a term of five years from the date of my death …" He also left her his Rover motor car. He left moneys to the Eye and Ear Hospital in Dublin as well as to the Royal Hospital for Incurables; and then as an afterthought, in a codicil which he signed ten days after the will itself, he left the residue of his estate also to Papa.

'Almost the first thing Papa did was to go straight into the Ulster Bank in Tullamore and close his account', was how Mamma always commented on the legacy.

'Why?' we asked.

'He had applied for a loan to buy cattle only a month previously and they had turned him down. It was a decision the manager lived to regret, I can tell you, and all the more so when Papa transferred his account to the Bank of Ireland.'

*

The speculation which the conditional nature of Old Elliott's bequest gave rise to provided occupation — almost to the exclusion of anything else — for every member of the family, even the most distant cousins, during the months that followed his sudden and unexpected demise. Hopes were raised, discussions held, letters written, alliances formed — affidavits were even prepared — all with a view to deciding upon whom Rathcormick would devolve in the event of Papa being unable to procure or obtain, by one means or another, some legal male issue of an appropriate kind. As the months went by and Mamma and Papa with baby Alice showed no signs of moving to Rathcormick and the Widow Nancy, instead of packing up, occupied herself exclusively by driving around the countryside in her Rover motor car, the eventuality that the will might ultimately be overturned seemed more and more of a likelihood. Then towards Christmas, and after several weeks of rumour, the news leaked out that Mamma was pregnant and conjecture, which had been of a general nature up to then, became specific: would the baby be a boy?

It is not often that the nativity of a child occasions as much woe — gloom is not too strong a word — among so many people as did the birth of my eldest brother. Mamma and Papa were naturally overjoyed by his arrival but it is fair to say that they were the only ones; everyone else in the family was inconsolable in their sorrow although, when it became known that the baby was delicate, disappointment momentarily turned to hope. Thomas Elliott, as he was called, was born with what approximated to a cleft palate and could not easily feed from breast or bottle so that his survival — much less his capacity to thrive — lay very much in the balance until Mamma developed a painstaking technique of feeding him by a dribbling method using a light metal spoon.

'What a time I had with Elliott,' she always said. 'The hours it used to take me to get him to drink even a saucer of milk. None of the rest of you were anything like as troublesome. It was touch-and-go for him for the first few months, I can tell you that.'

But as the months went by it became apparent that, although a struggle, Elliott would survive and when, exactly two years after Old Elliott's death, Mamma and Papa felt confident enough to accept the bequest and move to Rathcormick, he was already out of danger. Not that they were prepared, even at that stage, to leave matters to chance; eighteen months after Elliott's birth, Edward, healthy as a blade of grass in springtime, sauntered into the world by way of being a spare. But it did not take him long to realise that his existence was already superfluous as it was perfectly obvious — to little Elliott as he lay in his cot as much as to anyone else — that Thomas Elliott was indeed the heir, the male issue, that Old Elliott had required, nay, demanded. From that day forward no other candidacy was ever advocated, no other contingency even considered, as it was all too clear that the case was closed, the matter settled: the succession of Rathcormick had been secured.

All of this happened, as it seemed to me when I was a child, long before my time. Rosina was born — although not for almost four years after Edward — and then David, then Raymond, then Alan and, when Mamma was almost forty-three, me. I have only hearsay, stories and photographs to go on as to what life was like at Rathcormick in those early years.

Alice had a white rabbit. I know that because when I wanted one years later Mamma, based on her experience of Alice's, would not hear of such a thing:

'After a week you would be tired of it and then who would be left to feed it?' she said. 'Me. That's who.'

Elliott and Edward had pet goats. At a later stage, I had a pet goat too but mine was purely functional and was used to suckle the orphaned lamb (or lambs) that I would be given every year in an effort to interest me in farming. Elliott and Edward treated their goats as ponies and harnessed them up to specially made chariots and rode around the place like Ancient Romans on their way to the Coliseum. Photographs show the pair of them standing in the makeshift carriages holding the reins and looking like Charlton Heston. When the time came to go to away to school, Alice went to Sligo and Elliott and Edward were sent to what many people would think of as the best Protestant secondary school in Ireland: Portora Royal School in Enniskillen. By their own accounts, they learned little or nothing there and when they were about sixteen, Papa decided that they had been in school for quite long enough.

'What good is all that Latin and stuff going to be to them when there is a life cut out for them here?' he said. 'If I take them home now they could be a great help to me and they would also learn something practical.'

Every year on Speech Day at Portora (if Elliott and Edward were to be believed) the headmaster exhorted the assembled school that it was neither here nor there if they learned nothing at all because, wherever they went in the world, they only had to announce that they had been to Portora and every door would be open to them. Elliott was not sure about this, in fact, he did not believe a word of it; but Edward, convinced of its validity accepted the recommendation as very sound advice.

The Widow Nancy showed no sign of packing up

And that was the difference between the legal male issue which Old Elliott had deemed an essential requirement and the heir-to-spare whom Papa had judged an advisable precaution.

2. Three Centuries

Rathcormick is not one of the great houses of County Meath, not by a long shot. It is essentially a mean house, a farmhouse — no more, no less — gable-ended, with three storeys above a basement, and two small, low rooms leading off a hall or landing on each floor. The stairwell, poking out behind with straight flights of steps at right angles to one another, is also basic, avoiding all fancy in favour of the practical. The windows here, in contrast to all the others in the original house, open to the south so that there is a warmth about the stairs that is only found in those rooms which were later additions towards the rear.

There is no definite clue as to when exactly the house was built but it probably dates from the first or second decade of the eighteenth century. That was before plain farmers like my forebears developed the modicum of interest in "taste" which would have persuaded them to introduce an innuendo of architectural worthiness — a hint of style and ostentation — to the edifice rather than leave it devoid of all ornament as they did. The walls, of stone and rubble and rendered on the outside, are about four-feet thick and it is only the stone of the window-sills which has been cut to shape. Other than that, there is little evidence that even a stone-mason, much less an architect, impeded the construction in any way. The house is described in Lewis's *Topographical Dictionary of Ireland* of 1836 as "the Seat of T Potterton, Esq." but there is no allusion to its architectural style. And that is probably for the very good reason that it has none to speak of.

Presumably in cognisance of this, Old Elliott made, what would have been called in the eighteenth century, "Improvements" to the place. While most of these were appropriately modest and dictated by comfort rather than fashion, the exception was the handsome limestone Doric portico with which, in an uncharacteristic act of flagrant pretension, he embellished the hall-door. As a result, and after being so very reticent in its appearance for two hundred years, Rathcormick became, if not quite handsome, then at least moderately venerable.

While Rathcormick itself could never be described as a mansion, by the same token its lands could only with exaggeration be called a great estate. In *The Civil Survey* of 1654-56, they are described as "Rathcarmuck, half a plowlande" and the acreage is given as two-hundred-and-sixty of which one-hundred-and-sixty were arable, eighty in pasture, and twenty in bog. The location is described as "bounded on the east with the lands of Moyrath and Kildalkey, on the west with the lands of Ballynadrimna and Rathkenna, on the south with the lands of Corballis and a river on the north with the lands of Baskinagh and Ballynadrimna". Like the rest of Ireland, the farm was first mapped by Sir William Petty as part of the Down Survey in the 1670s and then by Bernard Scalé in a *Survey of the Lordship of Athboy* which dates from 1767. This volume is now in the National Library and it is a large-scale presentation version of Scalé's map that hangs in the hall at Rathcormick. By the time of the first Ordnance Survey map in 1836 the different fields had been fenced much as they are today and the one in front of the house, the Lawn, is shown landscaped with hardwoods. Beyond the Lawn is the field called the Round O because of the circular earthen mound capped by trees that is to be found there. We called it a fairy ring, and were always warned against playing there, but it is marked on the Ordnance Survey map as a fort; more precisely, it is a rath, the rath of Cormac. There was once a holy well on the lands dedicated to St Dympna. It had almost dried up by the mid-nineteenth century and was nowhere to be seen in our time. It may have been in the field called Tubber, *tobair* being the Gaelic word for well. Following on from the Ordnance Survey came Griffith's Valuation in 1854 and there Rathcormick is described as six-hundred-and-twenty-two acres, of which five-hundred-and-thirty-two were occupied, on a lease from the Earl of Darnley, by Old Elliott's father, Thomas Potterton. In his will, Old Elliott specifically mentions three-hundred-and-twenty-four Irish acres; but that was only the extent of the farm which by then was held, untrammelled by the inconvenience of either a

Rathcormick is not one of the great houses of County Meath

lease or a landlord, freehold or, in Irish terms, "in Fee Simple". These are the fields that, following the Wyndham Act of 1903 which enabled tenant farmers to buy out their landlords and which became law in 1909, Old Elliott had purchased outright from Lord Darnley.

And then to the family: what of Old Elliott's testamental contention that his "forefathers had lived and died at Rathcormick for over three hundred years"?

Three hundred years? No. According to *The Civil Survey*, Rathcormick was in the possession of "Sir Luke ffitz Gerald, Irish Papist" in 1640 and it was from him that the lands were confiscated — on account of his being a Catholic — following the 1641 Rebellion. *The Book of Survey and Distribution*, which dates from the 1660s, lists "Rathcormucke" with the information that, following the confiscation, two-hundred-and-eighty-three acres, one rood, and eight perches of the lands were distributed between the Duke of York and George ffitz Gerald while three-hundred-and-sixty-five acres went to Thomas Bligh. George ffitz Gerald had to testify his loyalty to the Crown before being reinstated on the lands of his father but when he died in the 1670s "without heirs male of his body" — as Old Elliott was to do two-hundred-and-seventy-years later — his estate reverted to the King. Passing to the Catholic Duke of York, later James II, they were sold following his defeat at the Battle of the Boyne. By a deed dated 24th June 1703, Thomas Bligh purchased for the sum of £6,850 almost three thousand acres in County Meath, including the three-hundred-and-sixty-five acres of Rathcormick which had previously been allotted to him. The father of the first Lord Darnley, Bligh was by then MP for Athboy and, on 28 July 1710, he granted a lease "for a term of three lives" to John Potterton of Rathcormick of "all the lands of Rathcormick and Rathkena ... containing five-hundred-and-forty-two acres ... at a yearly rent of one-hundred-and-sixty-five pounds, twelve shillings".

The fact that John is described in the 1710 lease as "of Rathcormick" would imply that he was already in occupation when he signed it and this is borne out by family papers which record his father, Thomas Potterton, who was born in 1643 and died in 1718, as the first of the name to live there. It is always said in the family that 'we came over with Cromwell'; but this Thomas would have been too young to have served in Cromwell's army and it may be that he was actually the son of the first Potterton to come to Ireland. John, the first leaseholder, was my great — six times — grandfather. According to the *Index of Prerogative Wills in Ireland*, he died in 1738 and was succeeded by his son Thomas who, in turn, died in 1756. It was this Thomas who consolidated the family's fortunes by extending their holdings to include not just the neighbouring properties of Moyrath and Balatalion which they had held for almost as long as Rathcormick, but Corballis and Baskenagh, Pagetstown and Hardrestown as well. Exceptionally, as all other family wills perished in the bombardment of the Four Courts in 1922, a copy of Thomas's will survives. Made on the 22nd September 1756 when he was "very sick and weak in body but of perfect mind and memory", it bequeathed the "Leasehold Interest of the Town and Lands of Rathcormick with all the stock and corn that will be on said lands at the time of my decease" to his son John. That John seems to have been succeeded by his brother, Henry of Moyrath, and then by Henry's son, Thomas, who in a deed of 1794 is described as a grandson of Thomas and great-grandson of the first John. Next came another John who had seven children by his wife Lydia Bell, whom he married in 1804. Among them was Thomas — father of Old Elliott — and Richard, my great-grandfather. Old Elliott's father was master of Rathcormick for sixty-two years until his death in 1890 but, with him — as happened later with his son — the family's direct descent almost came to an end. He had no children by his first marriage and it was only with his second wife, Dora Elliott, whom he married when he was forty-nine that he had a family.

From the time of Thomas in the mid-eighteenth century the family, although always close-knit, was quite extensive with different members occupying neighbouring farms. This remained the situation throughout the nineteenth century: apart from Thomas in Rathcormick, Griffith in 1854 records William farming two-hundred-and-fifty acres in Balatalion, Henry with six-hundred-and-forty-seven in Moyrath, and Arthur with two-hundred-and-fifty-four in Clonylogan.

This is a respectable history: I am the tenth generation of my family, almost in a direct line, to have lived at Rathcormick. But what is so remarkable is that the family has remained so ordinary, so … undistinguished. Modesty has always governed our ambitions, plainness has been the salient feature of our demeanour, and while our motto is *Regardez l'Avenir* — Look to the Future — we have done this over the centuries by remaining low-key, low-profile, and above all low-church. John, who died in 1738, described himself in his will as a "gentleman"; but we would hardly have the temerity to call

Papa and Mamma, Alice, Elliott and Edward, Rosina, David and Raymond, then Alan, then me

ourselves that today and, even though Old Elliott's father was granted arms, we have never aspired to any social elevation at all, much less attempted to establish ourselves on the foothills of the Irish aristocracy as represented by an entry in the pages of *Burke's Landed Gentry of Ireland*. Old Elliott's father hunted with the Ward Union and is included in the group-portrait of the hunt by William Osborne which now hangs in the National Gallery. Other than that, even though Old Elliott mentioned pictures in his will which "are to remain in Rathcormick as heirlooms", we rarely if ever sat to be painted and we certainly never became artists and painted anyone — or anything — else. Some of the family went to Trinity as early as 1818 and others, at various times, became clergymen and, again, Old Elliott mentioned books as heirlooms at Rathcormick; but, as a general rule, we have tended to frown upon too much education or any public show. George Bernard Shaw described his own family as "downstarts" because they were the very opposite of the "upstarts" by whom he was often surrounded. The Pottertons, in a line stretching back over three centuries, have always been downstarts too.

Ironic, therefore, that the family name should be immortalised in the pages of what is perhaps the greatest work of literature of the twentieth century: *Ulysses*. When Leopold Bloom is in a bookshop on the Quays on June 16th 1904 he spies through the window "an elderly female, no more young" leaving "the building of the courts of chancery, King's Bench, exchequer and common pleas, having heard in the Lord Chancellor's Court the case in lunacy of Potterton ..."

The case was a real one and was actually heard that day. Joyce used as his source *The Freeman's Journal* for Bloomsday which reported that the Lord Chancellor would hear the case of one "Potterton, of unsound mind ..." in the High Court. But, with the destruction of the Four Courts in 1922 and the loss of the accumulated legal records of generations, the details of the

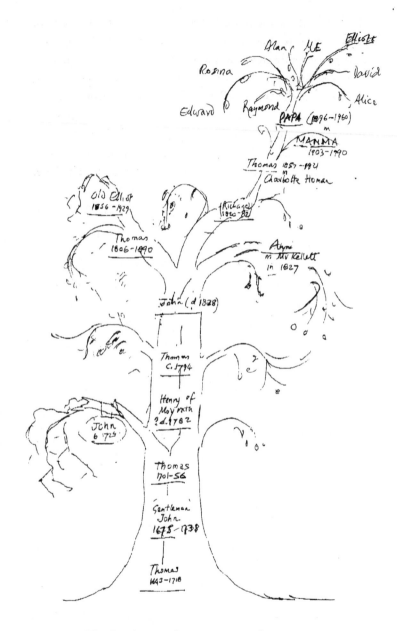

The family tree: downstarts over three centuries

case — and how exactly the lunatic was related to me as he or she certainly would have been — have been buried for eternity.

That is exactly how the Pottertons would have wanted it, and while there may be some satisfaction to be derived from knowing that the life the Pottertons led at Rathcormick and elsewhere did on occasion lead to their going insane, the absence of any acknowledgement of the fact, any record, any publicity, any proof, fits in exactly with how the family have conducted their lives down through ten generations and more.

·

3. A Proper Father

There was more to Rathcormick than the farm itself. There was also an auctioneering and land-letting business, established by Old Elliott's father during the agricultural depression of the 1880s when income from farming declined. Old Elliott, over the forty years of his stewardship of Rathcormick, had built this venture into a moderately successful enterprise. But when Papa heard that he had inherited Rathcormick — and over the two years or so that followed before he moved there — it never once occurred to him that he would be expected to continue this side of Old Elliott's affairs, much less make of it a going-concern. By the same token, it never occurred to Mamma that he would not.

Papa had no experience of office work; he had left school at an early age, and all he really knew was farming. He was also shy and not given easily to the ready conviviality that is the mark of a successful businessman, and as for the notion of standing on a podium and conducting an auction, the idea was about as alien to him as drinking a pint of Guinness or smoking a cigarette. Mamma had no experience either of book-keeping or typing, percentages or profits, lettings or valuations; she had

been governess to an English family called Bayley who lived —
with sufficient social trappings to suggest an unawareness on
their part that the First World War had either come or gone —
near Moate. But although her existence there had focused
exclusively on the nursery, it now seemed to her to have been
an ideal apprenticeship for the role she was ready to assume as
counsellor to the auctioneering apprentice that Papa — if she
had her way — was about to become.

'Old Elliott would expect us to continue the business,' she
said to him.

They had only been married about three years but,
nevertheless, the word "us" tripped off her tongue as though it
had been the practice of a lifetime.

The office at Rathcormick is an extension, a wing that
continues the facade of the house in the direction of the yard.
With a door opening into it from what was at this time the
dining room, it is just one room, but lofty enough to be two.

A proper father

The waiting-room adjacent to it, and part of the same construction has a maids' bedroom as its second floor. My earliest memory is of the old, leather-bound farm account-books which lined one wall, a huge, mahogany bookcase dominating another, and the desk beside the window. We called it 'The Black Desk', but it was an eighteenth-century Irish slope-front bureau — as solid and plain in its deportment as we ourselves — with drawers and a lid: the lid was always closed, the drawers always locked. A fireplace with a hearth fire is the principal focus of the fourth wall and above it — in my time at least — hung a head-and-shoulders portrait of Old Elliott himself. His kindly, moustachioed countenance gave an air of welcome to the room and, looking at the picture, it was easy to believe the epitaph on his headstone in Killaconnigan graveyard: "His Work and Charity shall remain a Monument to his Memory". The main desk, a mahogany knee-hole, stood almost in the centre of the room so that whoever worked at it — be it Old Elliott's father, Thomas, Old Elliott himself, or Papa — faced the fire. To the right of the fireplace was a smaller oak table which, over the years, remained the exclusive domain of the string of secretaries whom Papa employed to assist him and whose lives — once they set foot in Rathcormick — became inextricably, and often hilariously, intertwined with our own.

The office had a smell, an aroma. Not the smell of wood exactly but one derived from wood, as the scent of the wax that had been deployed for years to shine the mahogany furniture vied for supremacy with that which emanated from the preserved-pine of the shelving and the laths that lined the ceiling. The linoleum on the floor, and the polish that was used every Saturday afternoon to make it gleam, also contributed to the atmosphere and, even after half a century, I can smell the place precisely.

It was into this office that Mamma ushered Papa shortly

after their arrival at Rathcormick and in the early years — while he attempted to retrieve the business that had been lost during the hiatus which followed Old Elliott's death — she accompanied him. When her day's work was done and the children were all in bed, she typed his letters, filed his papers and, before Miss Davy came from Kildalkey on a regular basis to do the books, she did those too.

Over the years, and without necessarily setting out to do so, Papa made what might be regarded as a success of the business. What in his youth had been seen as timidity turned into wisdom, his diffidence into self-assurance; his former simplicity was now esteemed as unassuming while his innocence was looked upon as honesty. If he had been thought of as obstinate when he was young, he was now admired on account of his respect for a principle and his most salient characteristic — that of being old-fashioned — became known to all who encountered him as integrity.

He auctioned houses, farms, and furniture, and on summer evenings in June he toured the county, and adjacent counties as well, auctioning meadows: fields of long grass that would be cut for hay. He managed farms for some and organised their affairs for others; his clients included respectable widows, sundry smallholders, distressed shopkeepers and merchants, occasional foreigners, Land Commission evacuees from the West of Ireland, and the assorted detritus of the Anglo-Irish, most of whom were too ineffectual to do it themselves. He bought people's cattle and sheep for them — "stock" they were collectively called — at fairs in Ballinasloe and other towns on the periphery of the West and when they had fattened sufficiently — as they did very readily — on the succulent grasses of County Meath, he arranged for them to be sold. They were sent to Ganly's or Craigie's in Dublin.

During the day his peregrinations in his Ford Prefect, calling on people here and there, carried him quite far afield and, night after night, often until the very late hours, a succession of clients came to see him at Rathcormick. Some came on foot but most came on their bicycles, often having cycled from quite afar. A rare few came by car and all, once they had rung the bell at the back door, made their way to the waiting-room. Here, on winter nights, a fire always blazed on the hearth, there were comfortable armchairs, and, apart from the fact that smoking was not permitted, the atmosphere was so convivial that for most it was a social occasion. Many people, I believe, called for no reason other than a chat round the fire with everyone else and, when their turn came, some words of comfort about whatever was bothering them from T E — as they called him — himself.

Apart from their business affairs, on which Papa had become so adept at advising, many came to him with problems of a more personal nature. Often it was no more than a loan they would ask for; at other times, it might be help in finding a job. A dispute with a neighbour or, even more likely, a brother or cousin, was also an occasion when T E would be asked to intervene. Some came looking for romance — often Papa's secretaries (not to mention the occasional maid at Rathcormick) were pretty enough — while others had marriage on their mind. It was many the eligible bachelor — some fifty-year-old or other with forty acres to his name and a mother who

Papa's Prefect

had just died — whom Papa fixed up with a suitable bride; and when, in time, the same individual, now the father of six or seven, disappeared — lost to alcoholism on the building-sites of London, Liverpool, or Crewe — it was Papa who could be relied upon to find him and bring him back again.

Papa did not believe that "money was the root of all evil": drink was. And, as he went about his business in the rural Ireland of the Forties and Fifties, he found ample evidence to support such a contention. Believing, whenever possible, in prevention rather than a cure he devised the most ingenious methods for denying people access to alcohol. If anyone asked him for a loan, they were immediately suspect and he would generally respond by paying a visit to their family to ensure that they had enough to eat. By the same token, he never gave money to people at Christmas, but went round delivering hampers of food: Christmas cakes and plum-puddings baked by Mamma, and hams bought from Leonard's in Trim. Eventually, when Mamma objected that she could no longer cope with the scale of this operation, he gave people letters which authorised them to buy food up to a certain value at Spicer's, and he would go in after Christmas and pay the bills. Whenever he acted as agent in letting anyone's land, rather than pass the rent over as one would expect him to do, he retained it. Only when he was absolutely certain that the money would not be spent in a pub would he pay it out, and even then, only in instalments and often directly to his client's wife. The Pioneer movement owed many recruits to Papa who colluded with the parish priests of Athboy, Kildalkey, Ballivor, and elsewhere in making people "Take the Pledge".

In spite of his intolerance — and smoking, drinking, and gambling were his principal aversions — I believe that Papa's clients looked upon him as a friend and whether they were rich or poor, insignificant or very important, Protestant or Catholic, that is certainly how he regarded them. He summed up his feelings towards the end of his life when it came to making his will:

"I dislike a private funeral," he wrote, "and prefer to have my friends and neighbours of all denominations with and around me at the end."

When that end came his wishes were fulfilled although, as Catholics at the time were not permitted by their bishops to enter a Protestant church, the throng who loitered on the grass outside Kildalkey Church on a cold October day was considerably greater than the flock of family and friends who came to mourn within.

While Papa may have been regarded as a valued friend by most of those who came into contact with him in his business life, that is not to say that, as a man, he was friendly in the ordinary sense of the word — because he was not. He was serious and severe, strict and stiff, and nowhere was he more serious, more severe, more strict, and more stiff than in his own home and with his own family. As for demonstrating affection, his capacities — even by Protestant standards — were modest in the extreme. Occasionally, he would demand that we give him a "birdie" — meaning a kiss — but such a request was the exception rather than the rule and in general he found it easier to show a fondness for both his daughters — he thought the world of Alice, and Rosina occupied a very special place in his affections — than he did for any of his sons. Although he rarely raised his voice and never so much as slapped us, much less punished us in any more violent way, restriction and injunction, censure and complaint, were endemic to the way he dealt with all of us. This was so much in evidence when I was a child that it appeared to me that his entire existence was devoted to disapproval; and when I encountered other children's fathers, such as Uncle Ken or Mr Tyrrell, who did not behave that way, I had difficulty in thinking of them as proper fathers at all.

Diligence and hard work were central to Papa's ethos and he did his best to establish that they would also be the focal point of ours; recreation, even as a concept, was unknown to him and he always expected that it would similarly be a stranger to us. He was perennially active but, almost as a contradiction, he had no time for haste; he strolled or sauntered rather than walked and, when behind the wheel of his Ford Prefect, he rarely drove at more than thirty miles an hour. He referred to this as a 'good steady speed' and, as far as safety on the road was concerned, he observed but a single rule:

'Stay well out in the middle of the road,' he would say, 'where everyone can see you coming.'

It was not just while driving that, in Papa's view, danger lurked around every corner. Caution and concern were his constant companions and he saw potential catastrophe in everything from eating a mackerel to leaving live cinders in the grate after retiring to bed, from touching any of the berries on the bushes in the shrubbery to going out in the winter without being well wrapped-up. When he drove up the avenue and saw us playing croquet on the front grass, he stopped the car and rolled down the window to tell us he hoped we were being careful. It goes without saying that he regarded all the equipment on the farm, from a pitch-fork to a ladder, from the turnip-pulper to the threshing-machine, as potentially lethal; and, while he encouraged us to swim when we went to Kilkee, we were not supposed to go out of our depths, and he never rested easy until he saw us safely returned to the strand. Although it would have been normal living on a farm to learn to shoot, guns were totally forbidden and on the days when Carr, who was the head man, went out to kill the pigeons gorging themselves on the ripening wheat down in the Twenty Acres, we were instructed to stay inside. Horses, being but a short remove from gambling, were equally frowned upon. Although there was a pony at Rathcormick called Jack, a gentle relic of the war years when petrol-rationing often meant travel by horse-drawn trap, it was only David (and occasionally Alan) who ever rode him and then only when they knew Papa was away.

Papa disliked novelty in all its forms so that when his Prefect, its registration number AI 8369, became defunct, he bought another in an identical shade of green and although it had an equally distinctive and memorable number, ZN 1118, he hoped that no one would notice the change. He believed himself capable of driving only one make of car — it was the Prefect when I was a child — so that it was always Mamma who had to be chauffeur when it came to using the family saloon.

At Christmas, Papa also liked to avoid surprises. We had an elaborate ritual of present-giving which took place on Christmas night, lasted several hours, and involved the exchange and careful opening — the paper had to be saved — of as many as eighty or more beautifully wrapped gifts.

'How will we start this year?' Papa would say when we were all seated in a circle in the drawing room .

'By the youngest giving to the next youngest,' it would be agreed and, at that, I would give my present to Alan and wait until he had opened and admired it before working my way up the family, one-by-one, to Papa. This rite, repeated by all ten of us, reached a climax at a very late hour with Papa's presentation to Mamma. He would first have distributed his parcels to each of us but, as these had all been bought — and wrapped — by Mamma, his own surprise when we opened them was always as great as our own.

'Now, Papa gives to Mamma,' we would say.

He would reach under his chair and bring out what was clearly a bottle wrapped in a brown-paper bag. As he handed it to her, he would give her a birdie.

'I think you like this,' he would say.

'What can it be?' she would ask.

Feeling the parcel, she would avoid giving any appearance that she knew it must be a bottle and then, when she opened the wrapping and held up what looked like sherry, she would exclaim: 'My favourite. How did you think of such a thing?'

'What is it?' we would ask.

Without putting on her glasses, she would hold the bottle at arm's length and read the label.

"Sanatogen Tonic Wine."

Every year, he gave her the same present and her enthusiasm, upon receiving it, convincingly conveyed the impression that it was as nectar is to a goddess. In actual fact she never touched the stuff and, as proof of her distaste, copious supplies of it — souvenirs of Christmases past — lined the shelves of the pantry.

Souvenirs of Christmasses past

4. The Pursuit of the Practical

Alice, Elliott, and Edward are all so much older than me that I only knew them as relative strangers when I was a child, adults who appeared at Rathcormick from time to time. As I had little involvement with any of them, I was left to observe them from a certain remove and that is why my recollections of them are so very vivid. Rosina, on account of being delicate, was memorable in her own way. Raymond, and even David, being nearer to me in age were sufficiently similar for me to take much less notice of them, although I was always wary of David as I knew that my dog Rusty did not trust him. It fell to Alan, who was three years older than me, to be my daily companion but, as we had nothing whatever in common, this relationship was rarely a source of pleasure to either of us. It spite of that, we were reasonably fond of each other.

'It was Alice who brought you up,' Mamma always told me.

But that is not how I recall things. On the contrary, Alice was always somewhere else as far as I was concerned and, while I looked forward to her visits home and was absolutely desolate when she went away again, it would have been reckless of me to have relied upon her for my upbringing as she was so frequently and persistently absent.

Berridge House is where Alice spent her time. It was in Sussex and as the name suggested berries — I thought of ripe blackberries in the September hedgerows — Berridge House sounded a lovely place to me. I thought some of Mamma's hens also came from Sussex — they were called Light Sussex — and I imagined Alice at Berridge House surrounded by clutches of fluffy little yellow chicks.

Alice was learning Domestic Economy. The words conveyed nothing to me but whenever she came home she would bake the most delicious treats like chocolate éclairs, meringues, and caramel custard. She always iced the Christmas cake as well. Mamma would have made it in late October and applied the layer of marzipan but then it waited in a tin in the pantry until Alice came home and decorated it with white, royal icing. The icing itself and the way Alice deployed it was the main embellishment, but she always added a plaster snowman and a Santa Claus, 'to make the cake look Christmassy', she said. It was the same snowman and the same Santa Claus each year; they spent the summer months in the glass-press in the kitchen. After a while, I came to the conclusion that Domestic Economy must mean these sorts of treats. It also meant knitting: not just the relatively plain knitted pullovers and socks that Mamma made for us all the time, but complicated, even Fair Isle, knitting.

Whenever Alice came home, she would bring samples of her needlework with her: embroidered tea-cloths, cushion-covers, and fire-screens with flowers and animals, exotic birds, and ladies in crinolines all wrought most exquisitely. But in spite of the extreme realism of the designs, Mamma for some reason was always more impressed by the stitching at the back of the samples rather than the elaborate perfection of the front:

'Look at the other side,' she would say to Papa almost before he had a chance to admire fully the rabbits and robins which frolicked across a cushion-cover. 'There's not a single thread out of place, not one.'

Then as an added eulogy — and one which also commended itself to him — she would add: 'The work that went into it.'

At that she would lean over and massage the stitching with the tip of her index finger. Alice, looking pleased at the enthusiasm which her handiwork had engendered, would glance across at Papa in search of his approval and it was only with Mamma's next observation that the hint of a frown would trickle across her brow.

'Do you know,' Mamma would say, 'I'm nearly tempted not to use it on a cushion at all rather than cover up the back when no one will ever see it.'

While I was too young at this stage to appreciate the Famous Five books of Enid Blyton, I was already a devotee of the same author's more juvenile tales of the Secret Seven and I think it was on account of my familiarity with the world they inhabited that I imagined Alice's existence at Berridge House as an adventure shared with no more than about six or seven other girls. It was, therefore, with a sense that I had been betrayed — and my first-ever experience of disillusion — that I examined the enormously long, framed photograph of about one-hundred-and-fifty girls, all dressed identically, which Alice brought home with her when she came back from Berridge House for the very last time. And when she challenged us with the virtually impossible task of identifying her whereabouts among the group, my feeling of disenchantment was complete.

Nevertheless, and in spite of the shock, I still loved my big sister very much.

Although Papa had made it his excuse, in taking Elliott and Edward out of Portora, that they would be a great help to him while also learning something practical if they came home, neither of them were around for very long before he realised that the help they provided was of an indifferent kind. As regards mastering anything practical, their interest seemed to extend no further than wanting to drive or, as Papa described it, 'flither around the place wrecking the cars'. In actual fact Papa did not really want their help: Elliott, under his feet in the office all the time, was simply an irritation and Edward's attention span was, in Papa's view, so short that he could never be relied upon to complete satisfactorily any task assigned to him out on the farm.

Soon Papa began to ponder other plans, other options, and partly to get Elliott out of his way, and partly to train him for the future, he sent him to work in an auctioneering firm in Scotland. Located well away from the sordid and potentially corrupting metropolis of Glasgow and distant also from the perilous temptations of Edinburgh or even Aberdeen, the company was located in Dunfermline and, although enormous by comparison with Papa's own business, it had the same agricultural bias. Elliott spent several years in Dunfermline and my earliest recollections of my eldest brother were the photographs of him descending the steps of a Viscount at Collinstown Airport which accompanied his every return. With a belted mackintosh, a felt-brimmed hat, and the demeanour of a detective from Scotland Yard such as I had seen at the pictures, he cut a considerable dash.

Like Alice, Elliott always returned to Rathcormick with trophies of life beyond the seas. In his case, he excelled at woodwork and he used to make beautifully crafted wooden boxes that could be used as a tuck-box by any of us who were at school. On one particular occasion he presented Mamma with a compartmented and drawered miniature chest — worthy of Chippendale or Sheraton in the refinement of its cabinetry — that was intended as a store for her sewing materials.

'I'll have no excuse for not being able to find my thimble

now,' she said. 'Mind you, there are so many drawers I would nearly need a diagram to tell me which is which.'

Also, like Alice, Elliott was photographed with his colleagues and one Christmas he gave Mamma and Papa a similar long, framed photograph that rivalled in its panoramic extent the picture of Alice among the inmates of Berridge House. As with that photograph, the images of the faces were so small that to identify anyone was entirely a matter of chance, and it was only after considerable prompting that we eventually found Elliott secreted in the back row.

'Half Dunfermline must be in the photograph,' said David. 'They can't all be working in the one firm.'

'And who do you think they are?' said Elliott, 'the golf club?'

It was his way of reminding us that recreation was also part of his Scottish life.

With Elliott pursuing his destiny in Dunfermline, Papa now decided that Edward should become a vet and without any thought to the fact that Edward, no more than Elliott, had neither passed nor even sat any examinations which would qualify him for this or any other course of education, he set about sending him to the veterinary school at Trinity College. After making a few preliminary enquiries, he discovered to his dismay that in order to gain admission candidates were required to be familiar with basic Latin. While it could have been expected that he would then have abandoned his plan — with some sense of regret for his words, 'What good is all that Latin and stuff going to be to them?' — this discovery only served to make him more determined. To him, the regulation was merely an inconvenient and temporary impediment and, like all such impediments, it existed solely in order to be overcome.

To that end Papa turned, as he often did in such circumstances, to the advertisement columns of *The Church of Ireland Gazette* and, while disappointed by his perusal of the most recent issue and indeed by a couple of subsequent issues, it was not all that long before he came upon a notice which seemed like the perfect solution to his problem.

"Retired Schoolmaster," it read, "prepares pupils in History, Geography, English, and Latin for Littlego. Accommodation provided in family home. Apply: Mr T Tyner, The Ferneries, West End, Kilkee, Co Clare."

'It sounds ideal,' said Papa.

He had just read out the advertisement to Mamma.

'How?' she said.

'For Edward. It's only January now so he'd have time for a couple of months of grinds with this man and then get the Latin exam next May.'

'Do you mean, send him down to stay in … where is it … Kilkee?'

'Yes. I'll write off about it in the morning.'

In the event, Papa's plans were destined to failure, and although Edward was despatched within weeks to Kilkee, he stayed no more that a month: he never sat the Latin exam and he never became a vet. Even in respect to the more minor trappings of success, such as arriving home to Rathcormick with photographs and trophies as witness to his endeavours as Alice and Elliott did, Mr Tyner's tuition and the experience of Kilkee also fell on barren ground; and it was to be many years and his return from destinations far more fascinating than County Clare, before we would have the opportunity of savouring any exhibits of Edward's life and times.

But, when that time came, those adventures as described by him were to prove far more stirring and infinitely more exotic than anything either Berridge House or Dunfermline, Alice or Elliott, had ever — even between them — been remotely able to engender.

'It sounds ideal,' said Papa

5. Battle Lines

Kildalkey Church was not one of those giddy, Gothick structures which a body called the Board of First Fruits scattered about the Irish countryside, always in the most delectable settings, during the first and second decades of the nineteenth century. On the contrary, like Rathcormick itself — on the perimeter of whose lands it stood — it had a stern austerity that derived, on the one hand, from the sombre, black, cut-limestone with which it was built and on the other from the prosaic sobriety of its architectural style. An enthusiastic guidebook might have claimed it, in design if not in date, as "Early English". It had been constructed as late as the 1850s to the designs of the architect, Joseph Welland (whose plans for it are in the Church Library in Dublin) and it was consecrated in October 1856. It crouched behind a low wall — also in cut-limestone — on the road to Kildalkey but it was well set back, squatting indiscreetly in a crescent of trees. As it had neither tower nor spire, just a bell swinging loose in a bellcote perched on the west gable, it relied exclusively upon the existence of two yew trees gaping across the wall to make its presence known to passers-by. I now know that the church was dedicated to St

Mary but, on account of the fact that, in terms of religion, the name Mary was so potently associated with Roman Catholicism, we never referred to the church as Saint anything-at-all, and only ever called it 'The Church'.

In designing the structure, Mr Welland had denied himself the luxury of crockets, pinnacles, finials, gargoyles, or any of the other embellishments usually deployed to indicate spirituality in a building. Instead, he had elected to rely exclusively upon the use of the buttress — although not the flying variety — and the pointed arch. The windows, all six of them down each side and the three in the east end, were pointed; the entrance door (which was reached through a small porch) and the door to the vestry were pointed; so was the opening between the nave (which we called an aisle) and the chancel. As for any splendour or extravagance, that too was severely restricted and only the pair of lancet windows surmounted by a quatrefoil which punctured the west wall could be deemed to have been in any way unnecessary. A florid painted text above the chancel arch — "I am the True Vine" — was the only evidence of excess.

Although unremarkable in so many ways, Kildalkey Church had a singular distinction which set it apart: it was said to be built from "Weeping Stone". While in other denominations this phenomenon might have established the site as a place of pilgrimage, in the case of Kildalkey the trickles of water which streamed down the walls — inside and out, winter and summer — were thought of as far from miraculous. Instead of invoking the Almighty and expressing gratitude for such a manifestation, Papa — who looked upon Kildalkey Church as his personal property — periodically brought the church-decorating firm of Sibthorpe's down from Dublin to effect remedies for what he regarded as "a terrible problem".

Papa was what was described in his day as 'a great man for the church' — but as the church in question was the Church of Ireland, this encomium had nothing whatever to do with theology or even doctrine in which he, like everyone else in the Church of Ireland, had absolutely no interest at all. Instead, his practice of religion focused on the Scriptures, prayer, hymn-singing, and regular attendance at church: in other words, he was 'a devout churchman'. His children, not unnaturally, were expected to embrace his interests in this respect from an early age and I have to say I am glad we were. If nothing else, the words and music which constitute the Hymnal are among the most beautiful expressions of sentiment I know and to have gained in childhood a familiarity with the King James version of the Bible was a lesson in the use of the language for which only an introduction to Shakespeare's entire dramatic output would have been an adequate substitute.

But the church meant much more to Papa than the actual practice of religion. Politics were also concerned and in this arena he thrived. He was a lifelong member of the Select Vestry and also of the General Synod, and it was in these fora that he weighed into battle on any number of issues. He had two like-minded warrior friends, both bachelor gentleman-farmers, Richard Reynell and Ken Brabazon (we called them Old Reynell and Old Brabazon). If my understanding of events is correct, this trio seems to have opposed on principle the endeavours of every other 'great man for the church', certainly in the Diocese of Meath and, when called upon, in the rest of Ireland also. Indeed, only the activities of The Land Commission drew Papa's fire as swiftly as, for example, the frequent proposals to close some church or other on account of the ever-dwindling number of Protestants in Ireland. He was equally intransigent in his opposition to lesser issues, such as morning service in Kildalkey being infiltrated by the choir of St Anne's Cathedral, Belfast, merely by means of a recording, when no one local was available to play the harmonium.

In spite of Papa's many constraints, very little occurred during my earliest childhood to interrupt the harmony of life at parish level. Kildalkey was joined with Athboy and later with Ballivor as a single parish and Papa saw eye-to-eye with our clergyman, Mr Ruttledge, while Mamma and Mrs Ruttledge were as close friends as Mamma ever allowed herself to be with anyone. But when Mr Ruttledge left us to go to a church near Dublin (on leaving, Mrs Ruttledge gave Mamma all her geraniums) and Mr Webster arrived to take his place, a more ominous tone became apparent on the palette that was Kildalkey parish life.

On his first Sunday in Kildalkey Church, Mr Webster looked down at his congregation and, reading from the Book of Common Prayer, he warned:

'Repent ye; for the kingdom of heaven is at hand.'

With no sense that such an admonition might be premature, he continued:

'The Scripture moveth us in sundry places to acknowledge and confess our manifold sins and wickedness.'

At this point he spotted, seated in the front pew, Miss Higgins, whose life at Higginsbrook was of unblemished simplicity. Opposite her sat Mr Shillington.

'We have erred, and strayed from thy ways like lost sheep,' said Mr Webster.

He could not have known at this stage that Mr Shillington had contracted a mixed-marriage so that at the very moment when Mr Webster reprimanded, 'we have followed too much the devices and desires of our own hearts,' Mrs Shillington and his children were saying the rosary at Mass in the chapel in Kildalkey.

'We have offended against thy holy laws,' said Mr Webster.

'There is no health in us,' we agreed.

At that point his eyes fell on the two pews which we occupied, our well-scrubbed faces giving no indication of infirmity.

'Have mercy upon us, miserable offenders,' said Mr Webster.

He then noticed the happy countenances of the six Tyrrells squeezed in together across the aisle, and raising his eyes to the back of the church and seeing Mrs Liscombe and Mrs Lewis seated near the stove, he shouted:

'Today if ye will hear his voice, harden not your hearts.'

'Salvation will God appoint for walls and bulwarks,' he concluded on seeing Mr Rispin huddled near the heavy curtain which concealed the alcove that housed the bell-rope.

Reflecting on the scene — for that was the congregation in its entirety — as he made his way home to Athboy after the service, Mr Webster came to the not unreasonable conclusion that our worship would be greatly enhanced were we to attend Athboy church which, in addition to being centrally heated, had an organist and a much larger congregation, its ranks artificially swelled by the sundry, mainly American, missionaries who treated nearby Drewstown House as their home. Satisfied that such an improved arrangement might easily be accomplished by simply calling on Papa and Mr Tyrrell, and perhaps a telephone call to Mr Shillington and Miss Higgins as well, Mr Webster arrived home to his Sunday lunch happy in the belief that it was within his immediate power to improve the lot of his new flock so immeasurably.

Mr Webster drove a Simca and one afternoon shortly afterwards, when Mamma was up in the greenhouse re-potting Mrs Ruttledge's geraniums, the whirring sound of the car could be heard coming up the avenue. After it trickled to a stop on the gravel, Mr and Mrs Webster got out. They were shown into the drawing room by Molly and there they waited until Mamma and Papa joined them.

'Put on the kettle, please,' Mamma called to Molly as she came in from the garden through the breakfast room, 'we'll just have it on the trolley. Use the fruit-cake that's in the press in the pantry and do some brown bread and butter. The Belfast cups will be good enough.'

Mr and Mrs Webster stayed until about six. The conversation that took place was never discussed, and although Papa was often heard to complain about the arduousness of 'keeping Webster on his toes', Sunday worship in Kildalkey church continued with very few modifications for many years to come.

With the charitable disposition that is the hallmark of many 'devout churchmen' (of all religious persuasions), Papa 'could not abide that McCann'. By this was meant that he had a deep-seated loathing of the Bishop of Meath, James McCann, an eminent cleric by any standards who later became a distinguished Archbishop of Armagh and Primate of All Ireland. One of McCann's earliest outrages (Papa never referred to him as The Bishop) was to sell off the Bishop's Palace — a vast eighteenth-century mansion with magnificent gardens at Ardbraccan — so that he and his wife might go and live in a comfortable bungalow in the suburbs of Navan. There they became the envy of all the other clergy in the diocese who were still obliged to live in handsome Georgian rectories, with the result that McCann soon sold off a number of those rectories too. He followed this success with a rationalisation plan for the churches of the diocese which saw the closure of many whose congregations consisted of no more than two or three families and the introduction of a complicated system of worship on an occasional basis in others. From Papa's point of view, this was simply defeatism. Apart from anything else, the parishioners in the new "Unions", as the parishes were now optimistically called, were hopelessly confused by the complicated timetables for services and frequently ended up missing morning prayer altogether.

'Are we the first Sunday in Ballivor this month, or is it the third Sunday in Kildalkey,' Charlie Taylor would enquire when Papa, on seeing Charlie driving his cows along the road, stopped the Prefect and wound down the window.

Kildalkey Church
'Repent ye; for the kingdom of heaven is at hand'

'It's the afternoon service in Clonmellon,' Papa would reply, 'on account of the special service next Sunday in Agher.'

'C'mon up there,' Charlie would roar, bringing down his switch of a stick on the bovine rump nearest to him and, with a smile that signified his relief at knowing that he could safely avoid all four options, he would drive his caravan of cows on into his yard.

There were many other issues over which Papa came to blows with McCann: one of which must have been the elevation of Trim parish church to the status of cathedral, as they would never have agreed on such an important matter. The Diocese of Meath, by some oversight or misfortune, had no cathedral and a decision had been made to turn a parish church into one and thereby save the expense of building an entirely new structure. A case was made for the churches at Mullingar, Tullamore, and even Athboy, but Trim, although it is relatively small and very plain, prevailed. Papa must have approved because he presented (anonymously) a splendid carved mahogany chair to the cathedral in memory of Old Reynell, and he expressed a wish that a grave for himself and his family be established in the churchyard. If McCann was the loser in the battle — and it is fairly safe to assume he was — he wreaked revenge by turning the rectory in Trim into flats and building a new one — pebble-dashed with a red-tiled roof — right beside it. Papa said it was 'just a bit of a thing stuck on the side of the street', and demeaning to Mr Medlicott in his new-found status as canon of the cathedral.

Papa always conceded, and Mamma agreed with him in this, that McCann 'had a wonderful voice and always preached a splendid sermon', and when after his translation to Armagh, he was replaced by a genial Trollopian conciliator who agreed with everything everyone had to say, Papa would come home from Synod meetings disgruntled in the extreme, rather than flushed with excitement as he had done in the days of McCann.

'You couldn't beat McCann for a good fight,' he lamented sadly.

And he always referred to the new occupant of the see as 'The Bishop'.

6. Grey Matter

When I was just four, I joined Alan and Raymond at the Protestant national school in Trim. As I was not an easy child, Mamma must have been glad to have been relieved of me for six hours or so a day. 'A little weasel' was how I was often referred to in the family and I was that, and more. I was irascible and over-sensitive to the point of being disagreeable, puny and pernickety, peevish and complaining. Otherwise, I was a lovely little boy and the teacher, Miss Thompson, thought so too.

As all the others had gone there, she would boast that had she not been guaranteed a supply of Pottertons over the years, the school might well have closed down due to a scarcity of pupils. We were driven the eight twisty miles every morning and, according to whoever was at the wheel, the journey varied from one day to the next. With Elliott there was speed as well as safety; with Edward, speed alone was the prerogative; and when Papa drove us, safety was given such priority that the first lesson of the day would be well-advanced by the time we eventually arrived. In such circumstances, we were frequently not the only ones to be late, for if the Tyrrells, who lived between Rathcormick and Trim, failed to make it on to the road before Papa appeared, they would have to trail behind us all the way, while Alan and I crouched down in the back of the Prefect in shame and abject embarrassment.

The Tyrrells, Mary, Linda, Patricia, and Richard, lived beyond Kildalkey at Woodtown Abbott — which William Potterton had owned at the time of *Griffith's Valuation* in 1854 — and they were our nearest neighbours. They were also our friends and although we would never drop in on them, or they on us, we always loved going to Woodtown when invited there for parties. Mrs Tyrrell, who came from the North, was a most wonderful cook, and she brought a degree of perfection to most other aspects of life as well. She was much younger than Mamma which made her sufficiently different in our eyes for us to regard her as fun, while Mr Tyrrell — who, among other things, chatted easily, was known to laugh, wore a sports-coat, and occasionally drove his car at more than thirty miles per hour — was so different to Papa that the two might have originated on different planets.

The Tyrrells were not just our nearest neighbours: they were our only neighbours. That is not to say that lots of other people did not live near Rathcormick, they did; but as they were Catholic, we did not regard them — no more than they would have regarded us — as neighbours and as for mixing socially as friends, that too was out of the question. We read *The Irish Times*, they read the *Irish Independent* or the *Irish Press*: it was as simple, or as complicated, as that. When it came to primary schools, the sundry sequestered Protestants such as ourselves, who found themselves within a ten- or fifteen-mile radius of a town the size of Trim or Athboy, would make their way there by car each day, while Catholics, in droves, had only to walk or cycle to the nearest village or townland. Catholics at the time were forbidden by their bishops to attend Protestant schools, and on account of the fact that religion featured so prominently in the ambience and curriculum of both Protestant and

Catholic schools, no Protestant would have wanted to go to a Catholic school; that is the way it was and few people wanted things to be any different.

Although all primary schools were called national schools, Protestant ones looked different to Catholic ones. The latter, compact, solid, and rendered in concrete, dated mainly from the Thirties and resembled in architectural style the sort of house that came with a Monopoly set. A small, stone plaque some place on the exterior identified the buildings as a *Scoil*. As a general rule, Protestant schools (including Trim School) were about fifty or sixty years older, made of cut stone and built in an ecclesiastical style of architecture. The inscription on their exteriors was in English.

On my first day, Miss Thompson asked me what age I was. 'I'm four years, three months, and twenty-two days,' I said.

She clutched me to her side while making a noise, familiar like that of a hen on a nest, and attempting to prevent a grin, closed her mouth tightly and shook her head. The horizontal

The journey to Trim School varied according to whoever was at the wheel

coils of greying black hair which came down over her ears vibrated as she did so.

'And whose little boy are you?' she asked. 'You're mine, aren't you?'

As it was only Mamma or Alice who had ever said this to me before, I was nonplussed at Miss Thompson's impertinence, but in spite of that, as I stood beside her and she hugged me again, I found comfort in her body: it was plump, firm, clean, and, under her woollen dress, snug. I sensed then that Miss Thompson was my new friend but before that first morning was out I would learn, for the first time in my existence, just how fickle friendship could be.

'Now, we'll find a desk for you,' she said.

The high heels of her brown laced-shoes made a plopping sound on the bare floorboards as she moved down the centre of the room between the four or five rows of desks — each seating no more than four pupils — which were arranged on either side. The September sun came in through the tall, leaded windows and formed small diamond patterns on the floor and up the opposite wall where three huge maps hung. One was of Ireland — I recognised that; another, of an island about the same size was labelled Africa (as I would later learn); and the third, which — inexplicably — hardly showed Ireland at all, was of the world.

'Here,' said Miss Thompson when she came to the second last row, 'there's a grand place for you at the back of Infants. And Ursula will look after you. Won't you Ursula?'

Ursula Gibbs shuffled over in the seat, removing a large Jacob's Marietta biscuit tin as she did so and made room for me beside her. Miss Thompson lifted me into the seat.

'You're as light as a grasshopper,' she said.

Then, noticing Alan and Raymond across the room, she put her hands on her hips.

'This is the seventh Potterton who has been sent in to me to be taught,' she said.

Everyone turned around and stared at me.

'And I just hope that there's some grey matter in there,' she poked the crown of my head with her index finger, 'as none of the others had any. Otherwise, I'll just have to drum it in, won't I Ursula?'

'Yes, Miss Thompson.'

Miss Thompson now walked back up to the top of the room. There was a big iron stove there, the same as the one in Kildalkey Church, bottle-shaped but standing on legs with a bulbous bottom and a chimney-pipe which lead up to the rafters and out through the roof. It was railed off by a metal fire-guard and from one end of this, the end beside Miss Thompson's chair, swung two crook-handled canes.

'Now,' said Miss Thompson.

She knelt down and with both hands took hold of a little girl in plaits with round, wire-rimmed spectacles, and a metal brace across her front teeth.

'And who have we here?' she asked.

Stretching out her arms, she held the toddler away from her and squinted into the little face.

'I'm Patricia Anne Tyrrell, Woodtown Abbott, Kildalkey, County Meath, Ireland, Europe, The World,' said the infant, 'and I'm going to be five next birthday.'

'Well, Patricia,' said Miss Thompson.

She beamed.

'We have a seat here for you in the front row.'

'Such brains,' said Miss Thompson for all to hear.

She turned towards her desk.

'All the Tyrrells, every one of them, have such brains …'

Seeing Patricia Tyrrell take her place in the front desk, I realised that my status as Miss Thompson's best friend, and hers as mine, had been short-lived. When, a few days later, everyone was instructed to move to the back of the room and form a circle round the piano for singing-class and Miss Thompson, without so much as asking me to sing 'do, re, mi,' told me to take out my coloured pencils and draw a house, I sensed that my position was irredeemable.

'There never was a Potterton that had a note in his head,' she said to the entire school, lowering her bottom, so that it overflowed like jam from a sandwich, onto the swivelling discus that was the piano-stool. Sounding an "A", she plunged into the opening bars of "The Ash Grove".

In those first days and weeks, further indignities followed.

'When will I start Irish?' I asked Alan and Raymond.

The idea of speaking in an entirely different way appealed to me.

'You'll start soon enough,' they told me.

Their lack of enthusiasm could only be explained by the fact that they lacked enthusiasm for everything else about school as well. Then, one morning, Miss Thompson took all the Junior Infants aside.

'*Cad is ainm duit?*' she asked Eileen Hayes who had started at school one term ahead of the rest of us.

'*Eibhlin Ní Hea is ainm dom,*' replied Eileen.

Miss Thompson went to the blackboard and wrote out *Eibhlin Ní Hea*. When she had finished, she descended again towards the desks.

'*Cad is ainm duit?*' she said to Marion Lane.

Marion looked blank.

'*Muireann Ní Leighin is ainm duit,*' said Miss Thompson.

Then she repeated it, encouraged Marion to do the same, and wrote that out on the blackboard too. Continuing the procedure, she worked her way through Norman Davis and his twin Lesley, Ernest Mackey, and Eileen Redpath. Then she came to me.

'*Níl Gaeilge ar an ainm Potterton,*' she said, instead of '*Cad *is ainm duit?'* which I had expected her to say and then, in English, she repeated:

'There is no Irish for Potterton.'

I felt tears coming on.

'You just have to write it using the Irish alphabet. That's all you can do,' she said.

She wrote out Potterton on the blackboard. With its alliteration of three, flat-topped T's, it looked horrible; and then, when I had almost digested this disappointment, a further mortification awaited:

'And while your big brother David at least became Dáithi, and Raymond is Réamonn, and Alan, Ailín,' she said, 'there is no Irish for Homan either.'

Miss Thompson, who in actual fact excelled as a teacher, lived with her sister in a tiny stone-built house with pointed eaves, opposite the church and beside the new rectory, at the opposite end of St Loman Street to the back entrance of the school. While Mildred — for that was Miss Thompson's name — earned their living, Grace kept house and part of her responsibilities, which she carried out diligently, was to cook Mildred's dinner every day and pilot it on a tray all the way down Loman Street, in through the back gate of the school, up through the school-yard, and place it — exactly on the dot of one o'clock — before Miss Thompson as she nestled down to her desk in ravenous anticipation. It is doubtful that room-service in Claridge's, then or now, could be as efficient or as prompt, and it certainly could never have been more stylish: Mildred's tray came replete with white linens, silver-plate, a napkin in a ring, water in a carafe, and a posy of flowers in a vase. When Mildred lifted the silver-plate dome under which the repast had sheltered during its protracted progress through the town, the aroma which flushed through the schoolroom was nothing short of ambrosial.

Miss Thompson's teaching revolved around the three Rs.

'What does H say?' she would ask in her determination to teach us to read.

'H says Ha' was the answer.

Once we had learned what every letter had to say and had acquired the confidence to put the sounds together, we were able to read and also to spell; when it came to writing, we had headline-books from Brown and Nolan, which required us to copy out sentences — headlines — onto the series of blank, ruled lines which were printed beneath them. 'An ass is at the gate' was a statement which contained a sufficient number of A's for us to gain practice in forming that letter, and when we had succeeded, there were another twenty-five similar phrases to familiarise us with the remainder of the alphabet as well. The teaching of arithmetic, which involved memorising various tables followed by hypothetical discussions concerning apples and pears on a plate, required much more effort on Miss Thompson's part; but, by the same token, it extended greatly her opportunities for venting frustration, anger, and aggravation.

Trim School
Protestant schools looked different to Catholic ones

'If I have five apples on a plate and I eat two of them,' she would inquire, 'how many apples will be left on the plate?'

Hands would shoot up in the front row but, with an indifference that bordered on the callous, she would ignore them. Rising from her chair, she would re-address herself, this time towards Geoffrey Furlong who was seated at the back and who, she had observed, had not been listening for some time.

'Well, Geoffrey?' Miss Thompson would say.

'Say seven,' Billy Wilson, who had not been listening either, would prompt under his breath.

'Try four,' Freddy Davis would whisper.

Spoiled for choice, Geoffrey would answer 'six'.

Selecting one of her two canes and extricating its crook from the hole in the fender-top by which it hung, Miss Thompson would walk down the room.

'You're a dunce, Geoffrey Furlong,' she would say.

She would take hold of his ear and twist it.

'Your mummy and daddy are wasting their time driving you to school every day and I am wasting my time trying to teach you.'

She would twist further, and as she did so, she would notice Geoffrey's older brother Bobby in the next desk.

'The Furlongs have always been dunces,' she would say. 'Neither one or the other of you will ever know anything. Stand up and hold out your hand.'

Apart from her teaching responsibilities in the school, Miss Thompson also played the organ in Trim church.

'No one can play an organ like her,' Mamma would always say by way of a compliment; but on the sundry occasions that we went there, Alan and I were much more mesmerised by the way Miss Thompson wiggled her bottom on the organ-bench — in full-view of the congregation — than we were by the actual sound she managed to extricate from the instrument itself as she negotiated her way through the "Urbs Fortitudinus".

Mimicking this at home, Alan would sidle up on the undulating seat of the mahogany stool that went with our Collard & Collard and attempt to dislodge me:

'Move over there, Mildred,' he would say.

'Oh! Clifford, don't push,' I would protest.

Then I would wiggle my bottom in a poor imitation — on account of its tiny size — of Miss Thompson.

'I'm just about to begin the psalm,' I would say, 'and as you know, it's such a long one this Sunday.'

The Clifford we referred to was Mr Medlicott who, apart from being rector of Trim, was also manager of the school, and it was supposedly in that role — although he also taught us Scripture — that he came visiting every other day. We joked among ourselves that he was really Miss Thompson's boyfriend, a notion so completely preposterous to us as to be hilarious. Although Mr Medlicott was not very tall, and with the exception of a few grey wisps around his ears, entirely bald, he had a comely appearance that most people would have looked upon as handsome. He always dressed as a clergyman but instead of wearing a black suit, as was usual, he favoured a more striking, hand-tailored, dark-grey. This, when combined with the jet-black shirt-front and full ring of stiff, white clerical collar, enhanced his natural pallor and lent him a distinction that was quite singular. In summer, when he came to the school at lunchtimes and organised us into playing cricket, he permitted himself an even more pronounced elegance by substituting a cream-coloured linen jacket for the dark-grey of the winter months, so that even if the sun was not shining, Mr Medlicott's appearance always gave the impression that it was. Then, on the day of the annual school-outing to the strand at Bettystown in June, Mr Medlicott would be at his most debonair of all — appearing in grey flannels, a sports-coat, and an open-necked shirt, the collar of which would be folded down over that of his jacket. On this day he also wore latticed, brown-leather sandals; the Catholic priests who holidayed in a guesthouse near us in Kilkee wore the same but always in black. It would not be surprising had Miss Thompson viewed Mr Medlicott in terms of romance, because, in truth, he was as tempting as Clark Gable.

When Mr Medlicott arrived at the school to take Scripture class, Miss Thompson separated the school into two.

'All the infants on this side,' she said, 'Mr Medlicott will take fourth class up on the other. And remember, it's only just over a month till the exam. Isn't that so, Rector?'

'Just about five weeks, we haven't had the date yet. But they seem to be well-advanced.'

Miss Thompson looked at him disapprovingly.

'There can't be any complacency at this stage,' she said. 'Now Ursula, why don't you make a start by saying the Lord's Prayer?'

'Miss.' A voice was heard from the rear at Mr Medlicott's side of the room.

'Yes, Dickie,' said Miss Thompson, nodding in the direction of Dickie Parkinson.

'Is the Lord's Prayer the same as the Our Father?'

Although few of us understood the significance of Dickie's question, we were immediately aware from Miss Thompson's uncomfortable glance in the direction of Mr Medlicott that Dickie had touched upon an unwelcome topic; even if we could not be certain as to what it was in this instance, past experience had taught us to expect that Miss Thompson would be challenged by any question from Dickie.

Dickie Parkinson was different. His father, who had only one hand, drove a two-seater, open sports-car, and it was from this unlikely vehicle — unlikely because Mrs Parkinson, who was enormously tall was always slotted into the passenger seat — that Dickie would be deposited at the school each day.

Having collected her thoughts, Miss Thompson replied: 'There is no such thing as the Our Father, Dickie.'

The manner in which she said 'Dickie' implied that that was the end of the matter, but Dickie was far from satisfied.

'Well Mickey Tuite, who goes to the Christian Brothers, was able to ream the same words off pat to me the other day and he says that Brother Michael told him it's called the Our Father.'

'It's not the same prayer that Roman Catholics use,' Miss Thompson replied.

She was now quite flushed.

'It doesn't matter what they call it. Anyway, they only say half of it. When you get older you'll learn the doxology.'

Shocked as we were that Dickie knew someone who went to the Christian Brothers school, we were just as taken aback that his friend, Mickey Tuite, and indeed everyone else at the Christian Brothers', might be praying to the same God as ourselves. For that reason, we readily accepted Miss Thompson's explanation that something as mysterious as the doxology would one day account for it all, and when she turned her attention again to Ursula Gibbs, the sense of relief in the room was palpable.

'Now Ursula, begin.'

'Our Father ...' Ursula Gibbs began.

But before she progressed any further, there came a sniff and, throwing her head back violently, she groped under her seat for her biscuit tin.

Rushing to her aid, Marion Rowntree retrieved the tin and brought out a collection of sponges. By this time, Miss Thompson was on the scene and, taking out the towel which was always to be found in Ursula's school-bag, she spread it on the desk.

'Throw your head well back,' she said. 'Marion, hold that cold lid to the back of her neck. It'll stop in a minute or two.'

Ursula Gibbs suffered from nose-bleeds.

Indeed, scarcely a day went by that her nose did not bleed, and for that reason she came to school well-prepared with flasks of cold water, sponges large and small, and wads of cotton wool. These were the secrets of her biscuit tin and Ursula rarely complained, having stoically accepted that her education — indeed her life — was to be routinely interrupted by bouts of blood-letting. She never seemed delicate in any other way and pounded round the school-yard playing tip-and-tig as roughly

'And I just hope that there's some grey matter in there'

as the rest of us. In fact, quite remarkably, her nose only ever seemed to bleed when she was sitting quietly at her desk.

*

When the day of the Scripture exam arrived everyone, including Miss Thompson, wore their best clothes. Mr Medlicott arrived, accompanied by Canon Mayne who conducted the exam, and there followed a morning of interrogation which, depending on our age, covered The Creed, The Catechism, The Ten Commandments, Psalm 23, I Corinthians, Chapter 13, the Books of Exodus, Samuel, and Kings, and the Gospels.

'What is a parable?' asked Canon Mayne.

Miss Thompson's expression of anxiety gave way to pride as Mary Tyrrell's hand shot up into the air.

'We'll let someone else answer this one, Mary,' the Canon said, 'you've already done very well.'

When Patience Prentice raised her hand, Miss Thompson's tongue clicked loudly against her false teeth.

'Yes, Patience.'

'It's a heavenly story with an earthy meaning.'

A murmur of muffled laughter rippled through the room.

'Well done, Patience,' said Canon Mayne.

Mary Tyrrell's brow darkened with a look of uncertainty .

'Almost …'

Mary looked relieved.

'Can anyone help Patience?' asked the canon.

'Me,' said Billy Wilson.

By now, Miss Thompson was back at her desk. Leaning forward, she rested her forehead in her hand.

'An earthly story with a heavenly meaning,' said Billy.

'And can anyone remember any parables?'

'The Lord of the Vineyard.'

'The Mote and the Beam.'

'The Blind leading the Blind.'

'The Prodigal Son.'

'Ah! Yes, one of the most beautiful,' said the canon, 'and who will tell it to us? Mary, I'm sure you can.'

'A certain man had two sons,' Mary began, 'and the younger son gathered all together, and took his journey into a far country ...'

She knew the parable off by heart and, as she recited the words, Miss Thompson looked down the room.

With a distant look in her eyes, she glanced at Alan and then she looked at me.

7. Farming of the Future

The first time I ever saw a tipped-cigarette was when Edward came home from Canada. It was called a Lucky Strike and Edward had packets of them up in his room. Unlike the flat, cardboard packages in which Irish cigarettes of the time — such as Aunt Olive's Gold Flake — were contained, Edward's Lucky Strikes came in paper and cellophane cartons that had no lid; Edward just fished the cigarettes out of a hole in the top. But it was the filter-tip, as it was called on the packet, which was the real novelty.

Edward explained to Alan and me how it worked. He made us take a cigarette in our hands, then pointed out to us how white the filter-tip was. For a moment, Alan put the unlit cigarette into his mouth. Then Edward, using only his thumb and index finger to conceal the cigarette within the palm of his hand, tilted his head forward ever so slightly, looked at us out of the tops of his eyes, and shoved the cigarette into the corner of his mouth, rolling it ever so discreetly between his lips. Next, taking a silver lighter from his pocket, he flicked it alight and with a slow, circular motion appeared to just warm the end of the cigarette. He pulled in his breath — we heard the wheeze

— and as he did so the tobacco glowed. Tossing back his head, he blew the smoke out of the other corner of his mouth, then took the cigarette between the stained tips of his fingers.

'Look,' he said.

He held the filter, which we could see was now discoloured, towards us.

'That's the tar. What I am smoking is pure nicotine.'

My brother Edward was incredibly suave and glamorous. He had been in Canada and America for about two years, and even though he knew smoking was not an option in Rathcormick, he brought Mamma a present of an ash-tray on his return. It was made from a fossilised cactus tree. The bowl of the ash-tray, scooped out of the wood, was lined with a muddy-colour picture under glass of cacti in the Arizona Desert. Taking the ash-tray out of Mamma's hands as soon as she had opened the parcel, and before she had the opportunity to admire it, he weighed it up and down in his hand.

'Do you feel the weight of it?' he said.

'Yes,' said Mamma.

She was not certain whether it was supposed to be heavy or light.

'What age do you think it is?' said Edward.

'Well,' said Mamma, 'I suppose you got it in ...' She leaned forward to look at the caption on the photograph, 'Is it Arizona? Now, let me see. You were there in ... was it March?'

'No. But what age do you think it actually is?' he said.

Mamma frowned.

'I suppose ... about ...' she said.

'It's a fossil,' said Edward.

He gave it back to her.

'It could be ten, maybe twenty, million years old.

'Gracious ...' said Mamma. She dashed the ash-tray down on the table. 'That old. We'll have to keep it in the cabinet in the drawing room.'

Everything Edward had to tell us on his return was fantastic.

'You can drive for hours, days even, without seeing a living soul' was how he described something called the Painted Desert.

'Are there camels?' asked Alan and I.

We were thinking of the Old Testament illustrations in our bibles.

'Too dry,' said Edward. 'Too dry, and too hot. If you crack an egg on the bonnet of the car, it will fry within a minute. That's how hot it is.'

'Tch, tch,' we said.

We thought of the Austin A40 and how hot it could become when parked in the front yard on a sunny day, and with the exchange of a single glance, Alan and I resolved to experiment on the next warm day.

'Do you see that door I'm standing in?' said Edward, handing us a photograph of himself. He was positioned, with arms outstretched, at the entrance to what looked like a tunnel. We studied the photograph.

'It's not a door,' said Edward.

'And what?' we asked.

'It's a tree,' said Edward.

We peered at the picture more closely: there was not a leaf in sight.

'That's the trunk of a tree,' said Edward, 'a living tree. It's so wide that they have been able to run a road through it. I'm standing in the middle of it, that's where I am.'

I thought of the copper beaches at the front gate and wondered if their trunks would ever be large enough to divert the avenue through them.

'It's called a redwood,' said Edward. 'There are forests of them so tall that their tops are above the clouds.'

On his travels Edward had a suitcase which could be made larger or smaller by means of an elaborate mechanism holding the lid. The case was covered in stickers — Cunard, Aberdeen and Commonwealth Line, the Pennsylvania Railroad to name but a few — which documented a world that was about as wondrous to us as the man in the moon. Unpacking the suitcase in the spare-room after his return from Canada, he took out a white jumper with a picture of Niagara Falls across the front.

'Do you want it?' he said to Alan. 'Try it on.'

Alan pulled on the garment and then stretched his chest so that the full extent of the Falls and the over-laden passenger boat that bobbed treacherously beneath them was fully visible. *Maid of the Mist* read the legend around his waist.

'It's great,' said Alan.

'Would you like to see something?' said Edward.

He knelt down at the suitcase again.

'What?' we said.

He pulled out a shiny green tie, held it up and looked at it himself, then folded it over for us to see. On it was a picture of a girl posing full-length in a swimsuit. Having never seen such an image before, Alan and I were stunned.

'Put it on,' we said.

Looking at his reflection in the overmantel, he tied the tie, then turned round and posed for us to admire it.

'Wow!' said Alan.

I was silent.

'Are the children up there with you, Edward?' Mamma called suddenly from the bottom of the stairs.

'They're just coming,' he shouted as he ripped the tie from his neck.

'Run down quickly,' he said.

Putting his forefinger to his lips, he slammed the lid of the suitcase.

*

When Edward was twenty-one, Papa gave him a farm. It was beyond Ballivor and it had a white wooden paling along the road, entrance gates, and a straight avenue which led up to the house and farmyard. We called the place Gill's after the people who must once have lived there. Although Papa allowed Edward to farm Gill's — indeed actively encouraged him to do so — it was out of the question for him to be permitted to live there. As a result, Edward stayed on in Rathcormick and flithered up and down to Gill's in the car several times a day. In spite of the pleasure he derived from this activity, it was not all that long after gaining possession of Gill's that Edward came to the conclusion that, in order to farm it efficiently, it would be absolutely essential for him to spend some time abroad. This decision he based less on the agricultural potential of Gill's than on the prospects for entertainment and congenial company — of the sort which most young men find desirable — at Rathcormick: the former, by any standards, was considerable, the latter, in Edward's view, non-existent.

He announced his decision quite unexpectedly.

'Dairying is the thing of the future,' he said one day to Mamma.

'Do you think so?' she said. 'Your father has never been keen on the idea of a dairy herd. He says the risks and bother involved far outweigh the attraction of the steady income. And when the land is as good as it is here, store cattle and a bit of tillage are much the best.'

'There is not nearly enough land at Gill's to make tillage profitable,' said Edward.

It was the first time he had thought of such an argument, but as he mulled it over in the weeks that followed it seemed to be a very good argument indeed. As a result, by the time he plucked up the courage to address with Papa the topic of his going abroad, he had convinced himself that his real reason for wanting to do so was to familiarise himself with dairying rather than his original quest to relieve his boredom. His next proposition was equally unanticipated:

'The Danes have got it down to a fine art,' he said.

'What?' said Papa.

'Dairying,' said Edward.

It was his way of stating, although Papa could be forgiven for not understanding as much, that he had decided to go to Denmark.

Over the months that followed, Edward took to mentioning Denmark and the Danes with increasing frequency. His remarks would generally be prefaced by some complaint such as 'There is no money in cattle' or 'There's not the climate in Ireland for tillage' and then he would enunciate some theory or other in support his new-found advocacy of Danish farming methods.

'It stands to reason,' he might say, picking up the box of Calvita from the sideboard (then the only cheese widely available in Ireland), 'that, sooner or later, we'll have to make proper cheese in Ireland instead of this processed stuff.'

On other occasions his statements would be even more outlandish.

'Wait till you see, it won't be all that long before we'll all be eating Danish butter. And not just us, but the English and the Americans as well.'

As this was before fridges were generally in use, and as any butter, other than that which Mamma made every week, was unknown at Rathcormick, the notion that, at some time in the future, we would be obliged to eat something that had come all the way from Denmark did not seem, in spite of Edward's recommendation, at all attractive to us.

While Mamma was always interested in everything that Edward had to say and Elliott would always question him about his ideas — not because he wanted to hear the answers but merely to indicate by his reaction how foolish he thought

'Wow,' said Alan

they were — Papa chose to ignore the hints which Edward dropped with increasing and ever more dangerous frequency.

Eventually, inevitably, matters came to a head.

It was a November evening and Edward, more restless than usual, had plucked up his courage to ask Papa might he borrow the car to go to a social in Celbridge. Although a "social" was a dance attended exclusively by Protestants which took place in a church hall where tea and sandwiches were served and alcohol was entirely unknown, and although Celbridge, a simple and respectable village, was hardly Sodom or Gomorrah, Papa was not easily persuaded that either a social or Celbridge was a desirable destination and refused to let Edward go. There followed that rare thing, a heated argument, which culminated in Edward throwing down a challenge:

'It's no use,' he said, 'I'm only wasting my time at Gill's. There's nothing for it but to go to Denmark and see how things are done first hand.'

'And what's to become of Gill's while you are away?' said Papa.

'I'll set it,' said Edward.

'How would you set it for goodness sake? Don't you know that eleven-months land is all that anyone wants?'

At this stage, Papa was under the impression that the intended visit to Denmark would last about a month, but Edward had other plans and the idea of setting Gill's for a term of eleven-months fitted in with them exactly.

'If I went for about a year, I would really learn something,' he said.

And then, by way of demonstrating the seriousness of his intent, he added:

'I could even get a job on a farm if all came to all.'

Putting on his spectacles, Papa picked up the copy of the *Meath Diocesan Magazine* from the table beside him and, twisting in his chair so that the light was behind him, he started to read.

'You know very well that he has other things on his mind in the evenings,' Mamma said to Edward the following morning at breakfast.

'Mornings or evenings, it's always the same,' said Edward.

'It'll take time for him to get used to the idea that you want to go away. You can't expect him to agree to it all at once. You should have just said that you were thinking of going to Denmark.'

'I've been saying that for months,' said Edward. 'He doesn't take a whit of notice. It's like being in a prison here. There's no life and ... no ... fun.'

'There may not be much life or fun stuck on a farm in Denmark either,' said Mamma. 'And anyone who gives you a job is going to see to it that you work and, as for borrowing a car to go to a dance, that's not likely to be even an option.'

'I would be able to go into Copenhagen,' said Edward.

Mamma, who had by now finished eating, arranged her knife on the plate where her toast had been and pushed the plate aside. Lifting the cosy, she topped up her tea and positioned her cup and saucer in front of her.

'Pass up your cup,' she said to Edward.

She did not look at him, but as she poured the tea, she said:

'I would ask you to be very careful not even to mention Copenhagen to your father. He would go mad at the thought of it.'

In time, Edward had his way. Elliott undertook to look after Gill's for him while he was away; by some means or other, he found himself a job on a farm in Denmark, and, without mentioning Copenhagen, he set off. When he returned after the better part of a year, we were disappointed to hear from him that dairy-farming in Denmark was not nearly so advanced as he had been led to believe and, in fact, he had come to the conclusion that, considering the financial returns, it was much too labour-intensive to be practicable at Gill's at all.

'You should have seen the size of the fields,' he said, 'only little scuts of things. A bullock would be hard pressed to turn round in one.'

Gill's, by comparison, was like the Prairie, he assured us, and from then on, again with increasing regularity, this became his theme.

'In fact that's how Gill's really should be farmed,' he said one night.

We were all in the sitting room about to start a game of whist. Mamma was darning socks and Papa was at the desk looking for the cards. He had his back to the room but looked round at Edward's words.

'The Prairie?' he said.

He looked over the top of his spectacles.

'Will one of you put another sod of turf on the fire, please?' said Mamma. 'It's getting cold in here.'

But the months of freedom in Denmark had given Edward both courage and resolve.

'Cattle are the obvious thing for Gill's,' he said.

'I've told you that more often than I care to think,' said Papa.

'Yes, but not in the old-fashioned way,' said Edward. 'There would be a lot to be learned from seeing how things were done on a proper ranch: someplace like Montana or … Wyoming. That's how cattle should be managed. That's the way of the future.'

'And I suppose you're now thinking of going to America to see that,' said Papa.

He sat down at the table.

'Yes,' said Edward.

In the silence that followed, Elliott dealt the cards.

'Your lead,' he said to David when he had finished but other than that no one spoke, and even when Papa claimed nine tricks in a row in a hand of no trumps, an air of unease and apprehension hung over the room.

It must have occurred to Edward that he had gone too far as he never mentioned the Prairie again and, as for the notion of learning cattle-ranching in Wyoming in order to introduce it in Ballivor, that too was dropped. Instead, he opened his heart to Mamma and before long she came up with a plan which she felt would commend itself to Papa on the one hand and give Edward his freedom on the other.

'It's really terrible,' she said to Papa one day apropos nothing at all, 'the way we lost all contact with Uncle Tom and Uncle Jack after my Gran — who was an awful woman — made them go to Canada.'

As Papa did not know what to make of this statement, he said nothing.

'I'm going to get in touch with them,' said Mamma, 'and, if they are still alive, some of us should just go and see them. It's the only charitable thing to do.'

And so it was that with Gill's set as eleven-months land Edward — in the interest of charity — sailed for New York and on by train to Buffalo and across the border into Canada. He found Mamma's uncles, their wives and families, and for several months at a time, several years even, lived with them and became part of their lives.

When he eventually returned, an event for which we had prayed every Christmas night for years, Papa was so grateful that he would suggest to him on occasion that he might like to borrow the car and go to a social in Celbridge; but after Niagara Falls, the Maid of the Mist, California redwoods, and the Painted Desert, Celbridge held little attraction for Edward and he would tell Papa that he could not be bothered.

After a time, the boredom which Edward affected caused Papa some concern and he set to devising plans to remedy it by making Edward feel more useful. Since the year before he was married, when one of his heifers, Fantail of Ballycommon, had given birth to a bull calf which he christened Lord Offaly, Papa had kept a pedigree herd of Aberdeen Angus cattle. They moved with him to Rathcormick, switching their surname from Ballycommon in the process, and at a later date they were joined by pedigree Herefords. The better specimens from both herds were exhibited at the Bull Show in Dublin each year and framed photographs of Papa holding various bulky animals hung in the office: in the case of prizewinners, the silk rosettes which had been presented to them in their hour of triumph were attached to the frames. Their names — Mandarin, Mogul, Beausire in the case of the bulls, Mignonette, Modesty and Belise in the case of the heifers — were inscribed on the photos and details of their pedigrees were recorded — with all the thoroughness of Debrett — in the published annual herdbooks of the Aberdeen Angus Cattle Society or the Hereford Breeders Association.

Every year, when it came to registering the new calves, there was much discussion at Rathcormick as to suitable names and we would all make suggestions. But in spite of this apparently democratic procedure, Papa had a habit of dismissing most of our proposals, with the exception of those made by Rosina, and invariably ended up naming all the animals himself. It was, therefore, an enormous gesture on his part when, following Edward's return from Canada, he entrusted him with the task of recording the new additions to the herds.

'Just fill out the forms and send them off,' he said.

Mamma was stunned at the casualness with which he delegated the task, but when the registration papers lay, untouched, on the hall table for several days, she became irritated.

'Don't disappoint him by taking no interest,' she said to Edward. 'I want you to sit down and get it done today.'

Edward went into the dining room and, spreading all the documents out on the table, set to work. By dinner time he had finished.

'Have I time to drop down to catch the post in Kildalkey,' he shouted to Mamma from the hall.

'Well don't be long,' she said, 'I'm just about to teem the potatoes.'

Scattering gravel in its wake, the A40 shot past the windows and disappeared down the avenue.

It was several months before the new edition of the *Hereford Breeders Almanac* arrived at Rathcormick. When it did, its appearance was heralded by the most dreadful shouting after Papa had gone upstairs to collect the opened post from Rosina. Mamma rushed up the stairs, Elliott, followed by Rusty, came out of the breakfast room, and Miss Shannon called from the front hall.

'Is it something I've forgotten?' she asked.

'We're disgraced,' Papa shouted down the stairs.

Beausire of Rathcormick

He was in a rage and, what is more, he showed it in a manner that for him was completely exceptional.

'Disgraced,' he yelled.

He threw the brown paperback that was the yearbook down the stairwell; ducking it in its flight, Mamma ran up to the landing.

'Now calm down, my dearest,' she said. 'What could have got into you to upset you so much?'

She took him by the arm and they went into the bedroom. The shouting continued.

'I'll just have to get rid of the bulls,' he said. 'That's all there is to it. Just get rid of them.'

'Why on earth …?' said Mamma.

'But not before I put that brat on the first boat back to Canada. Take a look at the herdbook and see what he has done to me.'

Mamma came down the stairs.

'Let me see that,' she said to Elliott, who was standing in the inner-hall holding the battered volume.

'What is it?' he said.

She flicked through the pages until she came to those headed "Rathcormick" and then read through the pedigrees which stretched back over almost thirty years.

"Blue Banner of Rathcormick out of Blue Bess of Rathcormick by Caligula of Derrylea, calved 9 May 1946" was a typical entry. She read down the page and over to the next one and then, at the end of the section describing Papa's herd, she saw the offending words.

Under "Additions to the Herd for 1954" there was a list:

"Monday of Rathcormick, Tuesday of Rathcormick, Wednesday of Rathcormick, Thursday of Rathcormick, Friday of Rathcormick, Saturday of Rathcormick, Sunday of Rathcormick" was how it read.

'We're disgraced!'

8. A New Arrival

I was not all that old when I came to the conclusion that my brother Alan's company was not as genial as it might be and, as far as I know, my sentiments were fully reciprocated. Alan found me so tiresome that he had to resort to bullying me, and while I did not care for this at the time, I would say in retrospect that he was quite justified and that, in the longer term, he did not cause me any harm. Alan was a cheerful, outgoing, rugged little boy whereas I was hot-tempered, timid, and whinging. Additionally, I had a marked tendency towards being refined. The realisation that Alan was so very unsatisfactory as a companion made me think of other options, other prospects, and before long I came to the conclusion that my existence would be infinitely more pleasant if I had a younger sister.

Having thought about it for a while, I decided to broach the subject with Mamma. This I did one Saturday morning when she came into our bedroom with a bottle of castor-oil in one hand and a pot of raspberry jam in the other. As I knew we were about to be dosed, I decided to bring up the subject there and then; if nothing else, a discussion would delay the moment when we would be obliged to swallow the castor-oil.

'Mamma,' I said, sitting up in the bed.

'Mmm,' she said.

She put the jam down on the mantelpiece and started to twist the cork of the castor-oil bottle.

'Can you buy me a little sister?'

'What can have put such a silly notion into your head?' she said. 'Here now, put that towel across your chest and don't let me see you spit out even one drop of this.'

'All the others had a baby to play with, why can't I?'

'We'll think about it,' she said.

As she was about forty-eight at the time, she must have been fairly confident that the matter could go no further. But having mentioned the topic once, I found it easier to bring it up on subsequent occasions until, after some months of evading my requests, Mamma became impatient.

'You don't buy babies,' she said.

The firmness of her tone dissuaded me from asking the logical next question, but perhaps in anticipation of such an inquiry and as a means of changing the subject she then said: 'Perhaps we might think of getting you a dog.'

This suggestion I took to immediately and, as it was so very unexpected, so very novel — apart from Carr's collie, Rover, there had rarely been a dog at Rathcormick — all thoughts of buying a little sister vanished from my head.

'When will I get the dog?' I would enquire in the belief that its arrival was imminent, not realising that Mamma was hoping I would forget all about it and develop an enthusiasm for something else. Occasionally, she would make a token gesture of looking in the "Dogs" column of *The Irish Times*, and read out descriptions of animals that were "available to a good home … likes children", but she never replied to any of these advertisements. By the same token, when any of the others suggested that a puppy might be obtained from Veronica Clibborn, who won prizes for her spaniels at the RDS each year, or Mrs Lennon, whose place — according to Papa — was 'crawling with dogs', none of these possibilities were ever followed up. Finally, when I had almost given up on the notion, there came a surprising development.

The Wood-of-O, which had been Mamma's home when she was a child, was near Tullamore. It was reached by means of a very long avenue — punctuated by several sets of gates — which wound through trees to right and left. The house was long and low with a flight of steps leading up to the hall-door which was on the upper floor. The entrance hall — from which a staircase descended to the kitchen and other rooms — was flanked by a drawing room and dining room and, beyond them, bedrooms. To a small boy, the place was intriguing because, to all intents and purposes, it seemed to be upside-down.

Aunt Olive lived at the Wood-of-O with Grandpa Tong. She shared her life with a wire-haired fox terrier and she had a maid called Dolly Crotty; but when the maid, whom Alan and I thought was ancient, married a man who was also called Crotty, we did not think it was a proper marriage at all. Aunt Olive was addicted to Gold Flake and had a pronounced dependency on Mills and Boon: without exception, and throughout her life, she read four popular romances a week. By the time I was a child, Grandpa was quite elderly and Aunt Olive managed the farm. With the help of two or three labourers, she had cattle and sheep, made hay, organised tillage, kept hens and a pig or two, and had a few milking cows. I remember her making improvements to the farmyard (presumably after Grandpa had become too infirm to resist) and renovating the kitchen. She installed a Rayburn and had the well-scrubbed pine kitchen table enhanced by a Wearite top. At the same time, she converted an old bedroom on the lower floor into a breakfast room. Although Aunt Olive was quite proficient at organising all these endeavours, she was resolutely incapable of learning to drive a car, and in spite of the efforts which several people made to teach her — including, infamously, our cousin Moira — Grandpa's black Anglia remained in the car-house, unused and spotless as the day he had bought it, while Aunt Olive herself remained immobile — so to speak — until the end of her days. Not that she was dissatisfied with this state of affairs: on the contrary, she frequently expressed her contentment — as she frequently expressed her contentment at never having married — with the bicycle or pony and trap which she used as a conveyance on her weekly shopping and library trips into Tullamore.

Our visits to the Wood-of-O always took place on Sunday afternoons. The long drive brought us from Ballivor to Kinnegad, through Tyrrellspass, Rochfortbridge, Kilbeggan and then by back roads, avoiding Tullamore itself, over the Grand Canal which ran along the edge of the Wood-of-O, and finally — with Alan and I arguing as to who should open the gates — up the long avenue itself. My memory of those journeys is of the gatherings of men dressed in their Sunday best — blue

The Wood-of-O
Rusty's Birthplace (and Mamma's childhood home)

suits, white shirts, brown shoes, and Brylcream — who loitered at every crossroads on the way and who stared at our car as we passed. Their bicycles would be propped against a bank or hedge and sometimes they might be playing pitch-and-toss, but more often than not they spent their Sunday afternoons just lingering there, their Woodbines held within the palms of their hands.

We loved going to the Wood-of-O. The yard was more old-fashioned than that at Rathcormick; there was a huge chestnut tree near the house which, Aunt Olive told us, had once been struck by lightning so that part of its trunk — at quite a high level — was hollowed out into a natural house where Alan and I would play for hours on end. Although we were warned not to go near the canal, we frequently did so and, on wet afternoons, when Aunt Olive would produce a box of wooden bricks — relics of childhoods past — which she kept in a big desk in the dining room, we would build magnificent houses and castles. When we tired of that, there was a solitaire board of the same vintage, the secret of which defied us, wet Sunday after wet Sunday, year after year. As those afternoons drew to a close, we would have high-tea — a meat-tea as we called it — with a cold steak-and-kidney pudding, its pastry form moulded in a bowl and then turned out on a dish, with salads of beetroot and celery. When it came to about ten o'clock, we would face the long drive home. After we got an A40, in which there was a wireless (and also a heater), Elliott or David would turn on Radio Luxembourg and we would listen to *Top Twenty*; but if we got as far as the Hill-of-Down, and it looked as though we might be home before it got to Number One, the driver would slow down.

'Drive on a bit, for goodness sake,' Mamma would say as the Everly Brothers at Number Four gave way to Connie Francis at Number Three, 'or we'll never be home.'

In truth, she liked the programme as much as we, but on the

rare occasions when Papa was with us — it was exceptional for him to go to the Wood-of-O as he never forgot the way Grandpa Tong had dismissed him — we had to listen to Billy Graham.

It was on one such visit to the Wood-of-O that my yearning for a dog of my own was finally gratified. After the usual drive giving rise to the usual arguments between Alan and me as to who would open the gates, we arrived at the house. After we went in to say hello to Grandpa in his bedroom and returned to the dining room, we heard a great commotion on the staircase. Aunt Olive came into the room followed by two tiny puppies whizzing here and there and sending the door-mats in the hall flying across the lino in their wake. One of the puppies, white and woolly with brown and black patches on his back, jumped up on our laps one after the other and licked our faces as though we were ice-creams; the other, reddish-brown, whose breed was not instantly recognisable, charged around the room dizzy as a bluebottle, crashing into the furniture, jumping up at the window, and eventually hurtling into Grandpa's room where he disappeared under the bed.

'Get down, Twig,' Aunt Olive said to the woolly puppy who was now on Mamma's lap. 'Where's your manners?'

She chuckled.

'Olive, I thought you had agreed that when Trixie died, you would never get another dog,' said Mamma.

She pushed the puppy away from her nylons.

'Come here,' said Alan.

He lifted the furry bundle into his arms.

'Let me hold him,' I said.

For a moment we forgot that there was a second dog until Aunt Olive reminded us.

'Go and get the other one,' she said to Alan. 'He's called Rusty.'

Alan went into Grandpa's room.

'There's a good little dog,' he said as he got down on his knees beside the bed. 'Here, Rusty. C'mon, come out of there.'

He came back into the dining room after a few minutes.

'He won't come out from under the bed,' he said, 'all I can see are his eyes.'

'He's still a bit frightened,' said Aunt Olive. 'Dolly found him abandoned down on the bog when he must have been only a few days old. There was no sign of the mother. Clancy, in the yard, thinks there's a touch of a fox about him.'

She went into the next room.

'There's a grand little dog now,' she said as she came back with the puppy in her arms.

Rusty bared his teeth.

'That's the fox in him,' she said.

She put him down on the hearth-rug.

'You can see how nervous he still is,' she said to Mamma, 'but he'll get used to the children after a while and, after that, he'll be fine.'

By now, Rusty had calmed down. Adopting a pose reminiscent of His Master's Voice, he looked into the flames of the fire. Then, with one ear cocked — the other with a nick in it that caused it to lop forward permanently — he turned around to examine us. He had a winning face, but that was his best feature by far as his coat — even though he was still only a puppy — was rough and straight and, in colour, vaguely red. In choosing the name Rusty, Aunt Olive had described him exactly. Handsome he was not and nothing about him indicated that he ever would be. Charm, as was immediately apparent, had also eluded him. However, as he looked at us, his eyes conveyed such an intelligence that, had it been possible, he might have been descended from Solomon.

Alan and I played with the two puppies all afternoon. We took them out to the lawn and raced with them through the daffodils; we brought them up on the hay and made them jump down — like trapeze artists — from one rick to another; we bathed them in the water-trough in the cow-shed; and we hoisted them up into the tree where we made them lie down and pretend to be asleep. Eventually, Aunt Olive came out and called us in and we carried the exhausted little animals into the kitchen.

'Which one do you prefer?' Aunt Olive said to me.

'This one,' I said, lifting Twig into my arms.

'And what about Rusty? He's nice too,' she said.

'He's very snappy,' I said.

I rubbed the cut on my wrist where he had nipped me.

'He won't snap when he gets to know you,' she said. 'Would you like to take him home with you?'

'You mean for good?' I said.

'If you like him.'

I rushed up the stairs to Mamma.

'Aunt Olive is giving me Rusty,' I said. 'Can we take him home in the car?'

'Aunt Olive is very foolish to bother herself getting you such a thing.'

'But she didn't get him: he was found on the bog,' I said.

'If you really want him and promise to feed him yourself, I suppose you can keep him,' she said.

I was so excited that I had no appetite for my meat-tea. I fidgeted with the food while all the while casting glances under the table in the hope of seeing Rusty and swinging my leg to and fro in order to attract his attention. I took a piece of meat from my plate and held it down beside my chair in order to entice him, but it was Twig who bounced up and licked the morsel from my fingers. By the time the meal was over, I had begun to understand — even though our relationship was at such a very early stage — that affection, even in moderate amounts, would never be something that I could expect from Rusty, and by the same token, any other demands which I might think of putting upon him would also have to be carefully rationed.

When it was time to go home, Aunt Olive brought out a dog-basket.

'He has got used to sleeping in this,' she said, 'so you had better take it with you.'

'Where will it go?' I asked.

'We'll find a spot for it out in the forge,' said Mamma.

'He's a bit young to sleep outside just yet,' said Aunt Olive. 'He likes the heat of the Rayburn.'

Mamma's mood darkened. Apart from the illicit visits which Elliott's and Edward's goats had, notoriously, paid to the bedrooms on the top floor, Mamma had never allowed pets inside; and even when Aunt Jane came to live with us, bringing Toby and Topsy with her, she was only permitted to do so on condition that her dogs would never be seen in the house. Aunt Olive's notion, therefore, that 'this Rusty', as Mamma was already calling him, would be allowed to sleep in a basket in the kitchen seemed, in the context, preposterous and rather than discuss it further Mamma ushered us all outside to the car.

'We'll see what's what when we get home,' she said.

'Remember, he likes a raw egg,' Aunt Olive said as she leaned in my window, 'with a few breadcrumbs on it ... and the top of the jug of milk. And I've been giving him a Bob Martin once a week.'

From his position on my knee in the back of the car, Rusty stared at her with a look of utter disdain and, as we set off down the avenue, he scarcely said 'good-bye'.

As was usual on our arrival home, Papa came out to greet us and when I opened the car door Rusty jumped out, lifted his leg against the steps where Papa was standing, and ran off through the darkness into the laurels.

'Olive has given Homan a little bit of a dog,' said Mamma.

'And look at him now, wetting all over the steps. What she was thinking of I don't know.'

'The child has always wanted a dog,' said Papa. 'He'll be all right when he settles in.'

'Where's the basket to go?' said Elliott.

He pulled down the lid of the boot and grinned. The idea of a dog sleeping in a basket, when there were natural beds of straw or wool in practically every shed in the yard, seemed absurd. By this stage Rusty had reappeared and, in a second, run up the steps and into the hall. Before anyone could catch him, he explored the sitting room, making himself quite at home.

'If he wets in there, he is going straight back to the Wood-of-O,' said Mamma.

By the time we caught up with him, he was in the kitchen.

'I'll just put that down there for a moment,' said Elliott.

He deposited the basket beside the turf-box.

'It'll have to go out to the forge,' said Mamma.

By then seated in front of the Aga, Rusty, with no sense of awe, looked up at Papa.

'It might be a bit cold for him out there,' said Papa. 'Perhaps, just for tonight, it would be all right for him to stay in here?'

'Here?' said Mamma. 'Am I to come down in the morning and find his hairs in everything? Never in my entire life have I had a dog in the kitchen.'

Rusty ignored her.

'We often have a weak lamb in here for a night or two and it does no harm,' said Papa. 'The dog would be safer here for tonight …'

He noticed Rusty staring at him.

'Or … maybe a couple of nights,' he said.

'Better give him a drink of water, Homan,' said Mamma. 'Put on the kettle and we'll make a cup of tea. I'm famished after the cold of the drive.'

With a yawn, Rusty followed me into the scullery to explore. He drank a saucer of water and then, making himself comfortable, tucked himself into the basket where Elliott had left it beside the turf-box.

The basket, and that particular corner of the kitchen, was to remain his home for as long as Mamma lived at Rathcormick.

'Never in my entire life have I had a dog in the kitchen'

9. Thrift and Toil

One year, Mamma won first prize for her bottled pears at Trim Show. This was nothing unusual as she won prizes every year for jams, soda-bread, cakes, butter, eggs, honey, broad beans, beetroot, sweet-pea, gladioli, and above all, dahlias. Whether they were of the pompom, cactus, or giant-double variety, Mamma's dahlias always excelled.

'Aren't they almost the size of dinner-plates?' she would say to Papa when she had selected the examples to send to the show.

What distinguishes Mamma's prize-winning bottled pears in the memory is the fact that the following year when she had also entered bottled pears, she never got round to bottling any at all, and rather than disappoint the organisers of the show (or waste the entry-fee she had already paid), she sent in the same bottle as previously. They won first prize again. After that she sent them to Mullingar where they also won, and then to shows further afield where their success continued, and it was only after they had gained a third annual first prize at Trim that she retired them. After such triumphs, I am sure we never had the heart to eat them.

It was Mamma who kept the garden at Rathcormick. It was

at the back of the house, facing south, and its extent was much the same as is shown on the earliest Ordnance Survey map, that of 1836. On that map the planting — formal parterres of hedging — is also clearly delineated, but by our time a century later, all of this had been swept away with the exception of three box hedges which were by now gigantic. One of these, at the end of the tennis court, we called 'The Mulberry Bush' because it was round and at children's parties we played a game called 'Here we go round the mulberry bush'. The other two hedges, rectangular in shape and rising in peaks to about thirty feet, are as long as twenty yards and about a quarter of that across. They flank a narrow path which, when I was a child, led to nothing more significant than a lichen-covered urn. In spite of annual raids by Alan and me, small birds — sparrows, chaffinches, and tits — nested in these hedges almost in flocks. This part of the garden did not concern Mamma unduly, although she insisted that only Quirke be entrusted with the task of clipping the hedges every year: it took him almost a month. Mamma's garden focused on the middle path and the borders, stretching from the tennis court up as far as the vegetables, which ran either side of it. Delphiniums, Canterbury bells, Russell lupines, antirrhinums, sweet William and a great deal else besides grew there copiously; dahlias were marshalled into larger plots; and purple clematis intertwined with floribunda roses clung to the rustic trellis which, when Mamma had her way, extended its course farther round the garden every year. Aged apple, plum, and damson trees, wilful in their habits when it came to bearing fruit, stalked the garden, like stags on a mountaintop, here and there.

Mamma had green fingers and could grow anything to perfection; in fact, that was her trouble. She always grew far too much and what she grew was always far too perfect. Because she was so very practical, so very organised, she liked her garden to be practical and organised as well: all weeds, even pretty ones, would be vehemently rooted out, all edges would be trimmed, paths would be swept, rose-petals which had tumbled to the ground were considered an eyesore, chrysanthemums which had not been staked, a disgrace. It was only what Mamma termed the 'impossibility' of the size of the garden at Rathcormick which prevented it from being as perfect as she would have wished, but it was on account of this that it had a particular charm and enchantment.

Mamma never employed a gardener as such. Some of the men from the farm would come and do the heavy work for her whenever she needed it. And then there was Tommy Murray.

A sparrow-sized man, Tommy believed himself to be over eighty and he had worked at Rathcormick for almost seventy years. Indeed, so long was his tenure that Papa, having discovered by a close perusal of the by-laws of the Royal Dublin Society that the Society had a long-service medal for agricultural labourers, had some years earlier taken Tommy into McElhinney's in Athboy, fitted him out with a new brown suit, and driven him up to Dublin to claim his medal. But notwithstanding such an accolade, Tommy was — as far as Mamma was concerned — far from being satisfactory as a gardener.

'That Tommy Murray has been eating the peas again,' she would say.

She would be eating her Sunday dinner, and shaking her head, she would push a succulent-looking pile of peas to the side of her plate.

'I can just smell his old pipe off them,' she would say.

Although the men who worked in the yard were not expressly forbidden to smoke, as all of them did, it was understood that they would never smoke in front of Papa or Mamma and that no evidence of their habit, such as cigarette butts or used matches, would ever be left about the yard. This convention was rigorously observed and when, on occasion,

Papa would come upon Malone, or any others smoking, the man would attempt to conceal the cigarette behind his back and Papa, in turn, would ignore it. Tommy Murray differed in that he smoked a pipe, and as the effort involved in lighting it was considerable, he rarely settled down for a smoke until he was absolutely confident that the Prefect had sallied down the avenue. In winter, he would repair to the forge where he had created a comfortable perch for himself out of a bundle of potato sacks near the bellows, and there he would puff away. In summer, the rows of peas in the garden provided a more natural camouflage, and it was on account of the amount of time that Tommy spent there smoking that they developed the very distinctive flavour which, if Mamma's taste-buds were to be trusted, not only penetrated the pods as the peas withstood rain, wind, and sun but even survived their subsequent ordeal of being boiled in salt and water.

As the annals of the yearly Royal Meath Agricultural Show at Trim would confirm, Mamma brought the same industry to many other aspects of life as she did to her garden. But whereas the garden — with the exception of the occasional surplus vegetables which she would sell — could be deemed her recreation, her other activities — although generally initiated in the interests of thrift — soon assumed a commercial aspect which went far beyond what today would be regarded as pin-money. While the sale of eggs, and butter which she made, formed the basis of her personal economy, she also kept bees, pigs, even cattle — she had her own land — and whenever a sickly new-born lamb would be brought into the kitchen to be revived by the heat of the range and the comfort of a bottle of milk, she would add that to her stock. Reminding Papa three or four months later when it was sold that 'that lamb would not have lived had I not got up in the night to feed it', she would claim her cheque. She always kept two suck-pigs, saying that she would fatten them on the leftovers from the dining room and kitchen as well as an occasional bucket of milk from the cow-house; but when their diet had to be supplemented — as it always did — by sacks of pig-meal from Newman's in Athboy, she ignored the cost that that represented when calculating her profits, as it was Papa who paid Newman's bill.

In her bee-keeping — she had about four hives in the shrubbery down the avenue and the bees took the honey from the heather in the bog on the Athboy road — she relied, as she did for other endeavours, on Mr Sheppard.

A carpenter by profession, Mr Sheppard was a painstaking and sensitive soul who had to be "understood", but as so relatively few people did, he often had time on his hands and Mamma — who understood him perfectly — took advantage of this by having him attend to her bee-hives as he was also an

After such triumphs, I am sure we never had the heart to eat them

apiarist. She herself would have made up the wooden sections — she got them from Rowan's — before Mr Sheppard arrived of an evening and after a cup of tea, essential before Mr Sheppard could contemplate any activity, he would retire to the waiting-room. He would emerge almost half-an-hour later wearing the most fantastic costume and clutching in his hand a small smoking bellows — like a saint in an altarpiece displaying his attribute. Donning the colossal Panama — it had a cascading powder-blue veil — which was the *pièce-de-résistance* of his outfit, he would stride down the avenue as though he were off to Ascot, to return an hour or so later, triumphant, with the trays of honey.

All of Mamma's enterprises paled into insignificance, however, compared to her industry when it came to hens. She regarded these as the basis of any sensible woman's personal exchequer and, if she were to be believed, in the absence of Papa ever giving her an allowance or indeed ever paying for anything, she funded everything out of her egg-money. Clothes for all of us, things for the house, plants, seeds, and shrubs for the garden, petrol for the Austin, the Aga which replaced the range, and a carpet for Kildalkey Church. When fridges first became generally available, she bought a small one which was called, inexplicably as far as I was concerned, a Hotpoint and that was soon followed by a Hoover washing-machine. Then, at the time of Grace Kelly's wedding, when Papa eventually consented to us having a television, it was Mamma's egg-money which paid for the elegant, walnut-shuttered cabinet which found a home in a corner of the sitting room. There it housed the permanent snow-storm that blighted the lives of Dixon of Dock Green and Gilbert Harding, Sylvia Peters and Russ Conway, and even metamorphosed the Black and White Minstrels into an unsatisfactory uniform grey. Eventually, with her egg-money, Mamma paid for the building of the new dining room, and the antique furniture that went into it, and ultimately she bought her own car: a blue Renault Dauphine, a model then unknown in County Meath, which the men in the yard called her 'jet' and which Smith's in Trim had to import specially. So ingrained indeed was Mamma's belief in the necessity of 'egg-money' that when Alice was getting married the only advice her mother deemed essential to pass on to her was: 'Always keep a few hens, you'll find you'll need the egg-money.'

But Mamma did not just keep a few hens, she had scores of them. She would order what were called day-old chicks by the dozen each spring from the Elmbank Hatcheries in Cavan — Leghorns, Light Sussex, and Rhode Island Reds were favoured breeds — and these mites would be despatched to her in cardboard boxes by public bus, not just one bus, but two. A morning bus would take them from Cavan to Dublin where, after a few hours wait in the bus station, they would be despatched on an afternoon bus to Ballivor. Although technically only a day-old, the chicks would have had a lifetime of experience behind them by the time they arrived at Rathcormick, not that that meant their future was by any means assured. They would be lodged in a wooden house which stood on stilts up in the back paddock and although Mamma would have attempted to ensure that it was secure, safe, and hygienic (the inside walls would have been whitewashed with lime) before the arrival of the day-olds, a fox always remained a very real threat. The netting wire which was tacked over the windows and the new bolts and locks which fastened the door could rarely be relied upon to provide an adequate defence. But it was within the house itself that the greatest hazard lay, in the form of the galvanised-tin pagoda — heated by means of a paraffin lamp, insulated by miniature felt curtains around the inside, and euphemistically called an incubator — that was the day-olds' domain. Once there, their lives depended on the uncertain whim of the paraffin lamp, and the possibilities of death by suffocation, exposure to the cold or, the worst eventuality of all, being burned to death as part of a general conflagration which could destroy the entire hen-house, were very real. At one time or another all of these tragedies befell Mamma's day-olds and the prospect of such a catastrophe was always much greater than their likelihood of being treated as *hors d'oeuvres* by a hungry fox.

As the day-olds matured and their gender became apparent, the pullets would be segregated from the cockerels and the diet of the two differentiated. While it was oats, water, and greens for the pullets, huge saucepans of specially grown potatoes were cooked in the Aga for the cockerels: mashed up with separated milk, and an additional nutrient called Uveca which looked like cornflakes, this cocktail of carbohydrates was served up to them twice a day. By the time of Trim Show in the first week of September, the best of them — like Mamma's pears — were ready to be exhibited and thereafter, while the pullets were consigned to the hen-house and the life of egg-laying that was vital to Mamma's balance-sheet, the cockerels would be slaughtered — weekly, two by two — and would find their way, in a procession that lasted throughout the winter months, to the dining room table.

When Mamma read in *The Farmer's Journal* about a new method of more intensive egg production, her interest was aroused. It was called "deep-litter" and although it seemed quite extraordinary — intensive farming of any kind was still fairly unknown — it involved keeping hens in a hen-house without ever letting them out and regulating their lives largely by means of an electric light. By illuminating the hen-house for very long hours each day, the hens had longer days in which to lay, and in their resulting confusion were persuaded to produce two eggs (or more) a day instead of the usual one. Another feature of deep-litter — and this seemed a complete contradiction — was that although the hens were to be kept in the hen-house all the time, many more hens than would be usual in such a space might be accommodated. While this procedure would seem the norm for much of today's farming, it was a complete novelty forty or more years ago when electricity, which makes it possible, became available in rural Ireland for the first time.

Without mentioning her intentions to Papa, Mamma wisely realised that in order to introduce deep-litter at Rathcormick she should seek some technical advice, and someone called a poultry-instructress, an employee of the Department of Agriculture in Drogheda, was sent for with strict instructions to call only on a Wednesday (when Papa was in Dublin) or on a Saturday afternoon (when he was in his office in Trim). One afternoon a few weeks later, a smart, black Morris Minor came up the avenue and out stepped an attractive young woman in her late twenties. She was quite unlike anyone who ever came to see Papa. Alan and I were in the front yard and, being forbidden to ever rush out to the gravel to stare at guests, we hid in the Green Wood — the trees that concealed the yard from the gravel — and watched her ring the front-door bell.

'It's the poultry-structress,' whispered Alan.

'The what?' I said.

'You know,' he said signalling me to be quiet as Molly opened the door.

In time, Mamma came out the back door with the visitor.

'This is Miss McMahon,' she said when she came upon Alan and me. 'What do you say?'

'How do you do,' we said.

Miss McMahon spent most of the afternoon inspecting the front yard and then the range of stone sheds — the middle yard — which stretched up towards the back paddock where the new wooden hen-house that Mamma had bought only two years previously stood.

Without bothering to go inside and, indeed, in hardly glancing at it at all, Miss McMahon dismissed it without a thought.

'Much too small,' she said.

Mamma looked crestfallen.

When they returned to the front yard, they revisited the old engine-house. It was packed with parts of old machinery, broken-down wooden troughs, oil drums, even huge packs of wool that had somehow got left behind after the sheep-shearing a few years previously.

'This is the best,' said Miss McMahon.

'I wasn't so keen to have them so near the house,' said Mamma.

'You could have eighty in here without any trouble.'

'That number? How many did you say? Eighty? I was thinking of starting off just with the ones I have and then gradually building it up.'

'Doesn't work. You need numbers, otherwise it's not economical.'

'It'll be fairly difficult to clean this place out regularly when the floor is so uneven,' said Mamma.

Mamma's day-olds
Their lives depended on the uncertain whim of a paraffin lamp

'You only need to do that once a year,' said Miss McMahon. 'That's the beauty of deep-litter.'

Mamma was horrified.

It was some time before any obvious progress was made towards the introduction of deep-litter. The summer came and all that entailed: sheep-shearing, haymaking, the harvest, threshing; in the meantime the hens continued their carefree, outdoor existence unaware that by Christmas — if Mamma's plans materialised (and she had yet to broach the subject with Papa) — they would be "deep-litter hens", leading a "deep-litter life", and laying "deep-litter eggs". Mamma had had time to consider the project over these months, and she had come to the conclusion that the plans as outlined by the poultry instructress were perhaps not as extravagant as they had at first seemed. Once the shed was fixed up it would, after all, be as easy to manage eighty hens as twenty. As regards the increased yield that would ensue, she had written to the Monument Creameries in Dublin, who replied that they would be happy to give her a contract on condition that she could guarantee a minimum of fifty-dozen eggs a week.

One evening when Papa had come home earlier than usual, and settled down to his tea in the breakfast room, Mamma made a spur-of-the-moment decision that now was the time to seek approval for her plans. Without looking at him, she said:

'Do you ever think of doing anything with the old engine-house?'

'That place hasn't been used in years,' he said.

Momentarily confounded by the fact that his statement amounted to little more than a confirmation of what she herself had just said, Mamma decided to try a more direct approach.

'What about putting a few hens in there?'

'Hens? In the front yard? Messing up all over the place?'

At this, Mamma decided that she would have to be more resolute.

'Will you have another rissole?' she said.

She passed him the dish.

'I was looking at the house the other day and I felt it would be quite a good place for them.'

'Gracious, woman!' he said. 'What's wrong with the hen-house up in the back paddock? You only got that two or three years ago.'

Although realising that his question was entirely reasonable, Mamma had no intention of answering it.

'I'm thinking of going into deep-litter,' she said, 'which means that the hens would not be around the front yard as they would be shut up all the time.'

'Deep-litter? New-fangled nonsense. Just an invitation to fowl-pest, everyone knows that. How did you think of such a thing?'

'I always think it's an awful long trek all the way up to the paddock just to get an egg,' said Miss Shannon, with whom Mamma had already discussed her plans.

The interjection gave Mamma a moment to collect her thoughts and come to the conclusion that, in the circumstances, confidence rather than caution would now be best.

'I've had the poultry instructress here and she says that the old engine-house is the best place for deep-litter.'

She got up from the table and went over and drew the curtain slightly to prevent the glare of the sun.

'The turf-house and forge beside it already have electric light and it would be an easy matter to carry the wiring through. The water could be brought in at the back from the cow-house, and if the double doors are fixed up, it would make cleaning out the house very easy.'

'Do you realise, my dear, that you would have to put about forty hens in there to make deep-litter work?'

'Eighty,' said Mamma.

'What?'

'Eighty. The poultry instructress says the house would take eighty hens.'

'What on earth are you going to do with eighty hens? How would you feed that number? And the expense? Have you thought of where you'll sell the eggs? Ollie Bird certainly won't want them.'

'The Monument Creameries will give me a contract for fifty-dozen eggs a week,' said Mamma. 'And with eggs at three shillings a dozen, I'll have no difficulty coping with the costs.'

This statement put the matter on quite a different footing and Dada realised that Mamma's plans were already very far advanced.

'I wouldn't take any advice from that instructress one,' he said. 'She is probably some Dublin yoke who learned everything out of a book. It's likely the only poultry she ever saw were the ducks in Stephen's Green.'

There the matter rested. Papa believed — or at least hoped — that he had scotched the plan; Mamma's interpretation of their conversation was that he had given his approval for her to proceed.

'When Carr comes in with the milk tonight, would you say to him that I want a word with him,' she said to Molly the following morning.

That evening, when Molly heard the clanking of the milk buckets in the dairy, she went down. Carr was pouring the warm milk into the hopper on top of the separator and as he adjusted the two spouts — the small one for the cream, the larger for the separated milk — Molly said, 'The Mistress wants to see you.'

'There you are, Carr,' said Mamma when he came to the scullery door. 'Isn't it a lovely evening?'

'The swallows above in the big shed think so too,' said Carr. 'It'll be another grand day tomorrow, you'd know by the swooping of them.'

'Carr, the Master was wondering if, when you next get a wet day — although that looks unlikely for the moment — you might set the men to clean out the old engine-house.'

'The old engine-house?'

'Yes. I was thinking of putting a few hens in there.'

'Hens?'

'On deep-litter.'

'Deep-lither?'

On the day that Mamma had made her own initial inspection of all the sheds in the yard with a view to more intensive poultry-keeping, Carr had observed her progress; and the afternoon of the poultry-instructress's visit, on the pretence of filling a pothole, he had positioned himself on the avenue at the time of the visitor's departure. While not actually barring her way as she went out the front gate, he doffed his cap to her in such an elaborate manner that she stopped her car in the belief — quite justified as it happened — that he wanted to speak to her. Inquiring solicitously if she knew her way back to Athboy, it was no trouble at all for him to discover the purpose of her visit and the outcome of her lengthy deliberations with Mamma.

It came as no surprise at all to him, therefore, when Mamma asked for the engine-house to be cleared out; in fact he wondered why the instruction had not been issued months ago. In spite of that, he still affected an air of disbelief.

'Is it everything you'll be wanting out of the place?' he said.

'Everything,' said Mamma.

The fine weather continued for the next few weeks so that there was no chance for the men to have a wet day clearing out the engine-house. Replying to an advertisement in *The Farmer's Journal*, Mamma ordered sixty pullets — "ready layers" they were called — which together with the twenty hens she already had would make up the desired quota. The ready-layers were to be delivered towards the end of October which meant the deep-litter house (as the old engine-house had now become) had to be ready by that date, but when nothing had been done by the last week of September, after Papa went away for a few days to the fair at Swinford, she went out to the yard and put the men to work.

'Come out till I show you the hen-house,' she said to Papa when he returned.

She took him out to the yard. Drawing back the new bolt, she opened the door.

'Isn't it a grand use for the shed?' she said. 'Would you recognise it?'

'It's certainly a great improvement,' he said.

He knew he had been defeated but he also knew — from his experience of Mamma and her projects — that the deep-litter would be a success.

And so it was.

'We have deep-litter,' Alan and I boasted at Trim School when the Tyrrells announced that their father was going into Jerseys; and for years thereafter on Papa's weekly Wednesday visits to Dublin, space was made in the Prefect for the fifty-dozen eggs — and often more — that amply fulfilled Mamma's contract with the Monument Creameries.

10. Two Sisters

Around the time I was first able to read *The Irish Times*, one of the features which attracted my attention was a series of advertisements which appeared in the Saturday edition. There would be a photograph of some attractive (if slightly old-fashioned) young woman or other, and an accompanying text which informed the reader of her identity, appearance, and lifestyle. On one Saturday, "The Hon Judith Browne … tall, fair, blue-eyed … fond of country life and especially interested in riding and tennis …" might gaze from the page, followed the next weekend by "Miss Pamela O'Mahony (daughter of The O'Mahony of Kerry) … tall, dark, and brown-eyed … her many hobbies include fishing, tennis, and — her favourite — hunting …"

The young ladies who appeared in this way were all flowers of the Irish aristocracy, but as their species was in decline, those who survived to adorn *The Irish Times* were quite rare blooms and in the event the advertisements proved disappointingly short-lived. The point of them was explained by a quotation: 'I enjoy yachting, yet my skin never suffers from harsh winds or roughness,' one girl might boast while another — described as "completely outdoor in outlook" — would be more specific: 'I believe every face needs two creams,' she would warn.

114

This was the clue that the girls' "Passport to Beauty" was Pond's.

Although my sister, Alice, was about as far removed from the world these girls inhabited as it would be possible to imagine, she shared with them a dependence on Pond's and her dressing-table — no more, presumably, than Miss Browne's or Miss O'Mahony's — was never complete without a pair of matching jars. Putting a speck of white from one of these on my cheek, Alice told me it was 'Cold Cream'.

'The other one is Vanishing Cream,' she said.

Whenever Alice — who was almost twenty years my senior — was at home, she shared a bedroom with Rosina. This was the room above the kitchen which had been built especially to accommodate Old Elliott's sister, whom we called Aunt Jane, when she came to live with us. Having spent all her money on the Potterton Rest Fields for Horses in Rathfarnham, Aunt Jane

Two sisters

115

wanted to die in the home where she was born, Rathcormick, and in this she succeeded. When she passed away, her gloomy ambition satisfied, Rosina moved into the room and it was there that she, ultimately, died as well. Although associated with death in this way, the room was in fact the most cheerful bedroom in the house as it had a large window facing south onto the garden and another, looking out over the roofs of the yard, that caught the evening sun. There was a fireplace in the room where a fire would be lit during winter mornings when Rosina was in bed; but at those times of year when it was very cold, it was kept alight day and night. This was in spite of the hazard of jackdaws — refugees from the Green Wood — nesting in the flue and it was many a time that the chimney went on fire. Apart from Rosina's bed, the room also contained a double bed, a wardrobe, a chest of drawers, and, beneath a light suspended from the ceiling in one corner, a dressing-table. Made of walnut and as a result not a match for the other furniture in the room, it had a tall swinging mirror, drawers and compartments of varying sizes, and surfaces — like platforms — at several different levels.

Sometimes as a special treat when Alice was at home, I would also be allowed to sleep in this room, and next to the occasions when Papa was away and I was allowed to sleep with Mamma, sharing a bedroom — and sometimes a bed — with my big sister was the most comforting experience in the world. I would have been in bed for many hours before she would come upstairs and I would be awoken — as if to a different world — when, already in her dressing-gown, she would switch on the light, approach the dressing-table, and begin a ritual which transfixed me night after night as I peered over the bedcovers while pretending to be asleep. As an overture to the pageant which followed, Alice would take up her hairbrush. This was an implement with which I was familiar as Alan — having discovered how hard the bristles really were —

frequently used it on me as an instrument of torture. But Alice seemed to revel in its hardness as she carded, with vigour and determination, one tress after another. From a large, flowered bag she would extract further appliances: spools like honeycombs which, by means of her well-teased strands, she would deftly tie to her head and then grip in place with metal clips. Finally, she would stretch a net, robust enough to catch a shoal of mackerel, and lower it down over her head with all the ceremony of an archbishop donning his mitre. Now, sitting back on her stool for the first time, she would peer into the mirror and at that moment I too would catch a glimpse of her reflection; what I saw was no longer Alice but a creature who, like the bats that sometimes came into my own bedroom on the top floor, at once both fascinated and frightened me.

It was at this stage that she would reach for her Pond's. Hesitating momentarily at the dangerous choice between "Cold" and "Vanishing", she would thoughtfully make her selection, and with a finger-load which I was always certain must be "Vanishing", dab the blobs of cream on to her face: a blob on the forehead, a blob on the chin, and a blob on either cheek. Then, like Aladdin, she would rub and rub, only pausing occasionally to check in the mirror — as I imagined — for signs of her impending disintegration; but, night after night, the ritual ended with Alice still intact. When she eventually climbed into bed, she would read for half-an-hour, her knotted head resting uncomfortably on the pillow, and her face — its "Passport to Beauty" still aglow — directed resolutely at the ceiling.

For years (or so it seemed) I could never understand why Alice so desperately wanted to vanish, but as I had become privy to the riddle by the deceitful means of spying, I could never, ever, ask.

I have no idea how the years have treated those outdoor girls whose lives on the hunting-field, the high seas, or even the tennis court was so indispensably abetted by Pond's, but my sister Alice — now approaching her golden years — has to this day a complexion that is so clear it seems anchored in time. But whether it is the product of "Vanishing" or "Cold" — or, for that matter, Pond's at all — is a secret that only Alice herself may know.

*

There is some tragedy in most families; but when the tragedy is embodied in as beautiful a being as was my sister, Rosina, it becomes in a way acceptable without losing any of its poignancy. When she was born, almost four years after Edward and some twelve years before me, she was apparently healthy. Fair skinned, even more so than Edward, she was less sturdy than Alice had been as a baby but, unlike Elliott, she had no trouble feeding and thrived from the moment of her birth. She was christened Eileen (after Mamma), Anne (after Gran and Auntie Frank), and Rosina (after our great-grandmother, Rosina Rentzsch and, in the following generation, Papa's sister Isa Rosina). As these things sometimes happen, it became apparent as Rosina matured that she had many character traits in common with Aunt Isa: gentleness, kindness, and a simplicity that came from being entirely uncomplaining and selfless.

There are formal photographs of her with David (who was born after her) when she must have been about six years old. She has long, blond plaits and an alert expression and it is only upon close examination of the photo that it becomes possible to discern that she is slightly different, her head being larger than it should be.

In fact, Rosina was as much as three or four years old before it became obvious that she was handicapped. In certain ways she was highly intelligent but, in spite of that, some relatively simple activities defeated her and she seemed incapable of concentration. Nor did she have the energy of a child of her age. After visits to specialists, it was diagnosed — and these are the words that were always used — that 'she had been born with a bad heart.' Not a hole in the heart, not a weak heart, but a bad heart and there was nothing that could be done: she would be delicate for life.

Delicate is how she remained as she edged through her first decade and towards her teens and then, when she was about twelve, her condition escalated and she became seriously ill. Hospitalised in the Adelaide for months, there was no surgery or treatment available as a remedy, much less a cure, only drugs which, while eventually ensuring her survival, took their toll on her body. Mamma, and even more so, Papa — who lived for her, and she, as time was to prove, for him — were distraught and, in the absence of any other therapy, they resorted to what they trusted most: prayer.

'It was prayer which pulled her through,' Mamma always said and several years later, when Papa wanted to have Rosina confirmed, they arranged for a private confirmation service in the Magdalen Church which is where they had prayed, day after day, week after week, during the difficult hours of her most desperate suffering.

By the time I was a child, Rosina's condition had stabilised and she had a routine. She always had her breakfast in bed and when the post — which included all Papa's office mail — arrived, it was brought up to her. After her breakfast she opened the letters according to a system which Papa had taught her. Carefully and without haste, she slit each envelope with a paperknife, unfolded the contents and laid them in a basket, peered into the empty envelope — 'Make sure there are no cheques left behind,' Papa warned her — and then placed the envelopes in another basket. Before leaving for the day, Papa always came up to see her, sat on her bed, and talked to her about the contents of the letters as though Rosina had been able to read them herself. But Rosina, in spite of the many efforts that were made to teach her, was not able to read them, and never would be. Although clever in so many ways and capable of understanding a great deal, she was never able to master any of the Three Rs — reading, 'riting, and 'rithmatic — with which most children at that time began their education. She got up at about midday, and selected with care the clothes she would wear for the day as well as her jewellery; she had boxes of necklaces, bangles, and brooches which she kept most

Hesitating at the dangerous choice between 'Vanishing' and 'Cold'

meticulously in the drawers of her dressing-table along with other treasures — embroidered handkerchiefs, photographs in frames, greeting-cards, little pictures, and other trinkets which people over the years had given her.

She always laid the table for dinner: Mamma had taught her how to do that and, although she could not count, she did it in her own way according to a plan and rarely misplaced or overlooked anything. She had other routines as well but she was incapable of the energy that would have been required to help Mamma in the garden or even to have arranged flowers in the house. If there was any special activity or visit planned, Rosina was always considered first and a decision was made as to whether she would be up to the occasion or not. For a time, Ada Pigott came every other afternoon from Athboy and spent an hour or more attempting to teach her to read, write, and memorise Scripture. Alan and I, although at school all day by this stage, had to sit in on these lessons too and later, when a full-time companion-tutor came to live at Rathcormick, we had to profit from her tutorials as well.

On account of the fact that Alan and I never knew Rosina to be any different to the way she was, we accepted her as part of our lives and rarely gave it a moment's thought that she was not the same as other people's sisters.

'Our sister has a bad heart,' we would say, and that was that. On occasion we teased her.

'You're going to marry Tommy Gibson, we know it,' we said. But she was capable of teasing in return.

She knew that Alan's birthday was the same day as Mamma's and that mine was exactly a week before her own, and Papa always took her shopping for presents for us both. Nevertheless, she would pretend to us that she had quite forgotten and no matter how many leading questions Alan or I put to her in the week beforehand, by playing dumb she would convince us that she had not remembered the dates. She dissembled in the same way at Christmas:

'I'm just going to give you both a sod of turf, and that's that,' she would say to us over and over again and in a manner that was sufficiently persuasive for us both to believe her. In actual fact, she always decided of her own accord — and well in advance — what presents she wanted to get for every member of the family and, by keeping her ideas a secret shared only with Papa, she savoured the surprise when her gifts were opened.

By her mid-teens, when she had sufficiently recovered from the years when medicines of one sort or another were her daily diet, her appearance improved and her intrinsic prettiness emerged. She slimmed down and, over months of visits to Mr Morehead in Tullamore, which were as painful for Mamma as for Rosina herself, she had dentures fitted to replace the teeth she had lost through years of drug-induced decay. She had her hair permed; and, as her health improved, a complexion that was as translucent as a pitcher of buttermilk replaced the puffiness which in earlier years had disguised her natural skin. I remember her as a grown-up but when, not long ago, I saw a cinefilm of Alice's wedding and there was Rosina, I found myself looking at a beautiful young girl, her expression one of tenderness and hope.

By being always the focus of solicitude and concern, Rosina deflected attention away from me, the Benjamin of the family. As a result, I was never spoiled and I have always been grateful for that. But it is my memory of Rosina's general contentment with her lot — against all odds — that I treasure most.

11. 'One of our Own'

'That bloke would sicken you, going on about cows out on the pasture,' Papa exploded one day.

We were driving over to Craddenstown and tea with Uncle Jim.

'Can't he see that they are cattle?'

'I don't suppose the poor fellow has ever seen bullocks much before,' said Mamma. 'I mean, he was brought up in a town.'

'He told me, when I interviewed him, that he came from Hampshire,' said Papa.

'Yes, but a town in Hampshire. He talks about Lyme Regis.'

'I've already told him that you don't say cows except when they are cows and that the fields are fields and not pastures.'

'What did he say?' said Mamma. 'Do you think he understood?'

'He came to me with the advertisements for the land lettings in next week's *Meath Chronicle* and asked me if I wanted him to change the word pasture to field. I knew it wouldn't be at all a good idea to take on someone English. I never had difficulty like this with Miss Shannon and even Miss Cochrane, although she came from Dublin, knew not to say cows.'

'It's very difficult for town-people to learn the difference between cows and cattle and they never have a clue when it comes to bullocks and heifers. It's easy for us because we were brought up with it. He'll learn the difference in a while or so and I think if you explain to him that the lettings are for pasture land while the Lawn, for example, is a field, he'll get the hang of it after a while.'

'The same problem with him over setting the land,' said Papa.

Jerking forward in the seat, he put both his hands on the dashboard.

'Mind this bend,' he said. He stiffened and drew in his breath. 'If you don't soon slow down, you'll have us all in the ditch.'

Mamma changed into second gear.

'Setting what land?' she said.

'Any land. He doesn't understand whether it's letting or setting. That's what he told me.'

'Maybe I confused him by mentioning the ducks,' said Mamma.

'Ducks?' said Papa. 'What have ducks got to do with it?'

'I told him I got a setting of duck-eggs every year from Mrs Gasteen,' said Mamma. 'He had been out looking at the pullets, he called them hens.'

Mamma and Papa were talking about Mr Hannigan. When he first arrived at Rathcormick to take up the post of Papa's secretary, he said his name was O'Hannigan; but Mamma told him that 'we'd never manage that mouthful' and said she hoped he would not mind if we called him Hannigan. In the event, Mr Hannigan never learned the difference between cows and cattle, and when he returned to Hampshire, having only stayed a very short time, he was equally oblivious as to how a field was distinguished from a pasture. Pullets, hens, and cocks (which he referred to as roosters) looked one and the same to him, and although he might be excused for not recognising a hogget when he looked at the sheep out in Tubber, his persistent pronunciation of the female of the species as a 'you' — which was, after all, quite correct — instead of a 'yo' — which is what we called it — irritated Papa so much that he dismissed him abruptly one morning by telling him to catch the mail-boat as soon as he had packed his bags.

Mr Hannigan was one of a series of secretaries — each one more disastrous than the preceding — employed by Papa in the interim between the departure of Miss Shannon (a gem) and the arrival of Mr Denning (another gem). These secretaries always lived with us, occupying the small bedroom between the nursery (by then also a bedroom) and the boys' room on the top floor. They took all their meals with us, were required to play tennis, croquet, whist or Monopoly (above all, Monopoly) with us and, in general, were counted upon to become part of the family. These prerequisites, however, did not allow them scope for any familiarity: Papa's secretaries were always called solely by their surnames — prefaced by Miss or Mr — and they in turn, like the men in the yard or the maids in the kitchen, were expected to refer to Papa and Mamma only as the Master and the Mistress. Once they were installed at Rathcormick, they had little opportunity for escape — it would have been unheard of then for someone in such a position to have their own car — so it was essential that they would find the notion of an isolated life in the country among a family of boys and an invalid sister reasonably attractive. They were not permitted to smoke and, if they met all the other requirements, it was unlikely that they would have ever even heard of alcohol.

With such unusual criteria, it followed that it was not always easy for Papa to find secretaries and by the same token those who accepted such extraordinary conditions were, almost by definition, in some way extraordinary themselves. The advertisement for the post in *The Irish Times*, calling for a "lady office-general, live-in", would specify that it was a 'country position'. It would also declare: "C of I preferred". This reference to religion — to the Protestant Church of Ireland — was not intended as a ban on Catholic candidates but as a signal which, when read in conjunction with the words "live-in", would make plain what it was that lay in store for the successful applicant.

At this time in Ireland, most Protestants and Catholics observed their religion. They went to church every Sunday and most practised their respective faiths in the home as well. While we would say grace before and after meals, we did not bless ourselves as Catholics did; and while we often had communal prayers at home, we did not observe the angelus by stopping for silent prayer twice a day on hearing a chapel bell. Catholics, we thought, took the name of the Lord in vain. 'Holy God!' they would say with equanimity, and nor did they keep holy the sabbath day. Protestants observed it as a day of rest which meant that even playing tennis — much less cards or organised team sports — was out of the question, whereas Catholics reserved Sundays almost exclusively for sport. They played Gaelic football and hurling (which Protestants never did) and on Sunday nights, in what seemed like a terrible sin to us, they went to dances.

On a secular level, thrift, or Protestant meanness, was endemic to our way of life — from using up leftovers in the kitchen to "turning" bed sheets and worn collars on shirts — while waste and extravagance, synonymous in our view with a Catholic way of life, were deplored by us. There are countless other examples of how Catholics and Protestants behaved and thought differently and, as a result, a degree of segregation, accepted by most without any fundamental sectarian antagonism, became an inevitable social convention. We referred to another Protestant as 'one of our own' and Catholics, no doubt, had a similar euphemism for one of theirs. Protestants, as the expression went, 'dug with one foot';

Catholics, very decidedly, with the other. In the context of these customs, these restrictions, it is extremely unlikely that any Catholic would have been comfortable living among us at Rathcormick and it was for that reason — as much as our own possible discomfort in being confronted by Catholicism at such close quarters — that Papa sought, and always found, a Protestant secretary.

In spite of its unusual stipulations, the advertisement always attracted a wealth of initial enquiries, but when these applications were examined in detail and an attempt was made to make a list of candidates who would be called for interview, the number of possibilities would have been very greatly reduced.

'I couldn't stand anyone with a Cork accent around all the time,' Mamma might say when she saw the postmark on a particular envelope, and she would hardly bother to read the application that was enclosed. If a letter was untidy, it too would be dismissed.

'Look at the slovenly way she has written this: that one would be dirty in the house', was the excuse.

Anyone above the age of thirty was 'likely to be set in their ways' and they too would automatically be rejected; while an aspirant who enclosed a photograph of herself (as some occasionally did) was taken to be more interested in the "live-in" aspect of the position than the "office-general" part and that would be the end of that candidacy.

There had in the past been legendary occupants of the post. Miss Cochrane had been one; she could beat any of the boys on the tennis court and was unrivalled when it came to Monopoly. Then we had all loved Miss Shannon and were heart-broken when she left to marry Mr Dixon. In the event, it was the necessity of filling her loss and the irritating discovery that the available reserves of Irish Protestant girls had almost been depleted which led to the scope of the search being widened to include men as well as candidates from England. That critical decision paved the way for the colourful pageant of characters, including Mr Hannigan, which passed through Rathcormick before Mr Denning (who came from Longford) eventually became part of our lives and our greatest favourite of all.

'I'm Joe Glendenning,' he said, holding out his hand as he came up the front steps the summer evening that he arrived.

'That's an awful mouthful,' said Mamma. 'I'm sure you wouldn't mind if we called you Mr Denning.'

'Not in the least,' he said.

He was about twenty at the time and, as far as his appearance was concerned, the phrase 'tall, dark, and handsome' might have been coined specifically to describe it. But it was not just on that account that Mamma and indeed all of us instantly liked him: charming, obliging, adaptable, and considerate, he fitted in perfectly with our way of life. Even Papa, after a few years, came to trust him and rely upon him. So did Elliott but that may well have been because Mr Denning, although good at tennis, had the wisdom not to beat Elliott on the court with any degree of consistency. When, in time, Mr Denning resigned and left Rathcormick, we all missed him more than we could say as we thought of him as a brother and Mamma regarded him as a son.

Miss Pringle was the only exception ever to the general rule that secretaries should be under thirty; but, far from being set in her ways, she was blithely open to any new experience and, according to herself, loved what she called 'adventure'.

'I've always kept myself modern,' she said the afternoon she arrived, after Papa expressed astonishment that she had cycled all the way from Woking.

Removing her crash helmet, she propped her moped against the stone beehive outside the drawing room window. She must have been in her fifties, if not actually older, although her demeanour and conversation hinted at a rigorous deter-mination to seem girlish.

'It's so wild and green, just as I expected,' she said.

She looked down towards the Lawn and beyond it the Round O. Several chestnut trees and one or two beech, none of them more than fifteen years old, their youthful status confirmed by the palings which surrounded them as protection from the cattle, were dotted here and there among the older trees. The hedge, which divided the Lawn from Coran, had been newly coppiced and the gates, which led from one field to another, had recently been painted. Wildness, it was quite apparent, was not tolerated on this well-husbanded acreage and as for green, every blade of grass was tobacco-brown; it had been the hottest July on record with temperatures of over 70° for most of the month and an all-time high of 79° recorded in Mullingar on the 15th.

'The journey from the mainland was not as treacherous as I had supposed,' she said. 'Although the roads on the island can be very bad in parts, as I am sure you know.'

It was minutes before it dawned on Mamma and Papa that she was talking about Ireland.

'Quite precipitous in fact,' she said.

She let her eyes wander over the miles and miles of flat countryside which stretched out as far as one could see.

'The peasant children in the hedges by the wayside were quite startled by the noise of my Rudge,' she said.

Then she turned to Papa.

'But tell me, Mr Potterton, when did you first settle here?'

'Almost three hundred years ago,' he said.

He was oblivious to the fact that had he said 'three years ago', Miss Pringle would still have thought him a pioneer.

'Aha! There's an intrepid streak there I can see,' she said.

'Well no,' said Papa.

Even in his early years at Rathcormick, he had never exactly thought of his existence as rolling back frontiers.

'We came over with Cromwell.'

Unlike her conversation, Miss Pringle's dress and appearance, which was untidy in the extreme, made only a modest concession to modernity. She had greying hair which may once have been permed and she wore, almost as a uniform, a cardigan and blouse, a pleated skirt which fanned out as she moved, and thick knitted stockings.

'Brown is my colour,' she would boast in reference to this outfit. 'I've always known that, ever since I was a young girl. People often compliment me on it.'

During the day she wore flat, rubber-soled, lace-up shoes which made a noise on the oil-cloth that drove Mamma to distraction, but in the evenings when she joined us in the sitting room after tea, she changed into carpet-slippers. Rather incongruously, she also gave herself a dash of glamour at this time of day by the application of a scarlet lipstick on the approximate area of her mouth. Although far from obese, Miss Pringle was certainly not slim and, being parsimonious in her deployment of the corset, her hips wobbled when she moved while her bosoms seemed to have the same sort of fulsome looseness. Alan and I thought of her as a sort of coffee-blancmange and it did not take long for us to realise that we cared for her company as little as we liked the taste of the pudding she resembled. Our aversion may have had something to do with the very distinctive smell which, even after a day spent 'adventuring' on her moped over the roads of County Meath, was always with her. Mamma never referred to this in front of us but her announcement every Sunday evening that 'Mrs Rispin will be here in the morning to do the wash if you have anything, Miss Pringle', indicated that she was well aware of it; but when Miss Pringle replied — as she always did — that she 'had nothing that she couldn't manage herself', Mamma barely troubled to disguise her disgust.

Like any great explorer arriving on foreign soil — for that was how she saw herself — Miss Pringle immediately set out to civilise the natives.

'Now we'll dispense with that,' she said as she dismantled the new Remington dictaphone that Papa had bought for the use of her predecessor, 'it's Pitman's from now on. Do you know T E?' — by now she had become overbearingly familiar — 'Had there been no Pitman's, I believe there would have been no Empire.'

'It's not always easy for me to know when I can fit in dictation,' said Papa. 'When I have the dictaphone, it means I can do letters when I see the chance.'

'But it's the easiest thing in the world T E ...' said Miss Pringle, 'I'll come to you for shorthand first thing. Even when you are shaving.'

Papa was stunned by the suggestion.

One day when Miss Pringle returned from an excursion, she dipped into her bag — a large padded reticule made from Rexine — and drew out two pencils.

'Presents for a pair of dear little boys,' she said.

As the pencils had the novelty of each being red one end and blue the other, Alan and I — although wary at being called dear little boys by her — were happy enough to accept them but it was not long before we discovered what a mistake we had made. Returning from the office with a disused ledger-book, Miss Pringle handed us a few pages each and instructed us to kneel down on the floor.

'Now, we're going to draw a Union Jack,' she said.

Her voice wavered with emotion as she said it, and then like a soldier on the parade ground, she pulled herself up as though standing to attention and, as she stared at us to observe our reaction, it was obvious that pride eked from her every pore. But in expecting us to feel the same as she did at her mention of the Union Jack, Miss Pringle had made a miscalculation. The fact of the matter was that the flag meant nothing at all to us and the prospect of sitting down to draw it was about as enticing as if she herself had offered to pose in the nude.

Being a Protestant in Ireland was (and is) often thought of, by some Protestants themselves and by many Catholics, as synonymous with being English. But we, and other similar Protestants, never for a moment thought of ourselves as English. By the same token, it is quite common for all Protestants to be branded as Anglo-Irish. But we were almost as different to the true Anglo-Irish as we were to Catholics. When Brendan Behan defined an Anglo-Irishman (or woman) as a 'Protestant on a horse', it was evident that he recognised that there were some Protestants without horses — poor Protestants (of which there were many) and middle-class Protestants like our family.

The essential difference may have been that the Anglo-Irish owned their land whereas we were tenants in perpetuity. But that distinction would not necessarily account for the variations in customs, dress, accents, and interests, that existed between the two. Unlike the Anglo-Irish, we had no English relations, we did not go to school in England, and apart from two distant cousins who fought (and died) in the Great War, James Potterton (who enlisted in the 38th Foot Regiment at the age of eighteen in 1808) is the only Potterton recorded as joining the British Army. As far as lifestyle was concerned, Protestants like us appreciated comfort and really did think that cleanliness was next to Godliness (which we also held in very high esteem), and we savoured good food. These considerations were not at all important to the Anglo Irish who would have regarded them as mere impediments to the pursuit of more important activities such as hunting, shooting, and fishing with a sprinkling of gambling and adultery (as we suspected) thrown in.

We had perhaps more of an interest in the activities of the young Queen — at least in so far as *The Irish Times* reported (as it frequently did) on her doings — than Catholics did; and, at

the time of the Coronation, Miss Thompson and Mr Medlicott
contrived between them (in a way that Brother Michael in the
Christian Brothers would probably not have done) to relay the
ceremony by installing a wireless for the day in Trim school.
Molly, in the kitchen, would sometimes tease us by holding up
a Huntley and Palmer's biscuit tin in order to compare
unfavourably the image of the Queen on its lid (in diamonds
and a ball-gown) with a picture that she had found in a Sunday
newspaper of a bald and aged President Sean T O'Kelly at the
Dublin Horse Show; and on one infamous occasion the same
Molly actually went so far as to make a similar juxtaposition
using a press photograph taken during An Tostal.

'Even Cardinal D'Alton is bether lookin' than your auld
Queen,' she said.

Mamma read English magazines like *Woman & Home* but
that was because similar Irish publications did not exist and the
same was true for other areas of popular culture where the
absence of an indigenous product meant that Irish people were
obliged to look to England. 'Ireland's Nightingale of Song',
Rose Brennan, could bring tears to the eyes with her rendering
of "My Wedding Day" but when it came to the Eurovision
Song Contest we were obliged to cheer for England's Teddy
Johnston and Pearl Carr "Looking High, High, High" as
Ireland did not compete at all. The nearest thing to Irish
television were the efforts of Eamonn Andrews to conceal
What's My Line? from the curiosity of Gilbert Harding and
Lady Isobel Barnett which was on the BBC. The wireless
afforded greater possibilities and *Living with Lynch* was just as
good as *Life with the Lyons*, but it always took some time before
Radio Eireann's *Hospitals' Requests* would feature the songs we
could hear on Radio Luxembourg's *Alka Seltzer Show*. There
were of course exceptions and Vera Lynn singing a song about
Kingscourt, County Cavan — "Oh! to be in Doonaree," she
yearned improbably — was one of them. Alan, who was
enthusiastic about all sports, followed the FA cup and

supported Aston Villa: he had pictures of most of the players (as well as the English soccer league table) pasted to the walls of our bedroom. I, in turn, subscribed to the *Enid Blyton Magazine*; but, between us, that was the extent of our interest in England and, as for the Union Jack, contrary to what Miss Pringle believed, our knowledge of it was derived almost exclusively from illustrations in missionary tracts — such as we were given at Bible meetings — of black children waving it at each other while they marched, semi-naked, around the jungle.

Our ignorance in the matter was, however, lost on Miss Pringle who assumed that we would have understood the complexities of the design almost from the cradle. When, therefore, she emerged from the office after a quarter-of-an-

'Well done! I'm convinced you knew it all along'

hour and saw the pathetic red and blue boxes with which we had covered the paper, she was aghast.

'You start with the saltire of St Andrew,' she said.

She rolled her dentures in irritation.

'Everyone knows that.'

We stared at her bewildered and when she took my pencil from me in order to demonstrate, I started to cry.

'There now,' she said.

As she hugged me, Alan feigned concentration in the hope that he might be denied a similar privilege.

'It's easier than you think. Just draw the cross of St Patrick for me, surely you are familiar with that.'

I drew a shepherd's crook similar to that which I had seen St Patrick holding in a picture of him preaching on the Hill of Tara, but before Miss Pringle had time to examine it, Alan's design, which had a passing resemblance to a wooden gate, caught her attention.

'Well done,' she said. 'It's St George. I'm convinced you knew it all along.'

Over the next few weeks, there followed further sessions during which Miss Pringle attempted to have us perfect our technique and it was only when we appealed to Mamma to intervene that we gained any remission.

'The children are going to be busy for the next few weeks helping me get ready for Christmas,' she said to Miss Pringle in about October. 'They can go back to drawing again in the New Year.'

But by the time Christmas came, Miss Pringle had returned to Woking.

'I miss the W.I.,' she said after she had announced her resignation. 'There's nothing like that here.'

She moved to the edge of her chair as she said it and, adopting the mien of a soubrette, she smiled across at Mamma.

'The Mothers' Union is not for me just yet,' she said.

12. An Impractical Investment

Mamma often told me about the time when, before I was born, she and Papa drove Edward down to Kilkee. Having decided that lessons from Mr Tyner would be an appropriate preamble to his eventually qualifying as a vet, they made an appointment and set off on what amounted to a considerable journey. On arrival they stayed in a guesthouse called Duggerna.

'It's just two doors away from us,' Mr Tyner had told them, 'take the Strand Line once you come in from Kilrush and then follow the road all the way around the bay. Eventually, you'll come to a sharp turn — there's a sign for the Pollock Holes — and we're up there a couple of hundred yards.'

Mrs Hodgkins was waiting for them when they arrived.

'You should be comfortable here,' she said as she showed them into a bedroom on the first floor. 'I've no one else staying at the moment. The winter months are always very slack.'

'Is it always foggy like this?' asked Mamma, walking over to the bay window. 'I can't even see the houses on the opposite side of the street.'

'There are none,' said Mrs Hodgkins, 'just the cliffs.'

Bending down, she threw open the bottom window.

'Do you hear the waves on the rocks?' she said. 'That's the sea more than a hundred feet below.'

Mamma and Papa stepped back into the room.

'The spray often comes up over the road on account of the strength of the tides,' said Mrs Hodgkins.

When they had visited the Tyners the following morning — and settled the matter of Edward's education — Papa suggested that they might go for a walk down the town. Crossing the road, they took the footpath which ran along the sea-wall.

'I'm sure I saw the sea when we came in yesterday evening,' said Mamma, 'but with this mist, there's no sign of it now.'

She took out a head-scarf and tied it on over her hat.

'The tide must be out,' said Papa.

'It couldn't be out that far,' said Mamma.

'Sykes House,' said Papa.

He was looking across the street.

'They're really very fine houses,' he said. 'Some are just enormous.'

They passed the West Cliff Hotel — "Closed for the Season" read a notice in one of the windows — before coming to tennis courts and behind them, up from the seafront, the indistinct grey spectre that was the Hydro Hotel. A placard outside announced, "The King of Rhythm in Person, Joe Loss and his Orchestra" but pasted over it, on a diagonal, the by-now familiar sign: "Closed for the Season". Next came the West End Stores (J Doherty, Prop); it too was boarded up.

'We'll amble as far as the church,' said Papa.

That was closed also; a typewritten note attached to the door gave details of arrangements for the previous Christmas.

'There's not much life about it,' said Mamma, 'there mustn't be any services at all in winter.'

They made their way back to Duggerna.

'It's a lovely spot,' said Papa. 'The air is wonderful … and

137

the smell of the sea. I'm sure the weather wouldn't be quite as wet in the summer.'

The grey felt of his hat had turned black and his overcoat and shoes were soaked through. Mamma was also sodden. She had not said much during the last part of the walk.

Papa opened the gate to Duggerna and, as he did so, he noticed for the first time the sign in the window of the house next door. "For Sale", it read.

'What would you think of us getting a house here?' he said to Mamma later when they were having tea by the fire in the sitting room.

'Do you mean for a month in the summer?' said Mamma.

'Or to buy ...?' said Papa.

He drummed his fingers on the arm of his chair. Taking a handkerchief from the sleeve of her cardigan, Mamma blew her nose.

'I'm sure I've caught a cold,' she said.

'The one next door is for sale,' said Papa.

He took the tea which Mamma handed him.

'It would give the children a great holiday every year,' he said. 'The sea air would build them up for the winter and, if she was able for the journey, it would be grand for Rose too. We'd just come down for a month.'

'Do you realise that it took us almost a full day to get down here?' said Mamma. 'It's a desperate journey, all the way through Athlone and Portumna and, even when we eventually got to Ennis, it was another thirty-five miles. Mrs Hodgkins tells me that she gets a lot of Limerick people in the summer, it's all right for them, but Meath is far too far away.'

'We might just take a look at the house anyway,' said Papa. 'I'll ask Tyner if he knows anything about it.'

The next day, they looked at Lindenlea and by the time they left Kilkee at the end of the week, in spite of Mamma's anxieties, he had agreed to buy it.

'You have that bit of money of your own,' he said to her when it came to a discussion of the price, 'that would pay for it.'

'Do you mean the money Auntie left me?'

'Yes,' he said. 'That's what I was thinking of.'

'I was intending to invest that.'

'This would be an investment ...' he said.

And so it was that for the next twelve or fourteen years, Lindenlea became our home during the month of August every year and, even if the house was not the sort of investment Mamma had in mind when she inherited Auntie's money, the memories of the place and the times we had there are so potent that, had she purchased the Kooh i Noor, she could not have endowed us with a more propitious legacy.

The beautiful name, meaning the glade of the linden trees, was about as inappropriate for the place as its purchase was (in Mamma's view) impractical. Perched on the cliff-top, the likelihood that a linden might survive there was entirely improbable and the small patch of garden at the front of the house was home only to the carnations and pot-marigolds which flourished in the sandy soil. At the back, flames of rampant montbretia licked the dry-stone walls which ran the length of the garden towards a turf-shed and car-house at the far end and the only other vegetation (apart from grass) was the valerian which, like a bench of nodding bishops, held sway over those same walls along the top. Although facing south and always warm and sunny, we rarely played in this garden as it seemed so removed from the town and from the sea; but one memorable winter the storms were so spectacular that waves, unbelievably, washed over the house from the front and, in doing so, surprised the dormant vegetation — as well as Mr Tyner — with the random detritus of the ocean bed.

He telephoned us to report on the disaster.

'A whole chunk of the cliff up at Newfoundout has been

washed into the sea,' he said. 'You know where that is, just up from us here at the high-diving boards.'

'And Lindenlea?' said Papa.

'It's still there, I can tell you that. But you are going to have to replace quite a few slates and there are fish in the back garden.'

Alan and I longed for the following August when we could examine the damage in detail.

'Do you think the fish will still be in the garden?' I asked as we embarked on the last lap — Ennis, Kilrush, Kilkee — of the journey down six months later.

I thought of mackerel swimming, glistening blue and black, in and out of the turf-house.

'They might be,' said Mamma.

Lindenlea, like most of the houses of the West End, would have been built in about 1870 as a holiday home so that — following the completion of the West Clare Railway which made the town accessible — the wife and family of some Limerick merchant-prince might escape that city for the several months of summer every year. They would have been accompanied by their servants who would have been accommodated easily on account of the large number of rooms trailing out in a wing to the back. But it was the front rooms — the first-floor drawing room and the dining room below — with their bay windows which commended the place particularly to Papa and which gave the house its special character. From these, the sea was all-pervasive and the salt air was so pungent that our tin buckets and spades — if left there — would rust almost to extinction from one summer to the next. From those same windows, we looked out across the bay towards the ruffled line of white that was the northern shoreline. There, above the rocks, green fields were grazed by flocks of sheep and straggled herds of cattle and at times — as a sign of the weather it was said — these hardy creatures would edge their way, west, up the slope towards St George's Head from where cliffs dropped about two hundred feet or more into the Atlantic below. The house was always painted cream: its windows and hall-door as well as the decorative iron railings which shielded the front garden from the street were red, pillar-box red. While this paintwork was renewed — in order to contain the corrosion — almost annually, the interior — with the exception of the wallpaper in the bedrooms (one of which Mamma papered every year) — was never changed, nor had it been for decades. There was a dankness — a scent of water and of rust — about the place, particularly in the kitchen which had a stone-flag floor and lacked natural light; but when the windows of the front rooms were opened wide — as they were from the moment we arrived — the atmosphere was tempered by the reek of salt. When Papa bought the house, he bought the contents as well: linoleum in sumptuous patterns on every floor, iron bedsteads and marble-topped washstands in every room, and in the drawing room, above a marble chimneypiece, a huge gilt overmantel and, most incongruously of all, a family of Victorian portraits in gilded frames. Even after we turned this room into a sort of dormitory (so that as many of us as possible — Rosina, Alan, and I certainly — could benefit from the sea-air as we slept), the portraits stayed there, peering at us from among the waving palm-fronds which made up the design of the elaborate wallpaper that had probably been in the room since the house was built. Downstairs, we lived in the front room which was furnished with the dining-table, armchairs, and window-seats, and where each evening — although it was August — a turf-fire burned in the grate.

Life during our month at Kilkee, rather like life at Rathcormick itself, fell into two distinct phases, depending on whether or not Papa was present. During the first fortnight, when he was not, we were in Mamma's hands and once we had all helped to clean the place thoroughly and accomplished a few other annual chores — like painting the front railings and weeding the back garden — we devoted ourselves to the pleasures of the town. As country children, we were thrilled to be in such a metropolis and Kilkee in the Fifties was as exciting to us as Disneyland is to most children of today. Come rain or shine, we bathed every morning and went to the strand in the afternoon. Then there were random treats, such as shopping in O'Curry Street on our way to the lending library and perhaps a visit afterwards to The Cherry Tree, where we sat at a table and ate ice-cream sundaes. Some years Fossett's or Duffy's Circus came to the town and we went to that; and most years there was a funfair on the Esplanade and, possibly, we were also allowed to go to that. Consisting of little more than a few bumping-cars, a merry-go-round of trotting piebalds, and a carousel of flying chairs on chains, it was hardly Coney Island and the thrills it provided were fairly indifferent. The cars, by the time they got as far as Kilkee, had been so bumped that I was always under the impression that they were called bumping-cars because they looked like bumps and the flying chairs, which were specifically intended to be scary, achieved their purpose by being so dangerous that even Alan balked when he was dared by David to take a ride on them. Most of the time, instead of the funfair, we preferred the rival attraction of buying periwinkles from a street vendor whose cart was parked nearby. They came in a cone made from a newspaper and were extracted from their shells by a pin; but, like the ice-cream cones which we got from Murphy's Whipped Ice-Cream Parlour, Mamma only permitted us to eat them if we sat down someplace as eating on the street was not allowed. Occasionally, in the evenings, we went to the pictures and had fish and chips from Malocca's afterwards and sometimes we went to one of the plays (*Gaslight* was a perennial favourite) or music-hall entertainments which were staged in a hall up behind the West Cliff Hotel. We played pitch and putt and, less often, tennis, and in the evenings, when Alan and I were sent to bed, the boys went to dances in the Hydro.

As soon as Papa arrived, all of this excess came to an end. The older boys, David, Raymond, and possibly also Alan were immediately despatched to a Mrs Leyden for Latin grinds several mornings a week.

'What else would they do when they have so much time on their hands?' Papa would say when Mamma pleaded that they might be spared. 'They can't spend all day loitering about the strand.'

Then, as a further precaution against such an eventuality, he would plan different outings, different activities (most of which we hated) which he described as 'making the holiday'.

'Lisdoonvarna makes the holiday,' he would say in reference to the well-known sulphur spa about twenty miles from Kilkee where he obliged us drink the waters on at least one visit every year; but we loathed the all-pervasive smell of rotten eggs and detested the taste of the water itself.

Then there was the seaweed bathhouse. Although he never bathed in the sea himself, he was insistent — even when the weather was wet and cold — that everyone else did so assiduously; and, as though that was not enough, he made us all visit the seaweed baths — which, remarkable though it seemed, he had discovered a great fondness for himself — an experience that was agonising in the extreme. Architecturally they were somewhat similar to a Turkish bath, with steam rooms and cold rooms and pools, but the salient attraction were large domestic baths filled with seaweed which were made hot or cold according to the preference of the client (Papa preferred his tepid). Each bath was housed in its own cubicle and it was by immersion in the slime — there was no other word for it — and by remaining there for as long as an hour or more, that the clientele remedied, or at least benefited in one way or another, their well-being.

'The children will just use mine after me,' Papa would say to the attendant as he paid his admission charge, and then Alan and I would just hang around until he had finished and the seaweed was completely cold.

'Now hop in there the pair of you, it'll do you a power of good,' he would say. 'I'll come back in a few minutes to fetch you.'

With that, Alan and I edged into the bath and awaited his return; but, as he invariably found 'a most interesting person' with whom to have a conversation, he might be absent for as long as an hour.

Most mornings, he found some work for us to do — clearing up the turf shed was a favourite — and then in the afternoons, as he hated relaxation and could not see the point of just sitting on the rocks reading a book (as Mamma did) while we played on the sand, he would propose an excursion. Initially these might sound attractive and all the more so when Mamma would suggest that she would bring a picnic.

'Put the volcano into the back of the car,' she would say in reference to an aluminium chimney-like apparatus in which water could be boiled. 'We'll stop some place and make a cup of tea.'

But Papa would always have another agenda and we knew from experience that, even when he suggested something as enticing as an all-day outing to Rineanna to see the aeroplanes, there would inevitably be a drawback. It might involve paying a call on someone while we remained in the car for what seemed like hours on end, or else he was likely to encounter some total stranger (or family of strangers) and invite them to join us on our picnic. When we went to Spanish Point, specifically because the huge waves there were so much more exciting to bathe in than those in Kilkee, he would decide that they were simply too huge and forbid us to bathe altogether.

But the experiences which 'made the holiday' most in Papa's

view took place on Sunday evenings — he timed his own fortnight's holiday so that he had three Sundays in Kilkee — and involved what looked like a reasonably pleasant boarding-house which was situated on the seafront not far from Lindenlea. It was called Clar Ellagh and had its name emblazoned as the border of an enormous shield which was affixed, high up, to the facade of the building. But the real nature of the establishment — and its principal attraction for Papa — was hinted at by the large letters "CE" which occupied the centre of the shield and which any innocent passer-by might reasonably have assumed to stand for Clar Ellagh itself. While that was certainly the intention, it was not the actual fact and, more ominously, the letters CE stood for "Christian Endeavour". Clar Ellagh occupied several large houses and was indeed a boarding-house, and a very pleasant one at that. But it was diligently Protestant, and, while its holiday-making occupants attended church as a matter of course every Sunday morning (as indeed did we), they considered that to be quite insufficient and, as a result, each Sunday evening they organised a prayer meeting of their own at Clar Ellagh.

'What else could you think of doing?' Papa would ask each week if we tried, with one excuse or another, to avoid going to these meetings. 'Doesn't it make a lovely ending to the week?'

Lasting for two hours or more, the gatherings took place in a drawing room where the very few armchairs were quickly occupied by the elderly while the rest of us sat on the floor. What was called 'a few words', but was really a lengthy sermon, was delivered by some returned missionary or vacationing clergyman whose dress — a pale grey jacket — stressed the informality of the occasion. This would be followed by prayers but the core of the evening consisted of hymn-singing with certain favourites, such as "Will your anchor hold in the storms of life?" and "Rock of ages, cleft for me", being sung at every meeting (twice at some) on account of their being so very apposite to the venue.

'What's cleft?' I would ask Mamma as she rubbed Nivea into my shoulders as we sat on the rocks the next day.

'Run off and play for goodness sake,' she would say, 'and let me get on with my book in peace.'

Her Frances Parkinson Keyes lay open on the rug beside her. Doing as I was bid, I would scramble off over the craggy outcrops in the direction of the strand.

'Let me hide myself in thee,' I would sing to the rocks as I did so.

When Alice came down to Kilkee, as she did for a week or so every year, she would cook special treats. There might be lobster, which in actual fact we did not like all that much, and on one occasion she suggested gulls' eggs which she had learned about when she worked in a hotel in Cornwall.

'What sort of gulls?' said Alan and I when she first told us about them.

'Seagulls,' said Alice.

'You mean like the seagulls here?'

'The very same.'

'And where do the eggs come from?'

'The cliffs. That's where the seagulls hatch. The locals just climb down and get the eggs out of the nest.'

Alan looked at me and I looked back at him. And Mamma looked at both of us. She was sitting in the window helping Rosina shell broad beans for the dinner.

'You shouldn't tell the children things like that, Alice,' she said, 'and if I catch either one of you going anywhere near the cliffs, you'll both be sent straight home on the train without so much as a moment's thought.'

But the greatest treat of all which we ate at Kilkee did not depend on Alice's culinary skills, nor for that matter could it be described as a delicacy. It was mackerel. We bought them directly from the fishermen as soon as they came ashore in their currachs. Early in the morning, from her bed in the front room, it was possible for Mamma to see them — tiny specks of black disappearing and reappearing according to the swell of the sea — as they first came into sight well beyond St George's Head. As she rose and dressed, they became more real as they rowed their way the mile or more from the entrance to the bay back to the boat-house over by the East End. She knew that if she set off when they reached a point directly opposite Lindenlea, a brisk walk would get her across the strand by the time they hauled ashore; and she maintained she could tell by the sit of the currach in the water whether the catch that morning had been worthwhile. At times, some of us would accompany her, but more often she preferred to go alone — 'It's the one time of day when I can think,' she said — and she would return well before breakfast with enough mackerel, wrapped up in newspapers, for each of us. Occasionally we ate them immediately but more often they were reserved for midday; by evening, in Mamma's view, they were already too old.

The vegetables and fruit which we had at Lindenlea — runner beans, broad beans, cabbage, onions, tomatoes, apples, rhubarb, and plums — were all brought down from Rathcormick in an operation which rivalled in its scale and complexity a campaign of famine relief. Potatoes we bought locally.

'The Kerrs Pinks we got from that man out near Miltown Malbay last year were not that bad,' Mamma would say. 'I'll send out to him for a couple of sacks again. He's very good about delivering them and he generally brings me a crate of lettuce every so often as well.'

Joints of bacon and rashers from Leonard's in Trim were also brought down, but when it came to beef, it never occurred to us to eat it in Kilkee:

'What would beef be like when the land is only a bog?' Papa

would remark. 'We'll try a leg of lamb instead. There won't be much fat on it, we can be certain of that.'

But, in actual fact, we rarely had lamb as Mamma (who always referred to it as mutton) insisted throughout her life that it did not agree with her.

Apart from milk, which was delivered every morning by a milkman with a horse and cart, the rest of our fare in Kilkee came from the West End Stores. We always called it Doherty's, and then after it was sold one winter, we called it Haugh's. Mamma would leave a list into the shop once or twice a week and the shopping was delivered by a boy on a bicycle later in the day. Money never changed hands; everything we bought was written into a book and, at the end of the month, Papa went down and paid the bill. The only time we would drop into the shop was to buy ice-cream for pudding.

'Will you be safe to run down and get a block of HB?'

'Proddies, Proddies, we can tell...

Mamma would say to Alan and me as we dried ourselves on the strand after bathing, 'I'll go on home and put on the potatoes.'

'Can we get some Mi-Wadi as well?'

She would look at us.

'Please?'

'I suppose so,' she would say, 'but remember on the way home you're not to go near those Carneys. Walk on the other side of the road.'

She was referring to a family of freckled-faced red-heads who each year occupied a house on the seafront near Clar Ellagh and whose habit it was, whenever Alan and I passed on our own, to climb up on top of their railings and chant at us:

'Proddies, Proddies, we can tell; Kiss the Pope and go to Hell.'

We never understood fully what they meant by the words and Mamma only learned about the incidents accidentally when she overheard Alan calling me, as a term of abuse rather than endearment, 'a little Proddie'.

'Where did you learn that word?' she said, leaning out of the upstairs window.

Alan told her.

'Well, I don't want to ever hear you saying it again,' she said.

But she never explained why.

Lindenlea
'Where did you learn that word?'

13. Holiday Romance

The first time Uncle Ernie and Aunt Alice came to Kilkee with our cousins Clonagh and Aleck they stayed at Lindenlea. On all subsequent visits, however, much to the disappointment of Alan and I, as they were so generous and such good fun, they stayed at the Marine Hotel. There, presumably, they could get a drink and smoke a cigarette without encountering the stony stare of disapproval which greeted such decadence at Lindenlea.

'We certainly weren't going to stay at the Hydro,' Aunt Alice said. 'With all the noise from the ballroom every night, we wouldn't be able to get a wink of sleep.'

Had the Hydro Hotel been in South Beach, Miami, it would have been considered quite unremarkable, but as it was in Kilkee and the nearest thing to Art Deco of any building in Ireland, it was quite exceptional. Apart from its ballroom, it had tennis courts, a croquet lawn, a miniature golf course, and the promise of other unseen amenities which marked it out as a cut above any other attraction in the town. What is more, it looked wonderful.

Although I had never seen an ocean liner, I knew from the pictures of them I had studied on the labels of Edward's suitcase that this is what the Hydro looked like. Newly painted white every year, it was docked — or seemed to be — on a vantage point well up from the seafront and from there it gleamed and gloated condescendingly at every other structure in the town. Its windows, with red latticed exterior shutters that never closed, punctured its facade in horizontal lines creating the effect of decks from bow to stern; and when it came to the top deck, where — as it was actually a building — one might have expected to find a roof, there was none. As it was flat, it could not be seen. There was a tower of windows, positioned not in the middle of the facade but slightly towards one end, which rose several floors higher than the rest of the building. I imagined it as the funnel of my liner and floating from its pinnacle, not a coil of smoke but instead a flag: "The Hydro" it read.

The illusion of the Hydro being a ship became even more real after dark when light shone from its every window and the big-band sound of Johnny McMahon and his Resident Orchestra wafted, like the call of a wolf in the wild, out into the night air and down as far as the seafront. On evenings when Mamma had taken us to the pictures or out for a walk, we would stop on the way home and sit on the sea-wall and listen to the music.

"Oh the wayward wind," some crooner or other would warble, "is a restless wind/ a restless wind/ that yearns to wander."

We could hear the words perfectly as they throbbed above the wheeze of a tenor saxophone.

"And I was born, the next of kin/ the next of kin/ to the wayward wind," he would drone.

The fact that the lyrics made so little sense served only to distance even further the glamorous world of the Hydro from anything I could comprehend.

The boys went to The Hydro at night; not every night, but as many nights as Mamma could be prevailed upon to let them, and that was fairly often.

'There should be a clean Aertex shirt in the hot-press,' she would say as she gave her final assent. 'If not, you'll have to wait until the laundry comes back; but that won't be until Friday.'

But when Papa was in residence, getting permission to go to the Hydro depended on a great deal more than the availability of a clean Aertex.

'Why you won't sit down and play a round of Beg o' My Neighbour with the rest of us I don't know,' he would say. 'I can't understand what you see in that place anyway.'

The chances are that Papa understood perfectly well what they saw in the Hydro, and even if he did not it was to be made absolutely plain to him as he sat, reluctantly, on the rocks the following afternoon. He had only started on the Nevil Shute which Mamma had been urging him to read all week when his concentration was interrupted by the raucous giggling of a pair of girls as they made their way, dressed in nothing more than swimsuits, across the rocks in his direction.

I imagined the Hydro as an ocean liner

153

'Hi there, Eddie!' one of them shouted while waving her arms effusively.

Forgetting that no one had called him Eddie for almost thirty years, he stared, thunderstruck, at what he could only consider an apparition. But as the duo approached, it became apparent that they had not even seen him. Their sights were focused exclusively on Edward and David who were sitting on a rock behind him.

'Yous are the pair of boyos,' said the smaller of the two girls when they reached them.

Her black hair, sleek as a magpie's tail, framed her face with tight curls and the colourless white of her skin was pink, not from excitement or exertion, but from the sun, so that her shoulders and thighs glowed almost raw. Her friend, whose complexion — more reddish than fair — the sea air had doused with splashes of freckles was more outspoken:

'Yeah, what's your game leaving the pair of us standing like a couple of eejits waiting for yis above at the wall,' she said.

Edward and David reddened. Neither of them spoke.

'Dave, Eddie …' said the girls. 'Are yis pretending you don't know us. Get you!'

Towering above us as we sat in a group, they wiggled their bottoms like film stars.

'Yeah, get you,' one of them repeated.

'C'mon Cineva, we're only wasting our time,' said the other.

'Yis won't be walking us home from the Hydro tonight,' they shouted as they sauntered off in the direction of the shore, 'that's for sure.'

By the time they had disappeared — their giggling but a faint cackle across the rocks — Papa was buried deep in his book for the first time that holiday; and that evening, when the boys asked him if they might go to the Hydro, he was still too embarrassed by the encounter to risk any discussion of the subject by saying no.

Holiday Romance

I never went to the Hydro. Nor did Rusty — although, on one memorable occasion, he did go to church — but even without the Hydro he did manage to find other pleasures in Kilkee, and, perhaps even more than any of us, he adored the place. After his first year there, he would look forward to his holiday from one month of August to the next, and every year when it came to the last week of July and he saw fruit and vegetables being picked and packed in quantities at Rathcormick he would not let Mamma or me out of his sight lest the car should depart without him. It was not that he cared all that much for the bathing (in fact he loathed it) or, indeed, that he particularly welcomed the diet of fresh mackerel daily. Nor was he impressed — as we were — by bottled milk from the Kilrush Creamery: it was a very poor substitute in his view for the milk at home which was always warm, as Carr filled his bowl straight from the cow. Even Miss Jessup's cat, sunning herself provocatively in the Tyner's front garden, failed to interest him, and as for the Garda Sergeant in his uniform who lived the other side of the Tyners, Rusty simply ignored him. Rusty loved Kilkee for precisely the same as the reason the boys loved the Hydro. In a word, he loved it for the girls.

But then it was hardly surprising: the only other dog he ever saw for the remaining eleven months of the year was Carr's elderly sheepdog, Rover.

It was a tribute to the persuasive nature of Rusty's personality that he was ever brought to Kilkee in the first instance. He was never taken anywhere else and indeed rarely even set a paw in the car from one end of the year to the next. This state of affairs was largely of his own devising on account of the fact that, from the time of that very first journey from the Wood-of-O to Rathcormick, he suffered from car-sickness. As a result, the stuffy six-to-eight-hour drive to Kilkee was an agony for him and although I concocted many schemes as an antidote to his affliction — from making him fast for days beforehand to holding his nose permanently out the car-window — we would hardly have reached the Hill-of-Down (about ten miles away) before he would be vomiting copiously. At that time, a suggested remedy for car sickness was to sit on a newspaper, but my attempts to adapt this theory to Rusty's circumstances — I sat on the newspaper while he sat on my knee — proved as fruitless as all my other schemes.

Eventually, Mrs McManus, the chemist in Trim, was consulted. She thought for a moment or two and then, opening a glass cabinet, took down a small bottle of capsules from the top shelf and handed it to Mamma.

'Kwells,' said Mamma, looking at the label. 'Is that how you pronounce them?'

'A lot of people find them very good,' said Mrs McManus. 'You take one when going to bed the night before and another an hour or so before travelling.'

'But they are for Rusty,' said Mamma. 'Does it say they work on dogs?'

'You might as well try them,' said Mrs McManus. 'They're only one and six a bottle and it could well be that they would do the trick.'

Mrs McManus, as it transpired, was an optimist.

Rusty was more sick than ever that year in spite of the fact that, by the time we had got as far as Rochfortbridge, I had forced him to swallow most of the bottle.

'I can still see you stuffing the Kwells down poor Rusty,' Mamma would recall to the end of her days.

Whenever we arrived in Kilkee, Rusty would be trembling uncontrollably as a result of his ordeal. His eyes would be bloodshot, his mouth foaming, and he would be looking far from well. As soon as the car drew up outside Lindenlea, however, he would spring to life, demand to be released and, without even waiting for a drink of water, go dashing down the town with a glint in his eye. We would not see him again until about eleven that night when he would return and slink into the kitchen where he would collapse with exhaustion on the cold flagged floor underneath the unlit range. For a whole glorious month, with one or two exceptions, Rusty's every waking hour was spent in a constant pursuit of sex. He would set off as soon as the hall-door was opened in the morning, but at midday, when he knew Mamma walked down for her bathe, he would appear from nowhere without fail and accompany her down to the strand. While she splashed about in the sea, he would look round for what might be available, but then return with her to the house for his dinner. During the afternoon we would occasionally catch a glimpse of him, particularly if an expedition to the West End Stores for ice-creams was being organised, but very rarely did he ever spend any time with us. When he did, it was only to cause embarrassment.

'Is that yoke your dog?' some seven-year-old or other from Limerick enquired when Rusty positioned himself beside me as she and I built sandcastles together.

'Eh, kind of,' I answered.

As there was so very little about his appearance or even his demeanour that was immediately commendable, I would pray for him to run off and leave me alone. But Rusty was well-capable of reading my mind and, as if to teach me a lesson, he would lie down beside me, lift his hind leg, and proceed to lick his genitalia consolingly.

Although an annual holiday for Rusty and the attendant pleasures it afforded him had not been part of Papa's plans in acquiring Lindenlea, he did have in mind that it would benefit the rest of us, and in particular Rosina, to have a healthy holiday every year. Such was the success of this plan that after a couple of years it dawned on him that there were all sorts of other people in the world who would equally appreciate the experience.

Passing an institution called Mrs Smiley's Home on the

North Circular Road one day, he remarked to Mamma, 'That's a place that does a lot of good, I must call in and see them. We might have time on the way home.'

Mrs Smiley's home was a Protestant orphanage and when Papa went to see the warden he suggested to her that she might like to take her charges for a month to Kilkee the following June and stay in Lindenlea. She could have the house for nothing and, if she could borrow a bus, he could supply a driver — he had our lorry-driver, Keeley, in mind — to take them there.

'How many orphans are there?' he asked.

'Not as many as there used to be,' said the warden. 'Just nineteen at the moment.'

'The house would easily take that number,' he said. 'They could put some extra mattresses on the floor.'

And so it was that for several years Lindenlea became the summer outpost of Mrs Smiley's Home.

'Those orphans leave the place in a shocking mess,' Mamma would say every year after we arrived. 'As usual, I'll just have to spend the first week of my holiday cleaning up after them.'

Following the success (in his view) of the Mrs Smiley venture, Papa extended his search for further Protestant orphans who might also profit from a stay in Lindenlea. But as legal adoption had (at last) been introduced in Ireland in 1952, he found to his disappointment that they were in short and ever-diminishing supply. When, after a number of enquiries, he drew a total blank, he made an approach to a Catholic home for the deaf and dumb and offered them the same arrangement. Greeting him with some suspicion, the Reverend Mother in charge listened to his scheme.

'The girls here would go mad altogether if they were let out like that,' she said. 'I couldn't be responsible for them.'

Then, seeing the disappointment on Papa's face, she added:

'Perhaps one or two at a time could go, but no more.'

Later in the year, and with August again approaching, Papa brought up the subject with Mamma.

'We might take one of those deaf and dumb girls with us to Kilkee this year,' he said. 'She'd help you in the house and then, maybe next year when the Reverend Mother realises what a success it is, she might let us have a few more.'

The sixteen-year-old girl who spent that August with us, while not going altogether mad as the nun had predicted, proved to be an onerous liability. Accustomed from an early age to being part of an institution where she was surrounded by others with similar disabilities, she was disorientated in the extreme by the isolation of a holiday among a large family who understood very little about her and nothing at all of the sign language which she deployed as a means of communication. She caused alarm by disappearing altogether on several occasions and, one Sunday morning, when we went to fetch her from Mass, she was nowhere to be seen.

'In future, one of you will just have to go to Mass with her,' Papa said.

'Is that yoke your dog?'

There was always the fear that she would fall into the sea and drown, and on another occasion, David had to be despatched to investigate the cliffs on the far side of the road and search for her.

'Go now before the tide comes back in and washes the body out to sea,' said Mamma.

But before he had a chance to come back and report on the full extent of the calamity, Teresa had returned, smiling from ear to ear, her mouth wreathed in the tell-tale evidence of orange dye which established beyond dispute that she had been sucking an ice lolly.

Inevitably, Alan and I mimicked her mannerisms. When Mamma came out to the front one day to find us, amid squeals of laughter, conducting a conversation in sign language, we were given such a sound thrashing that thereafter we avoided the poor girl altogether. In the end, even Papa acknowledged that the experiment had not been a success:

'It would have been better with two or three of them,' he said, and then as though he was talking about a broody hen that was about to hatch, 'in that way, we would have got her to settle more.'

'It's the worst month's holiday I've ever had,' said Mamma, 'I've been at my wits' end most of the time. Writing notes for her every time I wanted to explain anything.'

14. A Friend in Need ...

While Papa had difficulty in expressing any warmth or affection on a personal level, particularly as far as his children were concerned, he more than made up for this deficiency when it came to dealing with strangers, and there was nothing that took his fancy more than being kind to someone whom he regarded as 'a deserving cause'.

When he went up to Dublin every Wednesday, he would park beside the Bank of Ireland in Foster Place. There he befriended a roguish character who, quite unofficially, went through the motions of ushering cars into their spaces and, having performed such a service, demanded a tip. Sensing that the money would soon be spent on a pint of Guinness, Papa sought to prevent this — or at least delay it — by giving the scoundrel what he believed was 'an interest in life'. As a result, the man — whose existence had hitherto been entirely carefree — soon found himself encumbered with a weekly sack of oats.

'Those pigeons haven't a bit to eat,' Papa would say as he opened down the boot of the Prefect. 'You need to sprinkle a bit of this for them every morning and evening. They'll get to know you after a while and there should be enough there to last you until I'm up again next week.'

Happy in the belief that he had done some good, he would set off for the day about his business.

At other times, his energies in relieving the hardships of those whom he believed to be less fortunate were much more exaggerated and complicated; and, with a campaign to export donkeys to the Isle of Man, they aspired to a level of utter absurdity.

The year that he and Mamma were twenty-five years married, Alice and Elliott persuaded the pair of them to go away on a short holiday.

'If you go in May,' they said, 'David and Raymond will still be away at school.'

'And I will come home for week and look after Rosina and Alan and Homan,' said Alice.

'Won't I be able to tide things over in the office well enough?' said Elliott.

He had just come home from Dunfermline.

'Go now, before the meadow-auctions begin.'

Mamma and Papa had not been away on their own since their honeymoon, and after much coaxing the decision was made and they set off for a week's touring.

'It wouldn't be a holiday if you just go to Kilkee,' said Alice and Elliott. 'Go someplace like Bundoran where you've never been before. And take the Austin instead of enduring the long journey in the Prefect.'

'It'll mean your mother will have to do all the driving,' said Papa.

'Well, I will,' said Mamma.

By now, she was quite looking forward to the trip.

'The week away did us a power of good,' Papa said when they came home again.

And then, by way of an excuse for the recklessness of it all and in spite of the odometer showing that Mamma had driven over five hundred miles, he added:

'Your mother was glad of the rest.'

'It was no holiday at all,' Mamma said later to Alice and Elliott. 'We had to drive out every day looking up this person and that. I was just sick of it. And there wasn't a single place where you could get a decent cup of tea.'

After the week in Bundoran, Papa was more easily persuaded to take other holidays.

'I might just take your mother away on a bit of a break,' was how he condoned the extravagance and, after trips to Portstewart one year and Kinsale the next, they eventually went as far as the Isle of Man. It was there that Papa met a man whose livelihood depended on giving children donkey-rides on the strand. As Papa reported the encounter, the man told him that he had four sons and that they were all on the buildings in Manchester.

'There's a grand living for them here,' he said 'if only I could get the asses.'

'I'll round up a few for you in Ireland,' said Papa. 'You can pay me back in a couple of years when you've had time to cover your costs.'

'Between me and the sons we could handle twenty-five,' said the man. 'As you can see for yourself, there's children enough wanting rides as would employ twice that number.'

Papa's word was his deed and when he next went down to the fair in Ballyhaunis he put out word that he was looking for 'a donkey or two'. Before that day was out, he had had the offer of seven and, by the time he was ready to come home the following day, he had bought those and a further four. Like the cattle, the purchase of which was the reason for his visit to the fair in the first instance, the donkeys were despatched on the train to the Hill-of-Down. They had to walk from there to Rathcormick.

'Just put them out in the Paddock,' Papa told Carr when they arrived. 'If you spancel one or two of them, that should make the others stay where they are. And make sure they have a drink of water.'

Over the next few weeks more donkeys appeared and before long tinkers took to arriving at Rathcormick with sundry asses and the occasional jennet while every evening the phone would ring with further offers, often from as far afield as Mountmellick or Borrisokane.

'It's like the National Stud up there,' Elliott said. 'All that's missing is Tullyar.'

'They seem to be content enough,' said Papa. 'The bit of feeding has given them a new lease of life.'

'They're in the lap of luxury is what I'd say,' said Mamma.

'They'll find it a bit of a change when they get to the Isle of Man,' said Elliott. 'Galloping up and down the strand all day long with every child in the place on their backs.'

'Donkeys like children,' said Papa. 'They'll be very happy after the hardship many of them have been through with the tinkers.'

'He'll never get a shilling out of the man for them,' Elliott said to Mamma later. 'That's for sure.'

'Well, maybe he won't,' said Mamma. 'But isn't he content enough just to have helped the poor man out.'

And so he was, although for several years thereafter he would sometimes say to Mamma, 'We might tip over to the Isle of Man and see how those donkeys are doing.' But it was never with the intention of exacting payment for them and, in actual fact, he never went.

*

Although the breakfast room in Rathcormick was quite small, it was there that we took most of our week-day meals, with Mamma sitting at the top of the table, Papa's secretary at the far end, and Papa to Mamma's left. With a huge window and a door that opened into the garden, the room was tucked in between the new dining room and the kitchen and like them it faced south. Rusty always loitered on the grass outside at mealtimes because that was where he was fed. By evening, the sun had faded from the room but the garden itself — the herbaceous border and the rustic trellis outside the window, the mown grass, and the dahlia-plot on the far side of the middle path — was in full light until the last rays eventually disappeared down behind the sheds in the yard.

One evening when we were all seated around the table Papa said to Mamma: 'You know that bit of an old cottage up there at the Stonyford near Rickard's?'

'Do you mean where the Gaffneys used to live?'

'Yes. You can hardly see the place now from the road with all the nettles up around it, and the tinkers made an awful mess when they camped there a summer or two ago.'

'What about it?' said Mamma.

She helped herself to one of the tomatoes from the glass-dish in front of her.

'Pass up the salad-dressing there, would you please boys?' she said.

'There's this couple,' said Papa, 'that came in to see me in Trim last Saturday and they want to live there. They're dead-set on renting it.'

'The poor people have to live someplace …' said Mamma, chopping the tomato, 'otherwise, it's the side of the road for many of them.'

Raymond handed her the salad-dressing.

'It would be a roof over their heads for the summer, I suppose,' she said.

'Well, it's not like that exactly …' said Papa.

There was a faint quiver of a smile in his eyes — an expression such as we only very rarely witnessed — and then he said:

'They say they've fallen in love with it.'

Mamma put down the salad-dressing. Resting her elbow on the edge of the table, she looked at Papa. David nudged Raymond and they began to giggle.

'It's the bridge,' said Papa, 'the old humped-back bridge beside the house. They say it's just like *The Quiet Man*. It was hard to fathom half of what they were talking about.'

'We saw *The Quiet Man* in Kilkee a couple of years ago, do you not remember?' said Mamma. 'But what's that got to do with Gaffney's old wreck of a cottage? Do you know anything about these people? Are they local?'

'They're Americans,' said Papa. 'I can't think what landed them up around here. They talked a lot of nonsense about the cottage being a dream come true — if they only knew — and that it didn't matter that there was no running water at the moment when they could 'access' the river. They wanted to move in straight away.'

'I'd be very careful about them, if I were you,' said Mamma. 'What did they look like?'

'They're young — they told me they had just been married — and very well-dressed. In fact, they were very polite and money seemed to be no object to them as they said they could pay a year's rent in advance if that was the system here.'

'Rent in advance for that place,' said Mamma. 'More likely you'd have to pay someone to live there at all.'

Looking around the table and seeing how amused we all were by his news, Papa became aware that he was enjoying himself.

'When I said I would look into it for them they were quite pleased,' he said.

Then, looking straight at Mamma, he added:

'When they were leaving the office they asked me if there was any place where they could buy me a cocktail.'

'They must be out of their minds,' said Mamma.

The young American couple who came into our lives in this

way were called Meredith. They were, as Papa had said, young and newly married and, although we had never heard the expression "East Coast WASP", the Merediths epitomised the genre. Mr Meredith, who was tall and good-looking, dressed in the same vein, but with an even more pronounced chic, as Mr Waldron and Mr McArthur whom most people regarded as the smartest men in County Meath. But whereas Mr Waldron and Mr McArthur wore faun-coloured cavalry twills, brown suede shoes, viyella shirts, tweed jackets, and yellow ties and socks, Mr Meredith varied this ensemble by the deft substitution of pale yellow corduroys and brown leather slip-on shoes with tassels. The latter were so exceptional that it is doubtful if Mr Waldron or Mr McArthur would ever have dared to wear them.

Mr Meredith, it almost goes without saying, was an artist or rather an artisan: he occupied his time in the manufacture of miniature horse-drawn carriages and, indeed, was so talented at this that it would not be an exaggeration to describe him as the Fabergé of his *métier*. While papier-mâché was his base material, he used real gold for the ornate Rococo frames, real leather for the interior upholstery, and real silk for the drapes. His lacquer was worthy of the finest *ébenist*, and the mythological scenes which he painted on the doors and blinds, while worthy of Boucher in their design, were on a scale so delicate that only a miniaturist like Hilliard could have challenged them in their perfection.

Mrs Meredith, who was writing a book, dressed like an American intellectual and had a resulting slatternliness about her appearance that did not commend itself at all to Mamma. She had the same unkempt seriousness about her demeanour.

'It's the real Ireland,' she said one day.

Mamma had just given her a jar of her green-tomato chutney.

'This is the real Ireland ...' said Mrs Meredith.

She clutched the chutney in both hands.

'This is what I've come here to find.'

In planning their love nest by the Stonyford, the Merediths imported a huge double bed from America. It had an upholstered headboard — serpentine shaped at the top — which was covered with a beautiful French *toile-de-Jouy* of cupids disporting themselves among architectural ruins in a manner that would have embarrassed even Madame Du Barry. This bed, as well as other unreasonable extravagances, confirmed what Mamma and Papa had suspected from the start: that the Merediths were 'totally hopeless and without a practical thought in their heads'. In that respect they were not all that unusual by County Meath standards — neither Mr Waldron nor Mr McArthur could exactly be described as 'down-to-earth' — but it was the Merediths' element of artistic creativity and their imaginative outlook on life that made them completely unique in our experience.

They in turn, although they had nothing whatsoever in common with us, seemed attracted to us as opposites, and Mr Meredith developed a habit of arriving at Rathcormick every morning for a chat with Mamma as she was doing the cooking.

'That fellow is here every day hanging around under my feet talking old rubbish', was how Mamma described these engagements. For Mr Meredith, however, the visits soon seemed to form the very mainstay of his existence.

As the Merediths' time in Ireland progressed, their antics became more and more outlandish. Nevertheless Papa persisted in his efforts to help them. When they announced that 'they wanted to see a bit of the country' and would be setting off on a tour, he asked them where they thought they would stay.

'Hotels,' they replied.

Horrified by the notion of such wantonness, he persuaded them instead to borrow Lindenlea for a couple of weeks and, although it was winter, they duly set off for Kilkee.

After a week or so, the phone went one night at about ten.

The Merediths planned their cottage by the Stonyford as a love nest

'Hold on for a call from Ennis,' said Miss Miggin from the Post Office in Kildalkey.

'Is that you, T E?'

Papa instantly recognised the American timbre but, in any case, Miss Miggin had already told him that she thought it was 'his American friend' who was on the phone.

'I've had a damnable job getting through,' said Mr Meredith. 'Something about the lines in Limerick going off at nine.'

'What are you doing in Ennis?' said Papa.

'We're staying in The Old Ground,' said Mr Meredith.

'What about Lindenlea?' said Papa.

'Arctic,' said Mr Meredith. 'Like the bloody Arctic. We moved in here after the first night.'

'When are you coming home?' said Papa.

'That's just the point, T E. You see we've run up a few expenses here and these people can't understand how easy it will be for me to wire them some money later on. But we've worked out a good plan between us. The manager guy has become a real pal.'

'And the bill?' said Papa, 'How much is that?'

'Just eighty-six pounds,' said Mr Meredith. 'It's just small bucks, but the thing is ...' Mr Meredith lowered his voice, 'I'm going to be able to make ten times that, if you're with me.'

'I think you should settle the account in the morning and come home straight away,' said Papa.

'They have this picture here in the lobby,' said Mr Meredith.

'Where?' said Papa.

'The lobby. Foyer. Hall. Call it what you will. Thing is, they don't realise that it's the real works. I offered them fifty, what do you say — quids — for it which would be a steal, but 'no go' I'm afraid. That's where Jimmy — my manager pal — comes in. I've persuaded him to let me have it for a hundred and he says that 'for luck' (Mr Meredith chuckled) he'll knock six quids off the check as well. Now what do you think of that for a bargain, T E?'

'It means that instead of needing eighty-six pounds, you now need one-hundred-and-eighty,' said Papa.

He pulled out the chair which was at the telephone desk and sat down.

'That's it. Exactly. And the picture of course. I'll have no trouble getting a couple of hundred … quids … for that. No trouble at all. It's just that I need — how will I put it? — an injection of funds to get me out of here with the booty.'

'I'll telephone you back in the morning,' said Papa, 'about ten or so.'

The following morning, when Papa eventually got through to The Old Ground, Mr Meredith had gone out for a round of golf, but he returned Papa's call that evening.

'I've spoken to the hotel,' said Papa, 'and I've sent them a cheque for a hundred pounds. Eighty-six to cover your bill, four to cover the latest expenses that you have run up, and a ten pound deposit on the picture. They're going to let you take it with you against my guarantee. Now I think you should both come home without delay.'

There the matter rested. We never again heard anything — either from The Old Ground or from the Merediths themselves — about the masterpiece from Ennis, and the Merediths departed Ireland, and our lives, about a month or two later.

Mr Meredith gave Mamma a carriage when they were leaving.

'It's a replica of one that belonged to the Empress Elizabeth,' he said.

'I'll have to look out for a couple of horses for it,' said Mamma moving the tiny shafts up and down. 'Meanwhile, we'll keep it in the cabinet in the drawing room.'

And there it nestled, as uncomfortable as the fossil that was Edward's ash-tray, among the collection of hand-painted

Worcester plates, Wedgwood coffee cups, and nineteenth-century Meissen which Aunt Jane had given to Mamma.

Often on a Sunday evening when we were sitting in the drawing room, it would catch Mamma's eye.

'I wonder what ever became of them?' she would say.

But we never heard from the Merediths again.

15. Under Siege

Quite unexpectedly, one year in spring, the congregation in Kildalkey Church was appreciably augmented when a new family arrived in the parish. Rossbawn was purchased by an Englishman, Mr Hardy, and shortly after he took up residence he appeared at Morning Prayer. He was chaperoned by an elderly dowager dressed, with a frail elegance, entirely in black and accompanied by a pair of exquisite young girls whose loveliness and poise — whose allure — was so singular in an English-rose type of way as to make it appear that they might have been spun from gossamer. After investigation, it transpired that Mr Hardy was a widower, the lady in black — whose mien suggested that she was a gentlewoman — was his mother-in-law, and the girls were his only daughters. To judge from their appearances, this unlikely quartet — lacking only a model for Mrs Bennett — might well have stepped from the pages of Jane Austen and, had that indeed been the case, Miss Austen would certainly have settled them in Cheltenham or Bath. Instead they found themselves in Kildalkey and, in the context of our dwindling parish numbers, Papa was delighted to see them.

Mr Hardy, the sort of Englishman who called a spade a

spade, was said to be rich as Croesus. But the precise origins of his fortune or indeed its exact extent, although much discussed in County Meath, was never established with any degree of certainty. Papa introduced himself to the newcomer immediately and a date was soon arranged for them all to come to Sunday dinner. But while this engagement proved to be a splendid success, it became clear as time progressed that, while the Hardy girls liked nothing better than an occasional game of tennis at Rathcormick and a romp round the garden with Rusty, Mr Hardy and Papa had about as much in common as a baby's bottom and a brillo pad.

Early on in their relationship, Papa attempted to interest Mr Hardy in joining the Select Vestry but this proposal was greeted with complete indifference; and when Papa suggested that 'he and the girls' might enjoy a Sunday evening missionary meeting in Rathmolyon, Mr Hardy's response went well beyond apathy to convey actual scorn. On another occasion, taking a packet of Players Please out of his pocket, Mr Hardy offered Papa a cigarette. Shortly after that incident — as though to compound the effrontery — Papa heard that his new friend had been seen having a pint of stout in Davy's pub in Kildalkey. As this was a perfectly natural occupation, indeed an essential part of life, in rural England, Mr Hardy could well be forgiven for not realising that it was far from natural in Ireland and that Protestants such as ourselves did not, by a denial of our own devising, go to the village pub. This proscription had nothing to do with drink (we did not go to the picture-houses in Trim or Athboy either) and even less to do with religion; it was a matter of social convention — social complexity — and the local pub remained the preserve of Catholics although, on occasion, one might catch a glimpse of the Anglo-Irish. Mr Hardy paid little heed to the refinements which such a protocol demanded and, by the end of his first summer in Ireland, he proceeded to an outrage so flamboyant, so provocative, that it was debated not just among Protestants at meetings of the Vestry and the Mothers' Union, but also by Catholics as they made their way to Devotions throughout the county: Mr Hardy sent his daughters to school at the Convent of Mercy in Trim.

Still, in time, and once the parameters of their relationship had been established, Mr Hardy and Papa developed a friendly, neighbourly accord so that when the newcomer's real reason for coming to live in Ireland became apparent — his passionate interest in horses and hunting — Papa was only mildly disapproving.

It did not take Mr Hardy all that long to settle into Irish life. Indeed he became settled so quickly that he soon embarked upon the task of looking for an Irish wife. Spotting an extremely attractive young lady in the neighbourhood, he proposed, was accepted, and within a month or two had shed the gloom of perpetual mourning that is the lot of the widower in favour of the satisfying gratification of early married life. His bride was less than half his age — but that was neither here nor there to Papa. She was also a Roman Catholic and it was on that account that Papa looked upon the marriage with disappointment and disapproval.

The source of Papa's antagonism stemmed from the fact that before the marriage could take place, the Catholic church required Mr Hardy — and indeed Mrs Hardy-to-be — to sign an undertaking that all children of the marriage would be raised in the Catholic faith; a rule, introduced by the church only in the first decade of the twentieth century, that was known as the *Ne Temere* Decree. This ordinance, which was strictly observed and closely monitored in its operation by the Catholic clergy — so much so that many Protestant marriage-partners were persuaded to become Catholic, to "turn" — was justifiably resented, not just by Papa, but by every Protestant in the country. It was seen as an intolerable intrusion on personal choice, as discrimination, and it was feared. Matters were not helped by the new Constitution of Ireland which de Valera brought into being in 1937 and which, as Article 44, included the clause, "The State recognises the special position of the Holy Catholic and Roman Church as the guardian of the faith professed by the great majority of the citizens"; and even though a subsidiary clause — an afterthought — "recognised the (Protestant) Church of Ireland ... and other denominations existing in Ireland", that was of little comfort or consolation to Papa. While this state of affairs and Constitution may have been just retribution for the Penal Laws of the late-seventeenth and early-eighteenth centuries which severely restricted the rights of Catholics, Papa could not see why, two-hundred-and-fifty years later, he should accept the situation without demur.

Having accounted for about ten per cent of the whole at the time of the foundation of the State in 1922, the Protestant population had dwindled by this stage to between three and four per cent, largely through voluntary emigration. In the context of the relative sizes of the two populations, it was well within the bounds of probability that a Catholic and a Protestant would fall in love and want to marry each other and statistics from the time show that thirty per cent of Protestant brides took Catholic spouses. In doing so, because of the *Ne Temere* Decree, Protestants were, in effect, subscribing to the ultimate extermination of their own people and, what is more, they had little choice in the matter. Their only choice, favoured by most parents including Mamma and Papa, was to avoid meeting Catholics in any context where friendship, much less love, might develop. The result was that Protestants isolated themselves within their own social spheres, their own institutions, their own traditions; *The Irish Times* was a Protestant newspaper, Guinness's, Jacob's, and other large employers were Protestant firms, the Adelaide was a Protestant hospital. Protestants were abetted in their isolation by the attitude of the Catholic church as the same bishops and clergy who enforced the *Ne Temere* Decree vetoed Catholics attending Protestant churches and Protestant schools. To add to this, many Catholics — with some justification, it should be stated — disliked and resented Protestants and disapproved of mixed-marriages just as vehemently as did their Protestant counterparts. Catholic resentment owed much to the fact that, while representing only a tiny proportion of the population, Protestants still accounted for about twenty-five per cent of employers and, in the same proportion, farmers with more than two hundred acres. When it came to such pillars of society as lawyers and bank officials, the Protestant ratio was as high as fifty per cent. As far as history was concerned, the majority of writers who gave Ireland its literary reputation — from Jonathan Swift to Sean O'Casey — were also Protestants; and, when it came to patriots and revolutionaries, Protestants could claim their share of these too — from Wolfe Tone to Robert Emmett to Roger Casement. In other words, although a very small minority, Protestants occupied a substantial niche in the history and life of the country.

We as Protestants, while incensed and shaken by the perfidy of the *Ne Temere* Decree and alienated by the culture of Catholicism which prevailed in Ireland at the time, did not feel unduly threatened or afraid on account of this state of affairs. As children at Rathcormick, while we were aware that we were different to the majority of people around us, we did not feel isolated but, shameful though it is to admit it, superior.

In his opposition to the *Ne Temere* Decree (which was eventually abolished by the Catholic Church a decade and a half later), Papa encountered universal failure except in so far as none of his children married Catholics. But when discrimination against him and his type moved from the spiritual world to the temporal one, from the sacred to the profane, and focused on that issue, that contention, which, after religion, has most preoccupied the Irish mind since time began, he could be relied upon to triumph; when it came to a question of property, a question of land, failure was not something Papa was ready to countenance.

While Old Elliott's improvements to Rathcormick, most notably the portico, had given the house a greater dignity — instead of being just a lanky farmhouse it was now, if not quite a Seat, at least a Place — both the entrance and the approach were still very unassuming when Mamma and Papa went to live there. Unusually for Ireland, where the most majestic entrance gates — the cost of which in the eighteenth or nineteenth centuries often bankrupted a family — are frequently attached to a house that is scarcely more than a hovel, the gates to Rathcormick — white and wooden with a paling to match — were so understated that a visitor might well have been excused for thinking that they led to a cottage. 'Gentleman' John Potterton, who probably built the house, and who died in 1738, had shunned the necessity of 'gates' and so had his only son, Thomas, even though it was he who had enhanced the family's fortune so considerably. Gates, and the grandeur that went with them, seem to have been equally unimportant to the next five generations and so it fell to Papa, the ninth generation, to endow Rathcormick with the preamble it deserved. This took the form of quadrant enfilades of cut-stone piers topped by limestone finials in the shape of cannon-balls and interspersed with iron railings that are about five feet tall. When this ensemble, which Papa acquired from some demesne that had been burned-out in the Troubles, was installed, copper-beeches were planted to either side and an extensive shrubbery (which included two monkey-puzzles) was created to shield the entrance avenue from the unsightliness of the back paddock and the distant farmyard beyond. The avenue itself is on an incline and, even after rounding a bend, it is only a colossal chestnut tree and a weeping-ash of comparable dimensions that attract attention; the house, reticent behind a Victorian laurel plantation, comes later. When it does, it is apparent that it frowns down upon the thirty or so acres called the Lawn which amble away from it. The pasture is separated from the sweep in front of the house and what we called the front grass by the covert means of a ha-ha — a device known to us as a sunk-fence.

In the case of the lands at Rathcormick, Papa also sought to enhance and improve upon his inheritance — or rather the inheritance of his eldest male issue — but in doing so he encountered an impediment which preoccupied and infuriated him so intensely that it made his skirmishes with Bishop McCann seem no more arduous than, at best, a round of no-trumps at whist or, at worst, a morning of Pitman's with Miss Pringle. This obstacle took the form of the Irish Land Commission, and although the odds were always greatly weighted against him, Papa rode into battle against the Commission on more than one occasion, adamant that victory would be his; and if not victory, then blood.

The Commission had been established in the 1880s as a

Rathcormick, the entrance gates

rent-fixing body, with the objective of relieving the lot of Ireland's tenant farmers — and that included our ancestors — vis-à-vis their landlords. But following the foundation of the State, its powers had been extended so that it was enabled to purchase land compulsorily. This it did so assiduously that larger farms and estates were depleted in size and their former acreage distributed, in holdings of no more than thirty acres with a new two- or three-roomed cottage attached, to smallholders from disadvantaged areas mainly in the West of Ireland. The divested landholders were compensated by the means of Land Bonds: monetary instruments which furnished a modest income but the capital value of which was practically nil.

With de Valera's ascent to power, the activities of the Commission were greatly intensified as it was part of his policy, enshrined in his new Constitution, "that there may be established on the land in economic security as many farmers as in the circumstances shall be practicable". That, to Dev, meant a countryside dotted with contented and self-sufficient cottagers, attired in homespuns, and farming a few cattle, a few sheep, a pig, and growing a few potatoes and a few oats — and all on thirty acres. As many of those so accommodated would come from Irish-speaking districts towards the western seaboard, they would converse — and pass on stories of old — in Gaelic and, it goes without saying, they would also be Roman Catholic.

Commendable as de Valera's vision was, Papa — who, like other Protestants, by a curious irony always voted for Dev — knew that his policy was not, and never would be, viable. Papa himself worked with land and saw at first hand the struggle it was for most of those small Land Commission farmers to succeed on such a limited acreage. He knew that the 'economic security' which Dev envisaged would always elude them and that the vision, attractive as it might be, was flawed.

It would be disingenuous, however, to claim that it was solely as a matter of principle that Papa opposed the activities of the Land Commission. He was as aware as everyone else, of the vexatious history of land occupation and confiscation in Ireland and the justifiable passions which the topic inflamed on account of the fact that Catholics, having been deprived of their land in the seventeenth century — like Sir Luke ffitz Gerald at Rathcormick — on account of their religion, were severely restricted when it came to holding it again until at least the end of the eighteenth. So effective indeed had the Penal Laws been that, although about three-quarters of the population were Catholic as the end of the eighteenth century approached, only about five per cent of the land of Ireland was in their hands. Papa was cognisant of the iniquity which this history represented but he also had something to lose personally. That something was Rathcormick itself, the lands of which had been rented and farmed by him and his ancestors for over two-hundred-and-fifty years. He believed, and there are many who might have agreed with him, that such a tenure conferred some rights; and, when push came to shove, he was prepared to defend those rights to the utmost.

As children, we were first made aware of the depth of Papa's passion in relation to the Land Commission when the hall-door bell went one evening and Molly came in to say that Mr Eivers was in the hall.

'Bring him in,' said Mamma.

Mr Eivers was carrying a large roll of documents under his arm and, after a few preliminaries, he was persuaded to unfold these and lay them out on the floor.

'I think this is the sort of thing you had in mind,' he said.

Mamma and Papa peered at the papers on which a reasonably accurate representation of a house was delineated.

Mr Eivers was an architect.

Alan and I craned over Mamma's shoulder.

'What is it?' I said.

'What does it look like?' said Mamma.

'I can see it's a house,' I said, 'but there's no upstairs.'

'It's a bungalow,' said Mamma. 'The bedrooms are all on the ground floor.'

Apart from Land Commission cottages, the sight of a new house was rare at this time in Ireland. Those which stretch along the Trim road from Kildalkey would not be built until a few years later and apart from Loman Street — where a batch of semi-detacheds had been completed the previous year — Dr Walter's residence on the Dublin road was the only recently constructed house in Trim; it was to be several years before Mr Malone and Mr Orr would build their flat-roofed houses on the Navan road. On account of this situation, it went well beyond being a novelty for Mamma and Papa to contemplate building a bungalow; it was quite simply abnormal.

'Where's it going to go?' said Alan.

'Don't ask so many questions,' said Papa. 'Down in the Bottoms if you really want to know.'

He was referring to the low-lying field at the very edge of the farm, near Kildalkey Church, and on the opposite side of the road to all the other land.

'What's it for?' we asked.

'Your father and I are thinking of going to live there and get rid of you all,' said Mamma.

That night, after we went to bed, Alan and I discussed the matter at length, and after considering many options, we came to the conclusion that Elliott must be about to get married. There seemed to be no other explanation for building a bungalow in the Bottoms.

'Do you think it's one of the Randall girls?' Alan whispered.

He was referring to a pair of sisters from Kells whose magnificent ball-gowns at a dance in Rathcormick the previous Christmas had proved conspicuously memorable.

'I bet it's Elizabeth Strong,' I said. 'It's obvious.'

But Elliott's possible marriage — which, in the event, proved to be several years off — was not the actual inducement to enhance Rathcormick with a dower-house. Much more ominously, the impetus had come in the form of a visitation from the Land Commission when their brazenness in making an exhaustive inspection of the Bottoms had alarmed and angered Papa in the extreme. This was on account of the fact that, only about six years previously, the Commission had taken by compulsory purchase some of the neighbouring fields and had distributed them, in allotments of thirty-eight, thirty-five, twenty-five, ten, and five acres, to some of the intending smallholders who were the subjects of Mr de Valera's dreams.

This area of Rathcormick, originally two-hundred-and-sixty-four acres which had been part of the lands since time immemorial, had not been included in the Fee Simple which Old Elliott had purchased from Lord Darnley in 1909. As a result, it was still held on a lease by our family in the 1950s as it had been since 28 July 1710. But, on account of the success of the Land Commission in carrying out the functions for which it was originally established, Lord Darnley had been bought out and the Land Commissioners themselves were now the landlords. In compulsorily purchasing part of the lands, the Commissioners sold the freehold of the balance — the Bottoms — to Papa. But their powers were such that they could at any time have effected the compulsory purchase of that as well. In response to this threat, Papa had conceived the plan of building a house on the land and thereby creating the impression that Rathcormick would one day have to support two households, an eventuality which, as he had six sons, was well within the bounds of probability. Far from being merely a bungalow, therefore, the proposed structure was conceived as a defence, a fortress, and as such it proved to be entirely successful.

Thereafter, Papa's battles with the Land Commission moved to a more novel arena entirely.

Towards Westmeath, on the way to Castlepollard, was a large house hidden from view by venerable beeches and oaks and standing on high ground. A modest entrance with simple cut-stone pillars supporting rusting white iron gates led to an overgrown avenue that wound up through tangled laurels and rhododendrons which, although only the common *ponticum*, never flowered. The clay in Meath is much too rich in lime. The house was one of those large, three-storey, square houses, rendered on the outside and with a large overhanging eave, that are not uncommon in Ireland. It was probably built around 1800 and, as it was not disfigured by anything that could be described as architectural merit or style, it remained reassuringly pleasant as a structure with a hall-door flanked by

Papa conceived the bungalow as a defence

lancet windows and the usual fanlight resembling a tattered doily above. The gravel sweep in front of the house had become a sward of grass and moss and underneath the giant single windows — their sills no more than eighteen inches from the ground — some hardy aquilegias and a few Michaelmas daisies, remnants of a herbaceous border, struggled to survive. At the sides of the house, grassy banks led down to basement windows and from this angle, where the friendly charm of the facade gave way to a chilly bleakness, the house appeared more sinister.

This was Cooper's Grove and it was here that Mrs Cooper-Pugh and her granddaughter Alexandra — who was my age exactly — took up residence every Christmas and Easter, and for several weeks each summer. Their visitations were not preceded by armies of servants to 'open the house' as would have been the case when, decades previously, Mrs Cooper-Pugh had married into Cooper's Grove; her husband, it was said, had been many years her senior while she had been no more than a child. Instead, Mrs Cooper-Pugh and Alexandra drove down from the modest house in a Dublin suburb where they passed the rest of the year in relative comfort, and camped in the huge drawing room at Cooper's Grove. They had beds on either side of the white marble chimney-piece, a black Aladdin paraffin heater in the centre of the room, and on the remains of a fine eighteenth-century mahogany side-table near the window, a Primus stove.

'I can never understand people with an interest in cooking,' Mrs Cooper-Pugh would say.

Making way for a blackened aluminium kettle, she would remove a saucepan of congealed baked beans from the Primus and, with only a moment's hesitation, dump it down on the pewter-coloured silver-plate tray which sat on the lid of a rosewood Bösendorfer grand.

Mrs Cooper-Pugh was Anglo-Irish by adoption — it was rumoured that she had been a dancer in London during her youth — and this explained the complete ease with which she was able to live in such deplorable chaos. As we were conventional, well-scrubbed Protestants, used to wholesome food and standards of hygiene which bordered on the obsessive, we found the general air of unorthodoxy at Cooper's Grove confusing and disturbing in the extreme. In the first instance, no part of the house other than the drawing room was occupied and, apart from the Aladdin and the Primus, the baked beans and the Bösendorfer, other aspects of the room's arrangement were quite unfamiliar to us: the mantelpiece, festooned with dusty, out-of-date calendar cards from the Meath Hounds, the Tara Harriers, and the Royal Society of Antiquaries, was unbelievably untidy; piles of *Country Life*, *Social and Personal*, and *Racing News* were strewn about the floor; and, while Mrs Cooper-Pugh and Alexandra sat on wooden stools near the fireplace, the large chintz-covered armchairs and comfortable-looking sofa were occupied exclusively by entire families of fox terriers.

Cooper's Grove was a substantial farm and it is safe to assume that, notwithstanding the marriage many decades previously of a Cooper daughter to a Pugh, it had been in the Cooper family for generations. Mrs Cooper-Pugh hoped it would stay that way and, more to the point, so did Papa. His interest in the matter — if an excuse was needed at all — stemmed from his friendship with Mrs Cooper-Pugh and the fact that he managed her affairs. Mrs Cooper-Pugh's hope had been that her only daughter, Virginia, would one day marry a gentleman, live at Cooper's Grove, and revive the old place; but Virginia, when she grew up, had other ideas. She married a gentleman all right, but as he sold Aga cookers for Masser's and lived in Clontarf, hopes that he would oversee a revival of Cooper's Grove soon faded while Virginia herself, once Alexandra was born, devoted her entire existence to the breeding of Airedales and ignored Cooper's Grove altogether.

This turn of events placed an additional onus on Mrs Cooper-Pugh and, when Virginia tired of the baby Alexandra after only a year or two, Mrs Cooper-Pugh took the infant to live with her, on the premise that failure with one generation did not necessarily mean that success would also elude her with a second.

'My grandmother has adopted me,' Alexandra would tell me.

We would have been sent out to play while Mamma and Mrs Cooper-Pugh had tea together, and as we penetrated further and further into the undergrowth, she would divulge details of the latest schemes which Mrs Cooper-Pugh had devised for her education and improvement.

'Alexandra is having elocution,' I would tell Mamma in the car coming home.

'And what about her riding? Is she still going to Iris Kellett?' Mamma would ask.

'Can I go to elocution too?' I would say.

'Don't talk nonsense,' Mamma would reply, 'you're affected enough as it is.'

But that evening she would, inexplicably as far as I was concerned, say to Papa: 'There never was a child that was given a better chance in life than Alexandra. Mrs Cooper-Pugh is terribly kind to her.'

Alexandra's progress along the sunny path which was intended to lead one day to the stewardship of Cooper's Grove had not proceeded all that far before it collided with precisely the same impediment as had led Papa to build his bungalow. This was an inspection of the farm by the Land Commission and a subsequent proposal to purchase compulsorily — and pay for with Land Bonds — Cooper's Grove in its entirety. The scheme was as a taper to a tinder-box and Papa, fuelled by a perverse disappointment that the bungalow had been so successful in making the Commission lose interest in his own affairs, went into battle on Alexandra's behalf.

Although she was no more that ten or twelve years old, he personally coached her for what amounted to a flamboyant appearance at a tribunal in Dublin when she swore under oath that it was her dearest wish and firm intention to one day farm every last acre of Cooper's Grove as her ancestors, for generations before her, had also done. Across the simulated courtroom, the team of civil servants was so startled by the assurance of Alexandra's performance in the witness-box that they overcame their natural prejudice towards someone like Papa and withdrew their case; meanwhile the arbitrator himself was so moved by the tableau as a whole — and not least by Mrs Cooper-Pugh's poignant recitation (also rehearsed by Papa) of her single-handed struggle to maintain Cooper's Grove through two generations — that he severely reprimanded the officials concerned for ever 'disturbing these good people' and ordered the claim to be struck off without further ado.

Papa showed no sense of jubilation when he came home. It was common sense as far as he was concerned that Alexandra would be allowed to come into her rightful inheritance.

Coopers' Grove
It was here that Mrs Cooper-Pugh and her grand-daughter,
Alexandra, spent several months of summer every year

16. The Best Beef in the Country

Granny Potterton — who eventually died in her ninetieth year — would come and stay with us sometimes, but her visits were never a success and she often insisted on being taken home again after only a couple of days.

'She just got into a huff and said she knew when she wasn't wanted,' Mamma would explain when Papa came home in the evening.

Granny got huffed quite easily. It was a pronounced character trait which she passed on to all her family, including Papa.

'There was nothing I could do,' Mamma would continue. 'I had no option but to pack her things and drive her straight back to Ardkill.'

Ardkill, near Carbury in County Kildare, is where Papa was born and brought up, the eldest of six. Granny, whose maiden name was Homan, lived there with Uncle Hubert. Her father-in-law, my great-grandfather, Richard, who was born — a younger son — in Rathcormick, had 'married into' Ardkill; his wife was Martha Sale and the Sales had lived there for generations. The house may once have been a glebe and that is what it looks like: very simple, two stories above a basement — the sort of house a child would draw. It was probably built about 1810. There is a farm attached which Granny herself farmed for years as my grandfather, Thomas, predeceased her by thirty-three years.

On one of her visits to Rathcormick when she was well into her seventies, Granny climbed to the top of Trim Castle and Uncle Arthur, who followed her up, had the greatest difficulty getting her back down again. Granny was always partial to an outing, and as she was interested in history, archaeology, and old things generally, the type of outing she liked most of all normally involved a ruin or two. It was rare for any meeting of the Kildare Archaeological Society to take place without her and she never missed their excursions.

'She could never sit still for a moment', was how Mamma described her mother-in-law. 'Always had to be gallivanting.

Ardkill, where Papa was born and brought up

191

Any old stone in a field was excuse enough for her to insist on being taken for a drive. Hubert, Ken, and Arthur had an awful time with her. Of course, Polly and Isa are exactly the same: always ferreting about.'

Granny's interest in outings and everything old occasionally brought her to destinations further afield than those visited by the Kildare Archaeological Society. In her younger days she had loved London, and when she came home she would tell about visiting the National Gallery. She always kept a peacock and peahen at Ardkill; they went well with her sense of style as they strutted about the sweep in front of the house.

'Awful noisy things', was how Mamma described them, 'and how she manages to keep a thing in the garden when they are so destructive, I don't know.'

But Granny Potterton managed to keep quite a lot of things in her garden (and also in her greenhouse) because she was a wonderful gardener. Unlike Mamma's garden, where order was imposed in every nook, Granny's garden teemed with naturalness, clutter, and romance; but what distinguished it as special, and indeed distinguished Granny herself, was flair. Granny Potterton did not just have good taste, Granny Potterton had flair.

Unfortunately I remember less about Granny Potterton's garden than I do about Granny Potterton herself and even that is not very much. Later in my life, however, I came to know her daughter Polly relatively well and, by all accounts, she was a replica of her mother. Instead of the Kildare Archaeological Society, Aunt Polly devoted herself to the Dublin Historical Society (and published papers in their journal). She was a fanatical collector of antique bits and pieces, and when it came to flowers and gardening, her expertise and accomplishment were greatly admired, even in Dublin horticultural circles. "Artistry" is the word which springs to mind in thinking of Aunt Polly. She brought the same artistry which she had inherited from her mother to everything she did and her home — cluttered, comfortable, and tattered to a degree — was always a delight on account of the unexpected and the unusual that was to be encountered there.

Granny Potterton was a large woman, very tall with big hands and feet. She always wore blue: powder blue, knitted, and in layers, accompanied by layers of beads in long strands that fell down almost to her waist. She liked clothes. I have a photograph of her with her three daughters-in-law, taken at Uncle Hubert's wedding when she was already elderly, and she is far more handsome than any of them. She outshone them all in other respects as well and, as a matter of policy, she let them know it. Like Aunt Polly, she could have an intonation in her speech which was not quite sarcasm but when used effectively — and Granny Potterton always used it effectively — had the capacity to make even the most innocuous statement sound devastating.

'You're marvellous the way you always manage to have fresh scones in the house,' she would say to Mamma, but in a way that had the desired effect of sending Mamma into a frenzy of resentment.

'What she had to be snobby about, I never knew,' Mamma always said about her. 'A more difficult woman never walked this earth.'

When she died, she was buried — alongside my grandfather and my great-grandfather — in the graveyard on the top of Carbury Hill.

'What a business getting a hearse all the way up there,' Mamma said when she came back from the funeral, 'a more awkward place would be hard to imagine.'

She moved the kettle over on to the plate of the Aga.

'But then when I think of it,' she said, 'I suppose it will be well-suited to her in that respect.'

Granny Tong was dead by the time I was born and the

member of Mamma's family who made the greatest impression on me — and indeed on everyone she met — was Auntie Frank. Like her mother, she had been christened Annie Elizabeth, but to avoid confusion between the two, everyone called her Frank. When Auntie Frank was only about twenty, she met a man called Leslie Knox at a tennis party and, before the afternoon was out, she had consented to marry him. The fact that he was a tea-planter and living in India (to where he was about to return) did not deter her in the least, and even though she had rarely been away from her home on a farm in County Offaly, it did not cost her a thought to promise to follow him. And that is what she did.

'When I think of it now, Pappy was awfully callous to let poor Frankie go off to India like that on her own,' Mamma

When Granny Potterton was well into her seventies, she climbed to the top of Trim Castle

would recall. 'And she not knowing a soul. Her bridesmaid was only another girl she met on the ship.'

'Why didn't she marry Uncle Leslie at home before he left and then go back with him?'

'Pappy wouldn't allow that. He thought it was just another one of Frankie's whims and that she would forget him as soon as he was back in India. But Frankie was very determined and in the end he had to give in and let her go.'

'Was no one worried about her setting off on her own? The voyage would have taken weeks.'

'Weeks! It was months and it was also months before we heard if she had arrived, much less whether or not Leslie was there to meet her. She might have got malaria or typhoid or anything and Leslie wasn't exactly the most reliable sort.'

'He must have had something.'

'Talk, that's what. He was all talk. Of course, he looked very dashing — as if anyone would put any store by that. But Frankie was very smitten. And, in the event, she always stood by him. But she has the climate in India to thank for being as crippled as she now is with arthritis.'

My earliest recollection of Uncle Leslie and Auntie Frank is when on one of their visits home from India, they stayed in Rathcormick. Uncle Leslie chain-smoked, stayed in bed for most of the day, and seemed (not surprisingly) to be addicted to tea. From early in the morning until the moment he appeared downstairs, Auntie Frank ferried trays of tea up to him in the spare room and, even when he was up and about, she maintained a pot of tea brewing on the back of the Aga all day long from which she replenished his cup at regular intervals until nightfall. I doubt very much if my Uncle Leslie had ever read the stories of Somerset Maugham, and it is even less likely that the illustrious author would ever have encountered him. Nevertheless, in both appearance and demeanour, Uncle Leslie was the living embodiment of a type of character which

Maugham delineated exactly: the spoilt, hot-tempered, weak yet strong, autocratic, and occasionally charming European who thrived on bullying the natives in some distant corner of the tropical globe. In appearance, he was also decidedly suave with the type of moustache that was called a Ronnie, sleek pomaded hair, and a precision about his dress which indicated the services of a valet or, at very least, a batman.

It goes without saying that Uncle Leslie and Papa had about as much in common as a tomcat and a terrapin, and that the weeks of Uncle Leslie's septennial furloughs which were spent at Rathcormick occasioned a strain in the household matched only by the bedlam which reigned whenever our cousin Moira (who was Uncle Leslie and Auntie Frank's daughter) stayed with us on her own.

Nostalgic for Ireland as they lived out their exile in India, Auntie Frank and Uncle Leslie had given both their children Irish names. Kevin, the elder, was fat and staid, but Moira was boisterous in the extreme. She had inherited from her mother such a sense of adventure and fun that to be with her — or anywhere near her — was a roller-coaster ride of the unexpected, the uncertain, and the unknown. Danger was unimaginable to her, thrills the mainstay of her existence, and recklessness was her alter ego. She was about the same age as Alan and, probably on account of the relative isolation of her childhood years in India, she had a resourcefulness when it came to devising the wildest of escapades which she put into practice with me, and more particularly Alan, as her accomplices. She got us to strip naked and go swimming in the swamp down the Lawn, even though it was only February and, in spite of an unexpected burst of sunshine, black frost still covered the ground. She excavated what she called 'a lair' by making a long, dangerous tunnel between the ricks of hay that towered about fifty feet up to the top of the hayshed, then summoned us to secret meetings there where she made us swear an oath of fealty to her — which, as she was so impressive, we readily did. Spotting the keys in the Prefect when it was parked in the front yard, she dared Alan to drive it and then, when he had it marooned and unable to reverse, she took the wheel herself, and before we knew what was happening, did a lap up the back yard, down the middle yard and, narrowly missing the piers as she hurtled through the arch, brought the vehicle to an abrupt and explosive standstill within inches of where we were waiting. At Mamma's instigation, Alice — in an attempt to turn her more into a little girl — gave her a home perm, but the last curler was hardly in place when Moira dashed out to the yard, hailed Alan and me, and brought us up to the loft where grain was stored.

'It's the Himalayas,' she said, with the certainty of one who had actually lived within view of the celebrated mountains themselves. 'Do you want to see an avalanche?'

Climbing onto a pile of oats, she scaled one of the peaks and then, shouting at us to watch, flung herself into the air. Coming down again, she landed on her bottom which set the slopes of grain in motion.

'Now you do it,' she said.

An hour or more later, when Alan and I were utterly exhausted, we went back into the house.

Mamma stared at Moira.

'Where on earth have you been?' she said.

Only about two of Alice's curlers were still intact — the rest had been lost on Everest — and Moira's head — its perming gel still effective — resembled a honeycomb of satiated bees. In place of the curls which Alice had so carefully created were grains of oats impacted like gravel on a road that had just been tarred.

Moira injected an element of rash exhilaration into our lives that even Alan, on occasion, found intimidating, a scar on his eyebrow serving as a permanent reminder of the time he was dared by Moira to jump from the top of the hay. But in spite of such mishaps we loved it when Moira stayed at Rathcormick and although Mamma found her antics terrifying — and she only ever got wind of some of them — she loved Moira's visits too.

After years in India, Uncle Leslie and Auntie Frank, Kevin, and Moira came home. They brought with them a pet monkey, and when they settled in Belfast, tied it by means of a long chain to a tree in their garden. We used to go and visit them, travelling up on the train from Amiens Street and, as there was still some form of rationing in the North, we always brought food: eggs, butter, home-made bread and, on visits before Christmas, a turkey.

'Take off your coats and spread them over those parcels,' Mamma would say to Alan and me as we approached the border.

'When the Customs Officer comes in, don't move. I'll hide the turkey under my fur coat.'

But on more than one occasion, in spite of Mamma's assurances that she only had 'a few Christmas things for her sister', everything was confiscated and we arrived empty-handed.

After a year or two, Uncle Leslie decided that he did not like Belfast and that they should all emigrate to Canada.

'Poor Frankie having to trail around the world after that man,' Mamma said when they left.

Then a few years later, Moira came back one summer and spent some months at Rathcormick. She was no longer the tom-boy but an appealing and pretty young woman and every bit as tempting as her mother had been before her. Not surprisingly, Mr Denning fell in love with her and, when she returned to Canada, he followed her. Making as his excuse that there was no future for him at Rathcormick, he left his job and, much to our sorrow, he left our family circle too.

*

Although Granny Potterton, Auntie Frank and Uncle Leslie, Uncle Arthur, and other more distant relatives were sometimes invited as guests to Rathcormick, it was unknown for any of us as children to ever ask a friend to come and stay. We had frequent children's parties, teenage parties, tennis parties — even dances — when the house would be thronged with guests but no one was ever asked to stay the night. This seems to have been more a convention — and it may have had something to do with the fact that Papa was so very stiff — than a deliberate policy, but the result was that on the very rare occasions when an outsider was introduced, their novelty value was at a premium. On no occasion was that premium quite so high as

Carbury Hill
A more awkward place it would be hard to imagine

when Elliott, about a year after he returned from Dunfermline, invited over a friend from Scotland.

Without ever being fulsome on the subject, he had from time to time mentioned Jennifer to Mamma.

'My grandmother was Scots,' was all Mamma said, 'and no woman ever worked harder.'

And then, when it looked as though Elliott was about to volunteer more information, she interrupted him:

'The Scots are always spotlessly clean,' she said.

Over the months, letters addressed in a confident, well-formed hand came every week or so to Rathcormick although occasionally the pattern was interrupted by the arrival of a postcard from Oban or Berwick-on-Tweed. Most times, Elliott would intercept the post before it was brought up to Rosina for opening, but when he failed to do so, Rosina would mistakenly open the letter and add it to Papa's basket of correspondence. Later, as Papa worked his way through the mail in the office, he would come across the letter — the writing-paper was invariably blue — replace it in its envelope and, without a word, put it down on the table beside Elliott.

After a time, Elliott asked Mamma if he might invite Jennifer to come and stay.

'How would Himself take it if I had a friend over on a visit?' he said.

'When were you thinking of?' said Mamma.

'September maybe. Now that he's got used to the idea that I'm well-able to look after the business on my own for the last two weeks of August while he's in Kilkee, he's always in better twig when he comes home.'

'Why don't you just ask him? That's the best thing. You know he never says no to you boys himself, whereas when I bring up anything with him there's no end of barging.'

'Maybe,' said Elliott. 'But perhaps, just this time, you might sound him out?'

'I'll try, but I still think it would be far better your saying to him that you have a friend and that her parents were very kind to you in Dunfermline, and that you'd like to invite her here in return. He won't eat you, you know.'

'I don't know all the same,' said Elliott.

Time does not relate whether it was Mamma or Elliott himself who brought up the subject with Papa but that year, immediately after we came back from Kilkee at the end of August, the visit took place.

When she arrived at Rathcormick she had a colossal bunch of flowers for Mamma which she must have bought in Dublin, but instead of being impressed by the thoughtfulness of the gesture, Mamma was flabbergasted.

'What could Elliott be thinking of to let the poor girl go and spend her money on flowers, when he knows that there are all the flowers in the world out in the garden,' she said.

Later in the afternoon, when Jennifer had unpacked, she came downstairs with a small crockery vase in the shape of a thistle and gave it to Mamma.

'I know that purple is your favourite colour,' she said and then, taking out what was obviously a box of handkerchiefs, she gave it to Rosina. Next came some shortbread in a tartan tin. It was labelled 'A present from Dunfermline' and she handed it to Papa.

'Elliott let me in on the secret that a bottle of Scotch wouldn't be quite the thing,' she said.

'You'll be longing for a cup of tea,' said Mamma, heading out towards the kitchen. Papa went into the office.

Turning to Alan and me, Jennifer produced two packets of huge round sweets.

'They're called gobstoppers,' she said. 'Try them.'

We opened the packets and popped a sweet into our mouths.

'Or krant shpreak,' said Alan.

'Wor tun ee,' said I.

We ran out to offer some to Molly in the kitchen.

'Would you like a gobstopper?' we said taking the half-sucked sweets out of our mouths to show them to her.

'Don't on any account let your father hear you saying something like that,' said Mamma.

She opened the tin that was on the table before her and took out a coffee cake.

'There's going to be trouble enough as it is.'

As it happened, Alan and I were thrilled with Jennifer who turned out to be a terrific sport. While Elliott was busy in the office, and when she was not playing tennis with David or Raymond, she entertained us with stories and all sorts of adventures that we had never before imagined. As there was no bicycle for her, she rode mine and popped me up on the crossbar when she challenged Alan to a race. She got us to take her out and show her the sheep and marched us through the stubble while counting the number of pigeons we managed to disturb. When she saw the Green Hill Pond, she promised us that there must be fish in it and that we would come back another day to catch them. The last of the hay was being brought in during the week that she was there, and after surprising the horses by offering them a lump of sugar (which they had never before been given), she joined us on the bumpy ride on the empty bogeys out to the hayfield with Quirke and Malone. On the return journey when the cock of hay had been loaded up, she hopped up at the back beside us, her feet dragging the ground like ribbons dangling from a bonnet, and laughed her way back in to the yard. But Jennifer's most memorable asset was the fact that she was a wonderful pianist. Without the encumbrance of a single sheet of music, she could play any tune we asked for and, more often than not, she could sing the words as well. With only the slightest prompting and without a thought as to whether Papa was in the office or not, she would sit down at the piano in the sitting room and play away. We were thrilled at the novelty of it and even Mamma seemed to be impressed:

'It's marvellous to have such a wonderful ear,' she said.

It was when Jennifer's visit seemed to be going very well that it came to an abrupt and memorable end. It was a Saturday dinner time about a week after she had arrived.

Raymond and David had not yet gone back to school, and although Alice was in England and Edward was abroad, there remained ten to be seated so that Rosina had set the table in the dining room. As Papa had to go in to his office in Trim for the afternoon, Mamma sounded the gong sharp at half-past twelve and told Molly to run out and ring the bell in the yard which would alert David and Alan (who were up in the back paddock) to the fact that the meal was ready. There was soup first, then when the plates were being cleared, Molly came in with the dinner — a steak and kidney pie, boiled potatoes in their skins, and peas — and set it down on the table in front of Mamma.

'I hope you don't mind kidney,' Mamma said to Jennifer.

She took up a knife to cut the crust on the pie. We could see through the glass sides of the pyrex dish that the juices were still bubbling from the heat.

'Not in the least,' said Jennifer. 'I love it.'

Mamma was at the head of the table and Papa was seated to her right. He leaned over for the jug of water and poured himself a glass.

'Pass that down to … em … eh …' he said to Raymond as he handed him the jug. He nodded towards Jennifer who was seated at the other end of the table.

'Will you have a potato?' said David.

He handed Jennifer the dish of Golden Wonders, their skins bursting open to reveal the full fleeciness of their insides.

'It's the very last of the peas, I'm afraid,' said Mamma. 'They might be a bit tough by now, but we quite like them that way.'

'Ugh,' said Alan screwing up his face.

Then, when everyone had been helped and Mamma had taken her seat, we all tucked in. There was no general conversation around the table, but Mamma was talking to Miss Shannon and Papa was suggesting to Rosina that, if she thought she would be strong enough the next day, they might go out for a bit of a drive. Low mutterings interrupted by sniggers came from the far end of the table as David and Elliott attempted to make Jennifer giggle over nothing at all. When these murmurings reached a crescendo, Papa's irritation became visible.

'I'll have a little mustard, if you don't mind,' he said to Miss Shannon.

Then, having speared a lump of steak on to his fork, he glanced down the table towards Jennifer and said in a loud voice:

'We get very good meat here on account of the land being so rich. It's not so good for mutton of course, but our beef is really the best in Ireland.'

Jennifer continued chewing for a moment or two and, when her mouth was quite empty and with all the clarity that her Scots accent could muster, she said:

'We get very good meat at home too ...'

The few days in the country had given her complexion an additional lustre so that the sweetness of her smile was heightened and it was with that smile that she now looked at Papa.

'You see, ma daddy's a butcher and he keeps all the best cuts for ourselves.'

The effect of her statement was so electric that, more than three decades later, Mamma still shuddered when she recalled the incident.

'It sounds funny now,' she would say, 'but at the time I was convinced that poor Papa was going to choke. I can still hear the way she came out with the word 'bootcha' and she being so anxious to please.'

After dinner, Papa spoke to Mamma, but before Mamma had a chance to speak to Elliott, he came to her and said, 'I know …'

He went over to the kitchen window and looked out. He had his hands in his pockets.

'Don't worry,' he said, 'she'll be gone by the time he gets back from Trim this evening.'

And so it was that Jennifer left Rathcormick. Elliott took her up to the boat that afternoon, the lid of the Collard & Collard was closed once more, Alan and I never caught the fish in the Green Hill Pond, and the best beef in Ireland was not mentioned again for some considerable time.

'I thought poor Papa was going to choke when she said it'

17. A Treatment for Tantrums

'You can throw that away without any further ado,' Papa said to Mamma one day after dinner.

He handed her a large, navy-blue, illustrated pamphlet with an embossed crest on the cover.

'Elliott and Edward between them learned nothing there.'

'I thought it was no harm sending away for the prospectus anyhow,' said Mamma. 'The school might have improved since the boys were there. There's supposed to be a new headmaster.'

'Well I am not letting any son of mine go to Portora ever again,' said Papa.

The time had come for Alan to be sent away to school and Mamma, on Papa's instructions, had applied for information from every Protestant secondary-school in the country.

'Mountjoy?' said Papa.

He picked up the next brochure from the pile that Mamma had put on the table before him.

'After the way that man Tate treated David, I wouldn't satisfy him by sending another boy there,' he said.

'Mr Tate was only doing his job,' said Mamma. 'You know that. And what was the man to do when he actually caught the young monkey, red-handed, with a cigarette in his mouth?'

'I'm not very keen on any of these Dublin schools,' said Papa. 'Alan would get to know no one who has any practical knowledge of anything.'

He discarded the prospectuses for St Andrew's College, Wesley, and The King's Hospital.

'That place!' he said. He held up a booklet, rivalling in its elegance the volume from Portora, which described the educational programme at St Columba's College. He fanned the pages and stopped to look at one or two of the photographs, and then peering across the top of his spectacles, he stared at Mamma.

'Do you really want a son of yours to turn out like Rexy Rankin?' he said. 'All the Rankins went there and a lot of good it did them. Teaching farming indeed, and the school stuck halfway up a mountain.'

'Now this seems like a nice enough place,' he said. 'Bishop Foy School, it's not too big and there's bound to be a lot of country boys there. We might tip down and have a look at it.'

'Why on earth would we want to send the boy off to school in Waterford?' said Mamma. 'It's the other end of the country.'

'A lot of pupils from there seem to go on for the church,' said Papa. 'It would be a good thing to have at least one son a clergyman.'

'It's difficult enough to get the children back to school even when they are nearby without sending them to the far corners of the world,' said Mamma. 'It would smarten Alan up to go to a Dublin school. There's this place Morgan's in Castleknock — so that it is not quite in Dublin — and it seems a good sensible school. If all came to all, he would be able to go back on the bus.'

And so it was that Alan was sent to Morgan's, but after

about two years, when he looked set to become a professional boxer (he came home at the end of each term with medals and terrible scars as evidence of his prowess in the ring), it was conceded that the choice had been disastrous.

The satisfaction of selecting a school for Alan led Mamma and Papa to think of sending me away as well and, as I was only nine at the time, their choice fell on a small boarding-school, Preston in Navan, which Raymond had been attending for several years. The school had been chosen for him because, as a small boy, he had an uncontrollable temper and when Mamma and Papa interviewed the headmaster, Mr Church, he assured them — without revealing that he himself was given to rages of the most frenzied and violent kind — that he was experienced in dealing with children of an irascible nature. Whatever Mr Church's method was, it became a subject of general consensus that 'he had worked wonders on Raymond' and, as I too had a pronounced leaning towards throwing tantrums, it seemed sensible for me to be subjected to a similar cure. And so, saying goodbye to Miss Thompson and leaving Rusty in as dejected and forlorn a state as he had ever been forced to admit to, I set off for Navan and the world of academe as represented by Preston.

The school was a big old heap of a building hidden away behind formidable gates in the very heart of Navan, with a gravel avenue that approached it from the rear. Its grounds, which were all to the front, were large enough for a hockey pitch and several tennis courts to be fitted onto terraces which stepped down, among flowerbeds here and there, from the main facade. Such was the seclusion of the place that once inside the precincts it was impossible to imagine or believe that the metropolis which Navan then was buzzed around on every side. This seclusion may have been a key element in the discipline Mr Church succeeded in imposing, as our experience of the outside world was limited to whatever we were able to observe as we stalked, two-by-two, up Flower Hill and out into the country on the extended walks which were an essential element of the school's agenda. Mr Church, along with Mrs Church and her sister, Miss Rockingham, lived in the rooms that overlooked the grounds; the dormitories and classrooms were at the back, the dining-hall in the basement. There too was the small yard, enclosed along one side by lavatories and with the Stick House (where firewood was stored) to the other end. This was the only outside space to which access, unsupervised, was permitted and it was there on Mondays that lines of navy-blue knickers — each bearing the name-tags of their owners, Catherine Hughes, Olwyn Onions, Jean Henderson, Gloria Craig — were exhibited in the breeze to dry. Exceptionally among Irish boarding-schools at the time, Preston was coeducational.

Raymond was Head Boy. He had been Head Boy for years as there were only twelve boys in the school and he was the oldest. There were sixteen girls. These quotas, which depended on the size of the dormitories, were fixed and although restricted, the small numbers were more than compensated for by the wide variety in the ages of the pupils which in a good year ranged from about eight to eighteen. The same diversity prevailed when it came to the Preston's curriculum: English, French, Latin, and Irish; algebra, geometry, and trigonometry; history and geography were all taught from elementary level to university entrance and, as if that were not astonishing enough, instruction in all these subjects was provided by Mr Church himself with the sole assistance of a kind and gentle Miss Dunbar. Neither physics nor chemistry was provided for at Preston, nor indeed was Art, but these omissions were offset by the school's reputation for Scripture while the musical accomplishment of many of the pupils, as well as their capacity for the waltz, gave Preston a renown which far exceeded, in the minds of many of the parents, the attractions and benefits of science. Music and ballroom dancing, taught weekly through the means of visitations from Miss Strong and Mrs Murray, gave the school a humanity which served to temper the rigour of Mr Church's regime.

Mr Church was an imposing figure: very tall, slim, silver-haired, masculine and with an hauteur about his bearing. While not excessively cruel, he revered discipline and sought to instil into boys and girls alike a reverence for order which matched his own. This he did by means of routine thrashings of the boys in his charge, which he performed publicly, and there was not a single person in the school who did not find him terrifying.

If Preston sounds the sort of school with which Jane Eyre in her younger years would have been familiar, that was actually far from being the case. It was certainly not Lowood, and although it would be fair to call Mr Church a disciplinarian, he had no Miss Scatchard to enforce his discipline along the lines which Jane Eyre experienced. Miss Rockingham, who had a tenderness and warmth about her personality, was both cook and matron; but, beyond all that, she was the mother which all of us were missing. She bathed us on Saturday nights, on occasion tucked us into bed, tended our cuts and sores, and when we got stuck after "Dear Mamma and Papa, I hope you are well …" when writing compulsory letters home, it was she who came to the rescue with the sundry items of "news" that Mr Church demanded. When in the kitchen, she contrived to turn the sparse ingredients which Preston's budget permitted into meals that were sufficiently disguised as to seem like food from home. On Sunday afternoons, she would often emerge — as though a truant herself — to share with us the collapsing remains of a chocolate cake which she had managed to whisk from the trolley while Mr and Mrs Church were still enjoying their tea.

Before going to Preston, I had for a time learned the piano. We had a shiny, black Collard & Collard which had stood unused in the sitting room since the time Mamma gave up playing before I was born. None of the others bothered with it and there was no atmosphere of music at home, but in spite of that, or perhaps because of it, I became convinced that I was musical, and after I pestered Mamma sufficiently on the topic, Mrs Rice was sent for. It was arranged that I would have lessons once a week, but almost as soon as these were underway, I realised that the scales which Mrs Rice seemed to think were essential to my progress were not at all what I had had in mind. I longed to play "Glorious Things of Thee are Spoken", the Twenty-Third Psalm, and even "St Patrick's Breastplate". After a while, I mastered a simplified version of "John Brown's Body", and surreptitiously I turned to a later exercise in my book and learned what I thought sounded like "Clementine"; but one day, when I was in the middle of the second chorus, Papa burst out of the office, identified the tune as 'an awful noise', and in ordering me to 'close the lid at once', instructed me to run out to the hen-house and collect the eggs. When Miss Pringle came she was more than willing to believe that I was musical and, although she was unable to play herself, she did teach me a one-handed version of "God Save the Queen".

All of this changed when I got to Preston. Miss Strong was one of those rare teachers who was so good at teaching that she acted as an inspiration to any pupil with whom she came in contact. She brought the best out of everyone she taught, so that children like myself, who were not in any way gifted musically soon developed a proficiency that was more than reasonable and, within two years, I had progressed to Second Grade. On account of Miss Strong, Preston was a musical school; almost everyone learned the piano and many people were extremely good; the grade examinations of the Royal Irish Academy of Music were part of the annual curriculum; and singing class on Thursdays was one of the highlights of the week. Unlike Miss Thompson, Miss Strong made no prior assumptions about anyone's voice, and indeed it was only with the greatest difficulty that someone like Raymond could persuade her, in order to be exempted from her instruction, that he had 'no voice at all'. She was a tiny lady — her growth had been stunted as a result of polio as a child — and, when she hopped up on the piano-stool, it was as though she were a sparrow, and when she started to play, it was as mellifluous as a lark.

The ultimate in musical accomplishment at Preston was an ability to perform two very complicated pieces. One of these, a largo and sonorous in the extreme, had fistfuls of resonant chords and required the most exhausting heavy-pedalling; the other, light as tinsel, trilled and tripped and, at its most exacting, demanded that the pianist should grope for the very palest of keys at the extreme top of the keyboard. The slow piece was called "Rendezvous", the energetic one, "The Robin's Return", and if one was to suggest a composer for either or both, it would be Brahms for "Rendezvous" and a meticulous imitator of Rossini for "The Robin's Return". To have heard Margaret Hughes — who was the best pianist in the school although Noel Nelson could perform anything by ear — play "The Robin's Return" or to see Dene Pickup's tall, elegant, figure seated on the piano-stool, her graceful fingers coaxing "Rendezvous" out of the ivory, was — for a small boy who longed to be musical — an inspiring experience.

When Bill Haley and his Comets brought out "Rock around the Clock" which introduced rock 'n' roll to the world, it was an instant success at Preston and before long we prevailed upon Mrs Murray to teach us the dance that, in the event, was to signal the demise of everything she and her profession stood for. With partners standing side by side and clasping each other, left hand to right hand and arms around the waist, we formed an orderly circle — like ponies on a carousel — around the main schoolroom, whose desks had been cleared to turn it into a ballroom. Then when Mrs Murray lowered the head of the gramophone and Bill Haley screamed at us to 'Shake, rattle, 'n' roll' we obeyed immediately, shunting forward and back, backwards and forward, in unison. Everything about Mrs Murray's version of rock 'n' roll depended on unison so that we might, for all the world, have been performing a quadrille; but in the context of the slow waltz, the quick step and the old-time waltz, rock 'n' roll was a wonderful novelty which immediately became a fixed attraction of Mrs Murray's Saturday night dancing-classes.

Apart from the dance itself, the signature hair-curl which Bill Haley sported on his forehead also made an impression on us and, with the aid of Tru Gel, we imitated it. This fashion was soon usurped by a fad for Davy Crockett hats — the song about the "King of the Wild Frontier" came out at that time — and we sent away for them to a London shop called Ellisdon's in High Holborn which advertised them in most of the comics which circulated around the school. Made of fur with a bushy tail hanging down the back, Davy Crockett hats were quite expensive and, in the event, proved to be entirely a luxury as Mr Church forbade us to wear them altogether. He pointed out, with some logic, that Navan was not "a mountain-top in Tennessee" which is where, according to the song, Davy Crockett was born. Ellisdon's also offered an illustrated catalogue of their other products and it was the arrival of this publication at Preston which led to the eclipse of Davy Crockett and every other craze that had gripped the school for some time.

For the most part, Ellisdon's sold joke products such as metal beetles — "just drop into a glass of milk and see everyone terrified" — or cushions which groaned when anyone sat on them; "Embarrass your Granny" was the guarantee. But one particular offering, the announcement for which occupied half a page, particularly caught our attention. "Hypnotise your friends," it said, "Anyone can do it." There followed a description of a booklet on offer which was "guaranteed" to teach the reader "even without previous experience" how to hypnotise people. Such an opportunity seemed too interesting to be ignored and, having organised a collection, we sent off a postal order without delay. In due course, a small, blue-covered paperback arrived in a plain envelope. *Hypnotism Made Easy* it was called and, having studied the volume throughout prep, one of the older boys, Russell, announced that he understood it completely and it was only a matter of someone volunteering and he would demonstrate in the dorm that night just how simple it was. All that was needed was a flashlight. When several boys volunteered, Russell went through the motions of assessing their suitability but his final choice fell upon a downy, twelve-year-old fairhead called Wood.

When Mr Church came into the dorm to perform lights-out that night, everyone was already in bed. Several boys even pretended to be asleep.

'Everything quiet, Nelson?' said Mr Church to the dorm prefect.

'Everything quiet,' said Nelson.

But for once, Mr Church was in the mood for a chat and he lingered at the door.

'Miss Rockingham tells me we'll be having the BCG next week,' he said.

'Yes, sir,' said Nelson.

'It'll be a bit of a disruption. But the doctor will bring a nurse with him from the hospital so that should speed things up.'

'Yes, sir,' said Nelson.

'Even still, they'll probably be here for the better part of the day by the time they vaccinate everyone,' said Mr Church. 'Very few people have already been done.'

'Some of the day-boys have,' said Nelson. 'Jackie Rowntree had it last week.'

'Is it terrible painful?' asked McKeever, who was always a sissy, from his bed in the corner.

'It makes a lot of people very sick,' said Mr Church.

There was a cheerfulness in his voice as he said it but then he became philosophical:

'It's extraordinary to think that TB will become a thing of the past,' he said.

There was a silence.

'Well, goodnight then,' said Mr Church.

He switched out the lights and departed.

The dorm was silent for at least ten minutes. What had seemed during the day like a great idea now became, in the darkness of the night, more frightening. What if anything went wrong and Russell, having hypnotised Wood, was unable to wake him up again? We remembered that the book said some people could walk on air if hypnotised successfully and we wondered what the people of Navan would say at the sight of such an apparition. As we lay there in the hush, many of us hoped the scheme would be dropped or, at very least, postponed.

After an interval, Russell got out of bed.

'Where's the flashlight?' he whispered.

'Now Wood, come and sit on this bed with your back against the wall and let your feet dangle over the side.'

He shone the flashlight on Wood's forehead.

'Close your eyes and let your body go limp. Now, tell me you're relaxed.

'I'm relaxed,' said Wood.

He stiffened on the bed and opened his eyes. The tension in the dorm caused us all to giggle.

'Everyone get back to bed until I have him completely out,' said Russell.

There was a seriousness about the way he issued the command and a gravity of tone about his next words — 'You're going to sleep, you're going to sleep' — which within a very short time convinced us that Wood was hypnotised.

'He's out,' said Russell.

He rested for a moment and then, shining the flashlight on the booklet, he turned over the page to Chapter Two.

"Elementary tasks for beginners" it was headed.

'Now I'm going to make him think it's a very hot day and that he is fishing down by the river,' said Russell.

'It's very hot, Wood,' he said.

And then he said it again and again until, in what seemed like moments, Wood had taken off the top of his pyjamas and, with the cord of a dressing-gown, was endeavouring to haul a fish up from the floor to the bed which he apparently believed was the bank of a river.

We all got out of bed and gaped.

'That's enough for tonight,' said Russell.

A wave of relief went round the dorm.

'I'm going to wake him up.'

He glanced at the relevant paragraph in the book and, having informed Wood that he was about to de-hypnotise him, began to slowly count down from ten. When Wood opened his eyes on cue, we gasped.

'You were hypnotised,' we said. 'You were really out.'

'Did you feel anything?'

'You weren't codding us, were you?'

'We'll do it again tomorrow night,' said Russell.

We all returned to our beds.

It was almost midnight and, in their quarters across the landing, Mr and Mrs Church had long since gone to bed and Miss Rockingham too, in her small room up in the attic, was also fast asleep. Somewhere on the opposite side of the building, Miss Dunbar, who was to be married that summer, was dreaming of organdie and tulle. In the dormitory, there came a knock on the door which separated us from the girls' dorm.

'Did it work?' whispered a voice through the keyhole.

'Yes,' said Russell. 'We'll tell you all about it in the morning.'

After that, until the end of the term, we had hypnosis in the dorm every night. It made a change from listening to someone reading aloud from Sherlock Holmes, which is what Mr Church believed that we were doing.

It was at Preston that I learned the facts of life. I already knew about the birds and the bees — or rather cattle, sheep, and pigs — as I had, at one stage or another, seen most of them being born at Rathcormick and, although some of the details remained a little hazy, I had a fair idea of what was what. I had not, however, managed to relate this information to the human world. I had played "I'll Show You Mine if You Show Me Yours" with a little girl friend while Mamma was having tea with her mother; but not having a younger sister, whose anatomy I might have examined more thoroughly, left me in a quandary when it came to several issues and, as a result, these remained unexplained. Being the youngest, I had never seen Mamma pregnant so that, when it came to the knotty problem of where babies come from, I was very undecided. Fairies, storks — there were none in County Meath — and cabbage leaves I knew were out of the question, but that was no help in explaining what Mamma meant when she told me that one of my friends was adopted. I could not see how that made him any different to me. One day, I overheard a plump tinker-woman at the back-door, in asking for 'a sup of milk and a haporth of drippin', tell Molly that she had 'another little crathur on the way' and hearing that led me to consider seriously for the first time other likelihooods which up to then I had regarded as impossible.

Preston put an end to all of this confusion. The school was a hot-bed of romance. Apart from the opportunities provided by Mrs Murray's dancing-classes and the possibilities inherent in a dormitory that was occupied by a group of boys of between ten and sixteen years old, there was ample scope for learning about sex in most of its forms and any reticence on the part of the very young was soon scotched by the example and instruction of those who were much older. In the first instance, the boys' dormitory was separated from the girls' dormitory by the sole means of a simple panelled door and when we, on both sides of this aperture, were not engaged in activities which were perhaps more usual in Ancient Greece than in 1950s' Navan, the door, which was always locked fast, became the focus of our interest. It had a key-hole and a gap at the bottom and these two openings permitted a copious exchange of billets-doux between those on either side. The requests, confidences, promises, arguments, and sundry points of information which

Preston was a hot-bed of romance

passed by this means from boys to girls and vice versa were legion; and, when it came to the keyhole, very few girls were averse to lingering for a moment or two in their nightdresses in the full knowledge that they were firmly in the sightline. As a general rule, there was much less demand for boys to do the same.

For my first term or two, my introduction to these goings-on proceeded along the most general lines, but as the Easter holidays approached, the extent of my knowledge was widened considerably when a thirteen-year-old siren, notwithstanding the difference in our ages, decided that she found me attractive. Clare was not the most beautiful girl in the school but, unlike most of the other girls who came from the country, she was from Dublin, was prodigiously well-developed physically, and had a natural preoccupation with sexual matters that marked her out as singularly advanced for one so young. All of this, she decided, she was prepared to share with me.

As Clare was not a girl to waste time, she made her intentions known very explicitly and one day, when I was taking off my cap and gabardine in the front hall, she approached me.

'You're my boyfriend,' she said.

I was not aware that it was possible to have a choice in the matter and so I did not contradict her; but in any case, as she soon told everyone else in the school, it seemed churlish to enter into a dispute. For a time, Clare was content with a relationship which amounted to little more than this unilateral declaration, and like most men in such situations, I was reluctant to take any action which would have disturbed the status quo. But after a few weeks during which, in return for holding my hand every now and then, she had promised me not even to look at any other boy, she decided to advance the affair to a more satisfying level.

The first intimation I had of this was one morning when

A Treatment for Tantrums

Miss Dunbar was in the process of explaining the hypotenuse to first class in the main schoolroom. The desks were divided so that there was an aisle down the middle of the room and those at kindergarten and first class level sat on one side, while second and third class sat on the other. When Miss Dunbar, having polished her glasses for a third time that morning, turned to the blackboard and with a screeching noise drew an isosceles triangle, I became aware that Clare, on the opposite side of the aisle to me, was attempting in a more vigorous manner than usual to attract my attention. Holding a note in one hand and *Palgrave's Golden Treasury* in the other, she indicated with a pronounced movement of her lips and an agitated shaking of her head that the note or the poetry book was intended for my inspection. Inserting the scrap of paper between the dark-blue covers of *Palgrave*, she leant down behind her desk and, with a determined swing of her arm, slid the volume across the floor in my direction. Scrambling down to get it, I removed the folded paper and glanced towards Clare.

'Open it,' she mouthed.

Ensuring that Miss Dunbar still had her back to the class, I unfolded the note.

"I bet you thruppence that you don't know what is an—" it read.

There followed a word beginning with "O", the pronunciation of which, even to myself, I was unable to articulate.

O-r-g-a-s-m was how it was spelled.

As I had no means of knowing what topic Clare was addressing — I assumed the word had something to do with the triangles with which Miss Dunbar had now covered the blackboard — I simply glanced across at her and smiled. Radiant with satisfaction, she beamed at me. There the matter rested as far as I was concerned and I slipped the note into the pocket of my grey flannels and placed the *Palgrave* under my desk with the intention of returning it to Clare at the break. However, it soon became clear from the agitated gesticulations which she sent in my direction that it was a correspondence rather than a simple wager that had been her intention, and so before Miss Dunbar had even begun to elucidate the Theory of Pythagoras, I found myself preparing a reply.

"I don't have thruppence," I wrote.

Tearing the page from my jotter, I took out Clare's book from under my desk and slipped the note between the much-soiled pages which described the burial of Sir John Moore at Corunna and dispatched the volume across the floor.

It was evident from her reaction that this was not the response Clare had expected, and frustrated in her endeavours, she decided to let the matter rest. However, a week or so later, she returned to her task. During the interim she had obviously reflected that her approach had been far too advanced and, in order to make any progress with me, it would be necessary to begin at a much more elementary level. The next letter I received — by the same means as the first — was altogether simpler and to the point and this time there was no possibility that I could confuse its contents with anything Miss Dunbar had ever attempted to explain.

"I know what you have you know where and it's called a penny," went the careful handwriting. "Do you know what I have and what it's called?"

This attempt to explain the pudenda was explicit enough and, furthermore, it was provocative because what I had "you know where" was not in my view called a penny and I replied accordingly. Bluffing, I also pointed out that I knew perfectly well what Clare had "you know where" but that I was not prepared to divulge to her what it was called. Ignoring this rebuff, Clare's next letter volunteered the information that what she had was called a purse; at the same time, she insisted that I had a penny.

After this, the correspondence — interrupted only by the periods when Mr Church was in charge — developed more rapidly and before long I had gained a great deal of information on matters I hardly knew existed a few weeks previously. It was a relatively simple step to understand that a penny got placed in a purse, although the result of such a deposit was more difficult for Clare to explain within the terms of the same analogy. Within a comparatively short time, her teaching became very advanced as she widened the scope of her instruction from simple sex to what now seems to me like advanced gynaecology. While I was happy enough to learn about the menopause, it struck me when I received a letter which focused — in lurid detail — on menstruation that the lessons had gone far enough and at that stage I put an end to our correspondence.

I believe that this came as something of a relief to Clare who, although resourceful, was by that stage finding it difficult to think of new topics to interest me. Thereafter her instruction took the form of "practicals" in the Stick House and for some months we settled into a routine and exploratory romance.

Curiosity rather than lust, and the satisfaction of doing something which I knew to be bad, was uppermost in my mind as I pursued these assignations. But it was diversion enough to assuage my previous tendency for throwing tantrums, so that the necessity of Mr Church drawing on the wide experience in dealing with irascibility for which he was renowned, became in time, irrelevant.

18. Partners

I taught Alan to dance.

It happened one Halloween when he had come home from Morgan's and I from Preston. He was very nice to me on the first day.

'We're having a dance at the end of term,' he announced to me after we had gone to bed.

'Where?' I whispered.

I was thrilled to think that we were now such friends.

'In the school you eejit, where do you think?' said Alan.

There were times when I tried Alan's patience and this was one of those times. Nevertheless, he soon recovered his equanimity.

'The Mercer's dames are being invited,' he said, 'and there's going to be a band.'

'We have dancing every Saturday night at Preston,' I said. 'Mrs Murray comes down from Dublin. It's only with a gramophone though. But we know how to dance properly.'

'Would you show me how to?' said Alan. 'I mean, I know how ... kind of ... but ... it's just that, for the dance, I'd like to be good.'

Thereafter, we spent the rest of the weekend together in Pat's

House. This was the house in the front yard which had once been the home of the head labourer and was now used as a dump for all sorts of debris from the house and farm. Alan and I made a clearing in what had been the kitchen and, clinched together in an awkward caress, we moved about in attempted unison.

'Slow, slow, quick, quick, slow,' I chanted as I reversed round the room in his arms.

'Say it out loud,' I commanded.

I recalled Mrs Murray's instructions.

'Out loud,' I repeated. 'It's the way you keep the beat.'

'Don't be daft,' said Alan. 'How am I to chat up a dame if I have to yell that all the time?'

'Up with your right elbow,' I said, 'up, up, up. Your arm must be straight out.'

Alan raised his chin.

'And don't be pulling me in to you.'

'How am I to push you around if I don't hold on to you?' said Alan.

'You're not supposed to push me,' I said. 'We're meant to glide.'

I tossed my head back languidly. Mrs Murray had often told me that I was a natural dancer.

By the end of the half-term, Alan had mastered the basics of the quickstep, the slow waltz, and the old-time waltz.

'I'll teach you the foxtrot at Christmas,' I told him.

But when the Christmas holidays came, he had lost interest, and when I enquired how the dance had gone, he was quite scornful saying, 'You don't know how to dance at all.'

After Mamma built the new dining room which, in spite of its scale and extent, Mr Sheppard had constructed single-handedly, she decided it should be inaugurated with a party before its decoration and furnishing was completed. When the new double doors, which separated it from the drawing room, were opened the entire room was about eighty-feet long and, as it still lacked a carpet, it had the natural appearance of a ballroom and so it took very little imagination for Mamma to decide that a dance was called for.

'The children' — Alice and Elliott were well into their twenties by now while Edward was abroad — 'were thinking of having a party at Christmas', was how Mamma raised the subject with Papa. 'After all, none of them had a twenty-first. With the petrol-rationing at the time, no one could get anywhere.'

'We could have a few people in for carol-singing,' said Papa. 'Miss Thompson could come and play. Or what about Beetles or a whist-drive?'

'None of those would be much fun,' said Mamma. 'They want a proper party. I thought of a dance. We'll make it evening dress.'

Papa's mind wandered to what a dance might involve and he thought of his friend Ken Brabazon.

'In that case we could invite Mr Brabazon,' he said, 'although we'd have to think who to ask for him.'

He had always considered it a waste — a waste of a Protestant — that Old Brabazon, who had a substantial farm and fortune, had remained a bachelor and he was always on the look-out to find him a wife. Mamma too would have liked to have seen Old Brabazon married, but it was nevertheless not her intention that he would find a bride at a dance in Rathcormick.

'He's much too old,' she said. 'The dance is for the young people.'

Elliott and David tittered. Alice picked up her book.

'We could ask Old Reynell as well,' said Elliott. 'And I'm sure Miss Reynell would be strong enough if she had a little warning.'

'What about the Hemingways?' said David.

Mr and Miss Hemingway, who each were about as old as Old Reynell and Old Brabazon combined, lived near Clane where Papa often visited them on a Sunday.

'And then there's Mrs Montgomery ... she can't have been to a dance since the Major died and they were still in India,' said Alice.

'If you're going to go on like this, there will be no dance at all,' said Papa. 'I don't see what's wrong with asking Mr Brabazon to the party.'

Thereafter, discussion of who might be asked proceeded along more orderly lines and a balance was struck between those whom Papa wanted invited because he thought they were suitable and those whom Alice and the boys wanted to come because they knew they were fun. First, from the relatively safe realm of 'family', came a wealth of names of various cousins and, after that, a list consisting of the offspring of bank managers, clergy, solicitors, doctors, and farmers like ourselves was approved without undue discord. Alice suggested some of her friends from Dublin, but as Papa disapproved of Dublin people in general and Dublin girls in particular, he voiced the opinion that they might feel a bit out of it before eventually consenting to their being invited. Emboldened by this decision, Elliott and David nominated some of the girls they had met at socials in Celbridge, but when names were mentioned Mamma indicated with a frown that they should desist.

'We'll just ask them,' she whispered, 'don't say anything now. It'll only lead to a huff.'

The dance, which was one of several that took place at Rathcormick during those years, was a great success. There was a Christmas tree in the bay window of the dining room and decorations all over the house; there was supper and then soup at the end; and there was a band. This was the Gold and Silver Dance Band which consisted of my piano-teacher, Mrs Rice, at the piano, her husband on the drums, and a pair of middle-aged identical twins who between them, as the night progressed, proved capable of playing as many instruments as would have put Billy Cotton and Band to shame. Called Greville, the twins came from Rathmolyon and apart from being identical they had the additional and unusual distinction of being albino. Wedged into the alcove beside the fireplace in the drawing room, the sound they generated was so stupendous that they might have been the Clipper Carltons, and when it came to their rendering of "Pretend", it almost seemed as if Nat King Cole himself were in the room. Papa was persuaded to take Mamma onto the floor for a dance early on. I had lots of dances, Alan would not dance at all, and Rosina, from a chair at the end of the drawing room, watched — quietly entranced and with no apparent sense of sadness — as girls of her own age, stiffly corseted in floor-length taffeta and tulle, discarded mohair stoles and stepped unto the floor, their strapless gowns defying caution and the cold. After supper, one Greville — it was impossible to know which was which — took the microphone and, in as plausible an imitation of Dickie Valentine as one could imagine, sang "The Finger of Suspicion Points at You". The lights were dimmed and Papa and Mamma found things to discuss in the sitting room while Molly and all the women who had come in to help returned to the kitchen. By now in our pyjamas, Alan and I leaned over the banisters and, at that moment, the Dublin girls and those from the socials in Celbridge came into their own.

At the end of the evening, after "Auld Lang Syne" and the national anthem, and after all the guests had departed, Rathcormick was quiet again. Mamma and Papa stood by the fireplace in the drawing room.

'Do you remember that Sunday afternoon when we first came here to see Old Elliott?' Mamma said.

'Yes,' said Papa. 'I do. It's hard to think it was nearly thirty years ago.'

Mamma put her hand on his chest and then, embarrassed by the intimacy of the gesture, she made as though she was straightening his lapel.

'I can still hear Nancy saying to me, in complaining about all the empty rooms, that it was a house that needed children,' said Mamma.

Papa looked at her.

'It's time for bed,' he said. 'It's been a very long evening.'

19. No Just Impediment

'Come here till I have a good look at you,' Alice said to me one Sunday afternoon.

I was home from Preston for Halloween and hanging about with nothing to do. Alan had gone off to Killucan with Papa and Rosina to call on Mrs Vandeleur; Raymond and David were out in the engine-house helping Elliott as he tinkered with the generator; Edward was in Australia; and Mamma and Alice, as I discovered when I wandered into the dining room, were sitting there beside the fire deep in conversation.

I went across to Alice and she put her arm around my waist. Pulling me towards her as she did so, she looked up at me.

'He's far too tall,' she said to Mamma.

'Do you think so?' said Mamma. 'Maybe if you had Ruth as well — she's still small enough — he wouldn't look so lumpy then.'

'The pair of them would be a show,' said Alice. 'Even if I am to have no one, they wouldn't do.'

She chuckled as she said the words.

'Too tall for what?' I said.

'Don't always ask so many questions,' said Mamma. 'Run off out now and find Rusty.'

'But it's going to rain,' I said.

'Well it's not raining yet, but if you don't go soon, it will be.'

After I left the room, I lingered in the breakfast room and thought about the conversation. I then went back to the door and put my ear against the keyhole.

'You will have to have Clonagh,' Mamma was saying.

'I suppose there's no point in asking Moira to come home from Canada,' said Alice.

'None at all,' said Mamma. 'You'll have more than enough to worry about without having to contend with Moira's antics as well.'

'What about Rosina?' said Alice. 'Would she be able for it, do you think?'

'We'll see what Papa feels,' said Mamma. 'I hadn't thought of it myself but it would be very nice. The best thing might be to ask her herself.'

When I thought I heard them moving, I shot out through the kitchen and, pulling on my rubber-boots at the back door, went into the yard. Wondering about what I had heard and what the discussion meant, I decided to ask Alan about it as soon as he arrived home. Later that afternoon, as the two of us made our way up to feed the hens, I said, 'I know something you don't know.'

It was the sort of statement which I knew Alan found intensely irritating.

'What could you know?' he said.

He stopped his bicycle and lowered himself from the saddle so that his left toe touched the ground. His right leg was still thrown over the crossbar, and in the trailer attached to the bicycle, were the two buckets of food for the hens.

'Just something,' I said.

Alan hoisted himself back up on the bicycle.

'Well it can't be anything worth knowing if you know it,' he said. 'That's all I can say.'

He stood up on the pedals.

'Push!' he shouted at me.

When we had dished out the food into the troughs and were bolting the hen-run again, he grabbed my arm and twisted it behind my back.

'Now what do you know, Mr Smartie?' he said.

He tightened his grip.

'Nothing,' I said.

As it happened, I was telling the truth.

'Tell me,' he said.

He twisted me down to the ground.

'What do you know?'

'Something about Alice,' I said. 'Let me go.'

'Is that all?' said Alan.

He released his grip.

'You mean that she is going to get married?'

He put the empty buckets back into the trailer and started to wheel the bicycle.

'As if that was anything,' he said, 'when the whole family has known for weeks.'

It was only that night in bed that the immensity of what had happened fully dawned on me: I had grown too tall to be a page at Alice's wedding. As I had looked forward to being one for years, my dejection was complete.

By the time I was next home, for the Christmas holidays, the talk at Rathcormick was of nothing other than the wedding. Cecil, her intended, came for a meat-tea one Sunday evening and it was on that occasion, when I slipped into the drawing room and found him and Papa alone there, that I overheard Papa say to him:

'Do you ... em ... smoke ... eh ... Mr ... eh?'

It was obvious, even to me, that Papa was interviewing his prospective son-in-law — he had positioned Cecil in the most uncomfortable armchair in the room while he himself was

'Do you…em…smoke…eh…Mr…eh?'

seated relaxed on the sofa — and so the enquiry was not as casual as the halting nature of its delivery suggested. As the engagement had already been announced at this stage, a dependency on nicotine, although a source of disapproval, was unlikely to prove a just impediment to the marriage. But had Papa discovered in the same interview that Cecil was, for example, a Freemason (Papa did not approve of Freemasons) or that his acreage was insufficient to support Alice even if she became extravagant, he would have had few qualms about insisting that she should set Cecil aside, annul her betrothal, and pursue some other avenue which would lead eventually to the altar.

To Mamma, such preoccupations, such anxieties, were a great deal less important than the actual arrangements for the wedding itself.

'The reception will have to be at home', was the first of her decisions.

'It must be at least a hundred years — even more — since there was a wedding at Rathcormick.'

At this, Papa became interested and, in the hope of discovering a wedding within the last century that might somehow alleviate the necessity of having to have another one now, he racked his brains to think when the last Potterton daughter could have been married from the house.

'It has to have been,' said Mamma. 'There was certainly none in Old Elliott's time. Unless you count Dora and Mr Tanner and that was hardly a wedding.'

'There's no need to bring that up,' said Papa.

'What?' said Alice.

'Old Elliott's sister, Dora,' said Mamma. 'She eloped with the policeman from Kildalkey, Mr Tanner. The family disowned her.'

'I'll go and get the family tree,' said Papa. 'That will settle the matter.'

When he had gone off to the office, Mamma said to Alice:

'Kildalkey Church is not going to be nearly big enough. It'll have to be in the cathedral in Trim but I'm leaving it to you to persuade him of that.'

'He'll never agree,' said Alice.

Papa came back into the room with some papers in his hand.

'There we are,' he said. 'I knew I'd find it. 1827.'

'Eighteen twenty seven what?' said Mamma.

'7 December 1827,' said Papa. 'Anne Potterton of Rathcormick married Richard Kellett of Ballinadrimna. These are the notes Polly made from the Parish Registers in Athboy. So it's a hundred and thirty years ago, almost to the day.'

'Well, isn't that interesting?' said Mamma.

She took up the tongs and moved the logs on the fire.

'Alice and I were thinking of a date in May,' she said. 'The daffodils would be over, but the narcissi would still be out and they'd make a wonderful scent in the cathedral …'

Papa stared at her.

'… and the lilac would be in blossom. I'll grow extra tulips specially in one of the vegetable plots.'

In the months that followed, Mamma made other decisions and plans with a similar enthusiasm and gusto. Books on wedding etiquette were purchased and perused, guest-lists were drawn-up and revised, the clergy were decided upon, a dance on the night of the wedding and a separate guest-list for that was planned, and, when it came to bridesmaids, their number — to include Rosina — was settled at five. With the reception to be held at home, a marquee was planned for the garden but, in spite of that, Mamma set about having most of the house redecorated. Dockrell's sent men down from Dublin who worked away for weeks. The pink canvas which covered the walls of the staircase from the lower hall to the top of the house was removed and the walls papered instead; a new stair-carpet, for all six flights as well as the landings, was laid down; the spare-room and the sitting room were papered and painted. In the garden, many more spring bulbs than usual were planted to augment the herbaceous borders of summer which would not yet be in bloom. A new trellis, running along behind the bed on the far side of the middle path, was erected; and Quirke was instructed to take extra care when clipping the box hedges and the Mulberry Bush. In the yard, where cars would be parked, all the doors to the sheds were painted, as were the front gates, the back gates, and the white gate which led from the gravel. The potholes on the avenue were filled with tarmacadam instead of the usual shovel of grit with which Malone filled them every other year. Easter came and went, the swallows returned to Rathcormick and their nests in the rafters of the Big Shed, Killballyowen won the Grand National and de Valera returned to power, triumphant, having ousted Mr Costello's inter-party government in a spring General Election.

That all of this was planned and accomplished in the few short months which intervened between the evening when Cecil assured Papa that he did not smoke and the moment he said 'I do' was truly remarkable. But in the event, Alice's wedding-reception never took place at Rathcormick at all, and when the time came for the engraved invitations to be posted, the phrase "afterwards at Rathcormick" was crossed out and the words "Gresham Hotel" substituted in Mamma's familiar and fulsome hand.

It happened very simply really. Papa had been to the Bull Show for the week, and although he had not even won a Highly Commended, he had sold several of his Aberdeen Angus very well and, as a result, he was in a good humour. One evening, the conversation was fairly light-hearted and we were talking about a dog called Laika which the Russians had launched into space in a sputnik. Apparently the dog had been trained, or so it said in *The Irish Times*, not to be greedy and to eat its food only in small portions at regular intervals so that there would be sufficient rations to last for the journey to Mars (or wherever) and back. In the event of the sputnik going astray — an eventuality which had by now occurred — the last meal available to Laika contained poison so that she could die comfortably rather than circle the planets indefinitely in a state of prolonged starvation. It was Elliott who suggested that if Rusty had been in the sputnik he would have had the sense to eat the poison on the first day out and not put up with further discomfort, and when we were all laughing at this, Papa suddenly said:

'And on that topic, where do you think everyone is going to go to the lavatory?'

The laughing stopped.

'Marquee or no,' said Papa, 'two lavatories — and one of them down by the back door and hardly fit to use — are not enough for one-hundred-and-fifty people.'

Mamma looked at Alice. She said nothing and nor did Alice. Papa continued:

'I don't see how you can have planned to have this reception here.'

Everyone was quiet. The association of Laika's plight as she pursued her celestial orbit high above us and the prospect of wedding-guests in a queue stretching all the way down the stairs and out as far as the gravel induced a sense of panic.

'We never thought of that,' said Mamma.

For the first time in months, she appeared deflated. She took up the notebook with lists of things to do which she now carried everywhere and flicked through the pages.

'You're right, of course,' she said. 'Do you think we'd better have it in the Gresham?'

Mamma wore black to Alice's wedding: a black dress, a black hat, black gloves, and furs. As the mother of the bride, she knew it was not the thing to do but she always wore black when she dressed up at this time and Cecil did not seem to mind. Nor did Alice whose own apparel was described in *The Irish Times* report of the wedding as "a classical brocade gown and a head-dress of Brussels lace which was worn by her grand-aunt at her wedding". The veil had been lent, at the eleventh hour, by a cousin, and although truly exquisite in its workmanship and beauty, it was of such enormous scale, density, and weight that it overshadowed in a way almost unbecoming every other carefully thought-out detail of Alice's ensemble.

When it came to the bridesmaids, it was typical of Alice's equable nature that, unusually for a bride, she permitted them to be arrayed more gorgeously than herself. Their dresses, acres of tulle coifed like meringues into floor-length confections of purple, primrose, and apple-green, were devised specially by Marjorie Boland. They were of such a frothy perfection and loveliness that they seemed inspired by the fashions of the Second Empire, although their true inspiration was more probably Victor Sylvester and the world of *Come Dancing* on the BBC.

Mendelsohn, Alice decided, was not for her. She chose Wagner, and with "Be Thou My Vision, O Lord of My Heart" and "Lead Us Heavenly Father, Lead Us", the service was conducted in a vein of religious sincerity. The effect was further heightened by the sight of so many clergy robed in the chancel and the poignancy — and triumph — of Rosina's courage, and Papa's concern for her, as she stood in the aisle throughout. When Alice and Cecil came down the aisle and passed under the temporary arch of moss, lilac, and narcissi which was Mamma's final *coup-de-theâtre*, there was hardly a dry eye in the cathedral. A red carpet outside led to a Rolls Royce parked at the gates and, after that, it was the Gresham.

Perhaps because I was so young, perhaps because it was Alice, perhaps because I had never been to a wedding before, perhaps, even, because I was not a page, Alice's wedding was to this day the most beautiful wedding I ever remember.

*It was typical of Alice's equable nature that she permitted her
bridesmaids to be arrayed more gorgeously than herself*

20. Trojan Endeavours

Elliott, unlike Edward, 'could make anything with his hands'.

At least, that was how Mamma always put it. What she meant was that he excelled at carpentry and was capable of understanding any machine down to the very last washer and gasket.

'He would have made a wonderful engineer,' she would say, 'if Papa had not gone and taken him out of school.'

When anything went wrong with the engine (as we called the oil-fired generator which supplied electricity at Rathcormick before the Rural Electrification Scheme brought in the ESB), Elliott was always able to fix it in no time. When he was not there, and before he came home from Dunfermline for good, evenings were often spent by the light of paraffin lamps as we would wait — and wait — for McEvoy to come up from Kildalkey to tinker away for hours before sorting out the problem. Papa had no clue at all about anything mechanical — he may never have lifted a hammer in all his life — so Elliott, it goes without saying, was an invaluable asset about the place. He cannot have been home for more than a couple of months before he had the engine in perfect running order, and the same was true of the pump which pumped water from what we called the Rat Tank in the yard up to a tank on the roof of the house. It always gave trouble so that the supply of water to the kitchen and bathroom was often precarious. But after Elliott's return, only the rare occurrence of a severe drought occasioned us to be left without water. Next, he turned his attention to the tractor. It was an old David Brown which seemed to function only on special occasions, but Elliott soon changed that. He also fixed up the binder, the plough, the harrow, and everything else around the place that was by way of being called machinery. In the days before the Hydraulic revolutionised farming, the mechanisms of the latter implements, many of them still horse-drawn, were fairly simple and often all that they required was an occasional squirt of grease; but it was only with Elliott's permanent presence that they received such regular attention that breakdowns became a thing of the past. He mechanised the grinder: a milling machine that was used for wheat and barley and housed in a shed in the front yard. By similar means, a gadget that was used for pulping turnips and mangolds was also made to function mechanically. Elliott's supreme innovation, and the one which caught Papa's attention, was a sort of conveyor belt which obviated the necessity of the men having to carry sacks of grain, one by one, up the stairs to the loft.

After a couple of years of such endeavour, and finding himself surrounded on all sides by technological perfection, Elliott considered that he was at something of a loose end. It was then he decided to buy himself a veteran car. Although it might have seemed more appropriate for him to have acquired a contemporary vehicle (which would at least have meant that he did not always need to ask Papa's permission to borrow the Austin to go to a social), he knew that such a move towards independence would occasion disapproval. His next choice could well have been a racing car as Papa's two brothers, Uncle Ken and Uncle Arthur, had successfully driven racing-cars when they were young. But Elliott — although always keen on winning — had very little interest in competitions and besides, he knew that Papa would simply not hear of such a thing. A veteran car, on the other hand, would give him scope to pursue his principal interest which was, after all, mechanics rather than speed; and, as such a hobby would be practised mainly within the safe confines of the engine-house in the front yard rather than on the racing track of the Phoenix Park, there was very little about it to which Papa could possibly object.

The car was a Trojan which appeared on its arrival by lorry at Rathcormick to be well beyond ever running under its own steam again and was, therefore, tailor-made to provide the challenge which Elliott required. It was a four-seater convertible with solid rubber tyres and solid spoked wheels, and unlike the Prefect or the Austin which had splendid running-boards, Elliott's Trojan had none. Its general shape, particularly when observed from the rear, was like a cup without a saucer while its engine was housed at the front in a gable-ended construction that looked like a church without a steeple. With hinged flaps to either side that lifted to reveal the motor, the church — or rather the bonnet — was lodged between a prominent pair of mudguards that sheltered the front wheels.

Elliott spent weeks, months and even years working on the Trojan. He referred to it exclusively by means of the pronouns 'her' and 'she'; and when he had cleared a space in the engine-house, where there was already a substantial workbench and room for all his tools, he erected her, like a public monument, on stepped wooden-blocks from which it looked unlikely that he would ever be able to dislodge her again. He worked on the engine every night, every Saturday afternoon, and, surreptitiously, on Sunday afternoons as well. He stripped her down and reassembled her and then he stripped her down again. He dismantled her bodywork, re-stuffed her seats, stitched her leather upholstery, and patched the canvas of her hood. In due course, trial runs ended in disappointment with

the Trojan refusing to travel even as far as the front gravel where
Mamma and the rest of us were assembled on the steps to see
her pass. After being pushed back into the engine-house and
lifted again on to her plinth, the process of stripping and re-
assembly would begin once again. Alan and I loved to watch
the meticulousness with which Elliott went about his task but
it was only David, who was also mechanical, who was ever
allowed to help. Mamma was also fascinated, and whenever she
spotted an engine-part on the floor that looked to her like brass,
she took it away only to return an hour or two later with it
gleaming.

'Didn't it take a marvellous shine?' she would say to Elliott.
'Give me that piece there and I'll see what I can do with it.'

Only Papa remained indifferent to the Trojan's gradual
transformation.

'You know that he can't see the point of it,' Mamma would
say to Elliott.

But the fact of the matter was that, although Elliott was his
eldest son and the heir through whom he had come into
Rathcormick, Papa only rarely saw the point of anything Elliott
did.

Elliott's ultimate goal in restoring the Trojan was that one
day he would drive her in the Veteran Car Run: an annual event
which took place in June when cars competed in a race from
Donnybrook Bus Garage to the Wicklow village of Rathdrum.
Initially, when the rusted parts of the Trojan lay strewn on the
engine-house floor, this seemed a very unlikely eventuality.
Later still, when dummy runs in the direction of Ballivor ended
with the car being towed home late in the evening, having been
stranded on the roadside not far beyond the crossroads, it
looked even less likely. But eventually the day dawned when the
Trojan was considered roadworthy, and with her bodywork
newly painted blue and yellow, she was transported up to
Dublin in preparation for the race.

This event was to take place on a Saturday afternoon which meant that, on account of his office in Trim, there was no question of Papa being able to attend. But Mamma, who was more excited than any of us, packed Rosina, Alan, me, and a picnic into the Austin and we set off on the unusual expedition of a Saturday morning trip to Dublin. The plan was that we would go first to Donnybrook Garage and see all the cars assembled there before the race began, and afterwards drive down to Wicklow, have our picnic, and wait on the side of the road for the passing sight of Elliott and David in the Trojan.

When we got to Donnybrook, there were hundreds of veteran cars parked along the road which stretched up the Dodder and, for a time, it seemed that we might not be able to find Elliott's car at all.

'We'll never see it among all of these,' said Mamma.

'There's a terrific one over there,' I said.

'That's a Riley,' said Alan. 'A Riley Redwing.'

'It'll make the Trojan look very second-rate,' said Mamma.

She took off the white cardigan which she was wearing over her summer cotton-frock and folded it over her arm.

'There it is,' said Rosina. 'Up there, just at the corner. I recognise the yellow wheels.'

'So it is,' said Mamma.

She started to hurry up the road.

'It's wonderful that they got this far,' she said.

'But the race hasn't started yet,' said Alan.

'I know,' she said, 'but I'm just glad that they made it as far as this.'

We ran up towards where the Trojan was parked.

'There seems to be no sign of the boys,' said Mamma. 'Can you credit that they would be so heedless as to go away and leave the car here all on its own. Just look at those people opening the doors and everything.'

We edged closer towards the car and, as we did so, two girls brazenly stepped up and plonked themselves down in the back seat.

'The cheek of them,' said Mamma.

They were dressed as Twenties flappers in calf-length dresses and cloche hats, carrying open parasols which they twirled impertinently on their shoulders. We had seen *Some Like It Hot* in Kilkee the previous summer and the girls looked to us like replicas of Tony Curtis and Jack Lemmon.

'Now they're having their photo taken,' said Mamma, 'with the two yokes in the striped blazers and boaters.'

'That's Elliott and David,' said Rosina.

'Where?'

'That's them. They're in fancy dress.'

At that moment, Elliott and David came over to us.

'We thought you'd be surprised,' they said.

'I wouldn't have recognised you for a moment,' said Mamma.

She turned towards the flappers.

'Is it Hilda …?' she said.

She leaned over the side of the car to shake Tony Curtis by the hand.

' … and Maud. Goodness! You both look terrific.'

We drove down beyond Bray, ate our picnic, and waited in the sun on the side of the road for what seemed like an awful age. The initial throng of cars turned to a trickle and, after that, it was only an occasional vehicle that wobbled down the hill in our direction. It was when we were on the point of making our way back to the Austin that the Trojan suddenly heaved into sight.

'There was a bit of trouble with her a few miles back,' David shouted at us. 'But she's doing grand now.'

Elliott was at the wheel, concentration etched on his face, but he scarcely dared glance in our direction, much less take his hands off the controls, for fear of further 'trouble'. The flappers were both recognisable in the back seat; but the faces which had giggled and grinned at Donnybrook had turned into agonised masks of blue. As they passed us on the road, they reached into their blankets and extracted their hands but when they attempted to wave, they could muster only a stilted jerk — like a puppet at the end of a string. The parasols, which had been such a feature of their ensembles, were nowhere to be seen.

The next day, when Molly came in from Mass just before breakfast, she brought the *Sunday Review* with her from Kildalkey.

'There's a great photo of Master Elliott and Master David in the paper,' she said when Mamma came into the kitchen.

And there it was. Elliott and David, Hilda and Maud, beaming from their seats in the Trojan.

'When you think of all the cars that were there, and that they should pick you,' said Mamma. 'But then you did look the best.'

She read the caption under the photograph, which

'They did look the best'

announced that Elliott and Maud were to be married the following month, and handed the newspaper back to Molly.

'Maybe we won't let the Master see that just yet,' she said.

She knew that Papa would not comment on the cigarette in David's mouth or on the presence of the two girls, but that a deliberate silence would convey his disapproval. But, more than that, she knew that he would be embarrassed and cross at them having their photograph in a newspaper.

'He wouldn't be interested in seeing it anyway,' said Elliott. 'He's never been interested in the car. Not from the day I got it.'

There was a tone, almost of anger, about his voice as he said it.

21. Changing Lives

When our cousin Clonagh was married early in the September which followed Alice's wedding, we were all invited. Aunt Alice, whom everyone loved because she made a point of enjoying everything in life to the full and regarded extravagance as a cardinal virtue, did things in tremendous style. The wedding, in the small country church of Ballyburly with a reception afterwards at Ballinla, their home near Edenderry, was on such a lavish scale (Uncle Ernie was rich) as to almost appear dissolute. While I recall nothing of the church ceremony, Clonagh's wedding reception was memorable on account of the delirious atmosphere of excess, the sense of good fun which Aunt Alice brought to it, and the general ambience at Ballinla where everything — down to the last stone of gravel on the avenue — was sheer and utter perfection.

Like Mamma when she was planning Alice's wedding, Aunt Alice had decided on a marquee, but rather than content herself with one, she had several and when it came to lavatories she had a superfluity of those too. In one of the marquees the reception took place, in another there was a bar, and in yet another a dance was planned for the evening. The purpose of an encampment of smaller tents scattered throughout the shrubbery was known only to Aunt Alice herself:

'I told Ernie we weren't going to stint when it came to our Clonagh's wedding,' she said when anyone enquired about them.

But, as Aunt Alice had never been known to stint on anything, this explanation was deemed to be very inadequate and it did little to stem the curiosity of the guests.

It was the presence of the marquee which Aunt Alice had designated a bar that led, by a curious set of circumstances, to an encounter which was to change the course of my life.

Elliott and David — Edward was still in Australia — were normal young men. They liked a beer, an occasional gin, they liked a cigarette, and they liked girls. Papa disapproved of all of these things, but rather than ever confront them head-on he simply turned a blind eye and limited his censure to more important issues, such as their wantonness in staying in bed late in the mornings. When it came to Clonagh's wedding therefore, Elliott, David, and possibly Raymond were faced with a decision as to whether or not they should enter the marquee which they knew to be a bar, while Papa was faced with a decision as to whether or not he should find them there. But the well-tested rules were applied, and Papa simply pretended that the bar did not exist; the boys, in the fairly certain knowledge that Papa was unlikely to come and root them out, spent a pleasant afternoon, drinking and smoking like everyone else, albeit surreptitiously.

Papa, in the meantime, found himself under canvas in another part of the gardens where, before long, he had struck up a conversation with a soft-spoken, middle-aged man whom he regarded as a stranger, but who was in fact the half-brother-in-law of Aunt Alice herself. This man was a secondary school teacher whose chosen subject was science, and by the time of his niece Clonagh's wedding, he had been so successful at teaching science in a series of Protestant secondary schools all over Ireland that he was now the headmaster of what had reasonable claim to being the oldest secondary school in the country: Kilkenny College. While it had not been the specific intention of Mr Colton to avoid the bar at the wedding — in point of fact, he often took a gin and tonic after a long day in his science lab — he had found himself at a loose end during the interval in the proceedings which followed the departure of Clonagh and her new husband, Hugh, on their honeymoon and the later arrival of the car-loads of younger guests who had been invited for that evening's dance. And so, like a Bedouin in the desert, he had wandered from tent to tent until he eventually encountered Papa who, under the mistaken impression that Mr Colton was also fleeing the bar, had struck up a conversation with him. It goes without saying that Papa's familiarity with Boyle's Law was fairly scant and that any discussion of Faraday's investigations of electromagnetic induction would also have drawn a blank, but despite these limitations, he and Mr Colton soon established common ground and a rapport developed between them.

As Papa later reported it, his opening foray had been:

'A lovely service, didn't you think?'

Mr Colton nodded. And then, looking straight at Papa, he beamed — and beamed. This was a mannerism he had perfected, which when used in the classroom, had the effect of lulling boys into the feeling that he was pleased about something when, more often than not, the exact opposite was the case. Like countless schoolboys, Papa took the expression as a general indication of openness and he proceeded.

'The Address could have been longer, I felt,' he said. 'Young people getting married need to be sent out into life with some sound guiding principles. They have to realise that marriage is not just …'

He paused as the sound of tables being dragged across the floor was heard from the neighbouring marquee.

'… not just … a party, not just … a dance.'

'I quite agree with you,' said Mr Colton.

'Did I hear that Mr Burrows is a Presbyterian?' said Papa.

He was referring to the bridegroom but his intention in asking the question was to discover if Mr Colton was a guest of the bride or the groom.

'His people, I believe, were originally from the North,' said Mr Colton. 'So he might well be.'

Papa was no wiser, but as he was formulating another line of enquiry, Mr Colton became effusive:

'Whatever he is, he's a lucky man to get Clonagh. From the day she was born, she has been the loveliest of girls and she'll make him a very capable wife.'

Papa was impressed by the stranger's use of the word 'capable'. Here was a man who talked the same language as himself.

'You know the Tongs a long time then?' he said.

'Gladys,' said Mr Colton. 'Gladys,' he repeated.

Papa was nonplussed.

'I'm married to Gladys.'

He scowled then as he generally did when he said something pleasant.

'Alice's sister.'

'Oh! Of course,' said Papa.

Mr Colton returned to the topic of his niece.

'And you may be sure that Clonagh will create a good Christian home,' he said. 'I see so many children whose parents have never even taught them the Ten Commandments, much less have them study the Old Testament. It's hard to know what chance, if any, such children will have in life.'

It was just at this moment, as Papa was deciding that he was really very impressed by Mr Colton, that Mamma came into the marquee, having found me loitering about outside. She had changed into a short evening frock.

'There you are,' she said to Papa.

Mr Colton got up and started to move away.

'As it's such a lovely evening, come out and have a look at Alice's borders, they've never been better.'

We went out and followed the path by the side of the house to the garden.

'You should just see her gladioli,' said Mamma. 'You'd almost think they were artificial.'

'That's a very sensible man,' Papa said as they reached the flower beds.

'That's Albert Schweitzer,' said Mamma.

'I don't know that I've met him before,' said Papa.

'No, I'm wrong. This one is Albert Schweitzer, the other one is Dr Fleming.'

She fondled the salmon-orange petals of a particularly luscious bloom.

'He said his name was Colton.'

'Him?' said Mamma. 'That's only Gilbert Colton.'

She took another flower in her hand.

'He's the headmaster of Kilkenny.'

As they continued down along the herbaceous border which was one of the splendours of Aunt Alice's garden, and Mamma further identified, correctly and incorrectly, the various species, Papa's thoughts turned to education.

'I've never been happy about Alan in that school,' he said.

'Alice's zinnias are not the best, I'd have to say that. Look at them!' said Mamma.

Later that evening, when the dancing started, Papa sought out Mr Colton again and the pair of them had a long conversation during the course of which Papa learned that Kilkenny College had been founded in 1538, that its alumni included, in the eighteenth century, Jonathan Swift, George Berkeley, and William Congreve, in the nineteenth century the novelist Michael Banim, and in the twentieth century a hero in the person of Admiral Beatty who had scuppered the Germans at the Battle of Jutland in the First World War. He also learned that this history was as insignificant to Mr Colton as it was to himself, and that as headmaster he was more concerned with the day-to-day running of the school and in securing satisfactory Intermediate Certificate results for the hundred or so boys, sons mainly of smallish farmers, bank managers, and shopkeepers in the Midlands, who attended. Mr Colton mentioned several words which Papa held in high esteem: 'discipline', 'honesty', 'hard-work', and 'good-manners'. These

The purpose of an encampment of smaller tents was known only to Aunt Alice herself

were his priorities and the ethos of his school: style, snobbery, sophistication, and culture, he indicated, he was happy to leave to others.

'What would you think of sending Alan to Kilkenny College?' Papa said to Mamma the next day.

'I suppose we could consider it for next year,' said Mamma.

'Or this,' said Papa. 'Term has only just started so you'd have time to get him kitted out if he went next week. I think I'll just drop a note to the headmaster of Morgan's. He'll fully understand when Alan doesn't go back.'

And so it was that Alan's educational future — and, as it happened, my own — was decided by the chance encounter between Papa, who was avoiding a bar, and Mr Colton who, very possibly, was searching for one. Perhaps, had Aunt Alice not been so very profligate when it came to marquees, my life — and Alan's — would have followed a different course.

Alan, who was born on Mamma's birthday, had turned fourteen that August. He was, therefore, at the in-between stage in his education when most parents would not have dreamt of having him change schools. But these formalities mattered not a whit to Papa whose habit it was to take any of us, on the slightest whim and with little warning, from one school and despatch us to another. Alan, who was of an obliging disposition, had no particular views on the proposed change in his schooling, so that when Papa asked him 'What he would think of going to Kilkenny?' all he said was: 'I'll miss the boxing at Morgan's, but as there are more boys in Kilkenny, the rugby is bound to be better.'

As to whether his scope for success when it came to the Intermediate Certificate in two years' time would be improved by the change in school, the thought never entered Alan's head. Nor was it a consideration that preoccupied Papa unduly, while Mamma's main concern was getting Alan ready and packed.

'It's a good thing that the blazers are black, the same as at

Morgan's,' she said. 'I've just had to change the crest on the pocket.'

'Where are my games' shirts?' said Alan.

He looked into the suitcase on the bathroom floor.

'You'll have to get those in the Monster House,' said Mamma. 'They have to be red and black, but these old togs of David's from Mountjoy will do you fine. With so much washing, they are nearly the right colour by now.'

Initially, Alan was regarded as something of a curiosity by the other boys on account of the fact that they had all been back at school for about a week by the time he arrived. Then there was the matter of age; while they had started their education in first class at the age of twelve, Alan at fourteen years old was entering only second class.

'I'll try him in second for a month or two to see how he gets on,' Mr Colton had said. 'But I'm sure he'll be able to move up to third by Christmas.'

As it happened, second suited Alan just fine. He had already done the year at Morgan's and so was vaguely familiar with much of what was being taught. So without having to devote much of his attention to what was going on he was occasionally able to answer a question with some degree of accuracy, but not often enough to jeopardise his chances of staying in second and being moved to the more taxing environment of third. Progressing from being a curiosity, Alan had little difficulty in quickly establishing himself with all the other boys; he was laddish, possessed a great deal of charm and a talent to amuse, and his prowess on the rugby field as well as the hockey pitch was sufficiently impressive to ensure that he was respected by boys and masters alike. In short, Alan was soon one of the most popular boys in the school.

When I came home from Preston for Halloween, I was anxious to hear all about Kilkenny, but as Alan had been invited home by another boy for the weekend, I found myself on my own, and when I asked Mamma how he was getting on, she became quite cross.

'The young rascal hasn't written a single letter since he went back,' she said. 'He could be on the moon for all we know.'

To fill the void, I took out the prospectus for Kilkenny College which I found in the drawer of Mamma's desk in the sitting room and studied it over the weekend with a mounting sense of envy.

The world it depicted seemed to me to be enchanted, and while the words 'halcyon' or 'idyllic' were not part of my vocabulary by this stage, only they could adequately describe the life that Alan, if the prospectus for Kilkenny College was to be believed, must now be leading.

There was little or no description of the actual school itself. Not a mention of the splendid Georgian building it occupied, and no reference whatsoever to the magnificence of the school's setting on the banks of the River Nore with the battlements of the great castle of the Dukes of Ormonde rising from the river on the opposite side. Dean Swift, Berkeley, Congreve — even Admiral Beatty — were equally ignored. Instead, the Prospectus introduced itself by promising "a sound education to Intermediate level for Protestant boys of all backgrounds". In the unlikely event of the prospective parent finding this definition of the school's ethos too general, it was amplified by the statement that "sons of military personnel posted abroad as well as of foreign diplomats serving in Ireland" attended the college together with "a small annual intake of pupils from England, America, and as far afield as Hong Kong and Australia". "A limited number of day-boys from the city and county of Kilkenny is also provided for," it said.

The curriculum that could be expected was as far-flung and wide-ranging as the cosmopolitan pupils themselves. Apart from the usual subjects which Mr Church catered for at Preston, Kilkenny offered physics and chemistry, German and

Greek, art and drama. Then there were several other subjects —
"classes which could be arranged in consultation with the
Headmaster" — such as Spanish and Italian, trumpet,
saxophone, violin, and other musical instruments, and
strangely enough, domestic economy. When it came to what
was headed, "Recreation and Leisure Activities", the
possibilities seemed to be enormous: rugby, hockey,
badminton, and gymnastics were the staple diet of the winter
months (when swimming and diving were also options); and
then in summer, cricket, tennis, and "a full spectrum of
athletics" took over. Rowing and canoeing were further
attractive summer choices. In the case of all sports, matches
were played against other schools and the college competed in
the Leinster Schools Junior Rugby Cup competition each year.
Plays were produced each Christmas term in the Berkeley Hall
where "the modern stage facilities were a recent addition to the
college's amenities". All new boys were given a music audition
and those with suitable voices became choristers at St Canice's
Cathedral. The college lending-library catered to the school's
curriculum with a wide selection of books on science,
literature, and the arts and, far from being locked up in the
school from one end of the term to another as one was at
Preston, boys at Kilkenny College were treated to "pictures on
the last Saturday night of each month" while debates or talks
took place on other Saturdays. Finally, there was a Tuck Shop
which sold lemonade, ice-creams, chocolate, and "a suitable
selection of comics".

The last page of the prospectus was taken up with a list of
the staff headed by "Mr Colton, B.Sc (Mod), MA, H Dip.Ed";
and, as this list was quite extensive, it made the combined
activities of Mr Church and Miss Dunbar at Preston seem
heroically ambitious if not downright reckless. The same might
be said for Miss Rockingham who performed the roles —
admittedly with ease — of matron, nurse, cook, and

housekeeper at Preston when these functions were fulfilled by four different women at Kilkenny.

After several sessions reading the prospectus over the Halloween weekend, I came to the conclusion that I was not being educated at all at Preston and that it was of the utmost importance for me to transfer to Kilkenny without delay. Although only eleven, I was attracted to the more international environment Kilkenny College promised, and the possibility of forming a wider circle of friends. And while the extended list of sports that would be available at Kilkenny held less attraction for me than art classes, drama, and debating, I persuaded myself that, if I were correctly dressed for games (as the photograph in the prospectus of boys playing cricket showed them to be), my sporting abilities would improve and games might well become enjoyable.

I recognised that it would be best to tackle the subject of a change of school first with Papa, and so on the Sunday morning when, in spite of a considerable frost the night before, which still lingered on the avenue, he suggested that we all walk down to Kildalkey Church, I volunteered immediately. When Raymond and David said they would wait and come down in the car with Mamma, I knew that I had my chance. Even though it was cold, he still walked very slowly, making a noise with his lips as he puffed for breath. He commented, more to himself than to me, about various aspects of the farm as we passed: a bit of fencing that needed doing here, a bullock that was lame on the hoof over there, and a piece of machinery that should not have been left out in a field somewhere else.

'I'd like to go to Kilkenny College with Alan,' I eventually said.

'I have been thinking of that myself,' he said. 'But, of course, it would depend entirely on what your mother feels.'

Mamma was easily persuaded — for one thing I would be able to wear Alan's hand-me-down uniforms — and although it was decided to wait and see what Alan said about the school when he came home at Christmas before making any final decision, the idea of sending me to Kilkenny that next summer term took root. When I went back to Preston after Christmas, it was for my final term.

22. In the Footsteps of Swift

On my first evening at Kilkenny College I encountered a boy whose name was Rideaux.

'I'm French for curtains,' he said.

He grinned as he said it and I assumed he was French. The following morning, when I met another boy who was called Lefroy, I concluded that he too came from France. Preston was very provincial, I thought to myself.

But in our next conversation Rideaux told me he came from County Laois — 'My dad works for Odlum's Mills' — and Lefroy, it transpired, came from no farther away than the lakeside village of Killaloe. Neither of them had ever even been to France. The same frustration applied when it came to boys of other nationalities. Even though the prospectus had promised Americans and Australians, there were none and after a few days I came to realise that the only "foreigner" in the school was an extremely timid individual called Beavis, who only came from Wales. As far as "the sons of military personnel posted overseas" were concerned, there was one boy, Benson, whose father had been a Colonel in the British Army; but he was now retired and lived about four miles away in Castlecomer. Then there was Bunworth who came from

Athlone. His father — and uncle — were indeed military and both were posted overseas; they were the Commanding Officers of the Irish Peacekeeping Forces in the Congo and, as a result, their exertions and adventures were reported in *The Irish Times* every day.

And that was as glamorous and as international as the cast list at Kilkenny College ever aspired to, in my day at least.

The academic curriculum also proved to be far less alluring than the prospectus had led me to believe and, apart from the additions of art and science, it was not much different to that at Preston. Music, which I liked, was the exception, but instead of being revered as it had been at Preston it was almost despised at Kilkenny. The organist from the cathedral, a diminutive and colourful character called Mr Skilton whose floating locks of greying hair and bow-tie were undoubtedly inspired by images of the young Listz, occasionally appeared on the off-chance that someone or other might wish to perfect their scales. But he very rarely encountered any custom and his main contact with the boys derived from his role as choirmaster. But, as most boys wanted to avoid being in the choir at all costs, Mr Skilton was often obliged to offer a bribe to potential choristers by promising occasional tea and cakes with him and his wife — who was equally minuscule and also a musician — in the Hansel-and-Gretel-like house they occupied, together with two grand pianos, in the cathedral precincts. I really wanted to become a chorister although, in order to make myself popular, I pretended otherwise. When it came to my turn to be auditioned, however, Mr Skilton found me as wanting in vocal ability as Miss Thompson had done several years previously. As a result, I was denied the opportunity of dressing-up every Sunday in the ruffled blue and white of a choirboy to trill my way through a sung Eucharist, and the choir-stalls which confronted each other across the aisle complementing so splendidly the Gothic vaulting that was one of the salient attractions of St Canice's, remained the elusive preserve of other boys.

On the basis that the prospectus did say that lessons in the "trumpet, saxophone, and other musical instruments could be arranged in consultation with the headmaster," I had persuaded Mamma to make arrangements for me to study the violin. I may have done this in the mistaken belief that, had I not done so, I might be the only boy at the school not studying an instrument, but as it happened I became the only boy actually learning one. As a result of weekly lessons with Mrs Connick, far from being looked up to and admired for my endeavours, I drew attention to myself in a way that, being the youngest of six boys, I knew from experience would ultimately prove unwise. And so, after a term or two of choosing between an hour's violin-playing beside the fire in Mrs Connick's comfortable sitting room — often followed by a glass of lemonade — or three hours of being jostled and thrown about on the rugby pitch in the mud and rain, I chose the latter. I had already perfected a single-note version of the opening bars of Dvorak's "New World Symphony" but that proved to be the full extent of my repertoire, and with my decision to leave Mrs Connick my music-playing came, regrettably, to an end.

Mr Hendy taught art. He also taught mathematics. He brought to the teaching of one subject the talents he had perfected in instructing the other so that his explanations of algebraic formulae were sufficiently artistic as to be vague in the extreme and his drawing of the polygon aspired to a virtuosity that even Leonardo would have only very rarely attempted. By the same token, he taught art with a mathematical exactitude that would have challenged such a master of the genre as the great William Morris himself; pupils were required to render the organic form of the tulip into a complex series of repeats and patterns with the aid of compasses and dividers. This was called mechanical drawing and design and it formed but one half of Mr Hendy's tutorials; the rest of the time was devoted to still life or object drawing. While both disciplines demanded an ability to apply a wash successfully, mechanical drawing required in particular inventiveness, precision, and a feeling for colour, while still life necessitated a more spirited talent and a genuine artistry together with a mastery of the ellipse. I took to Mr Hendy's teaching of art immediately — he was a very good teacher — and, without being a prodigy, I had sufficient talent to ensure that I was always among the top two or three boys in the class. My tulips were so far distanced in their design from the originals as to be deemed extremely successful and, when it came to colouring them in watercolour, my assured use of fresh, vibrant colours singled out my paintings from the slovenly purple, green, and brown slops that were the finished products of many of the other boys. My still lifes were — in Mr Hendy's view — less successful and, in their tendency to ignore the precise details of the model in favour of an overall "effect" which I judged more satisfactory, they often incurred his disapproval.

Although Mr Colton's science lab was one of the school's newest amenities, I soon found that, once the novelty of the Bunsen burner had worn off and the possibilities inherent in "immersing a body in a fluid" had been fully explored, science — either physics or chemistry — held little attraction for me. History I wanted to like but the manner in which it was taught in order to conform to the national syllabus — and its diligent avoidance of any English history other than that which detailed English treachery in Ireland — gave rise to a certain confusion. The War of the Austrian Succession, the Flight of the Earls, the Edict of Nantes, and even the Battle of Clontarf became a blur, while personalities — Turenne and Condé, Rinuncini, Gustavus Adolphus, Silken Thomas — remained no more flesh and blood than print on a page. The teaching of Latin was in the experienced hands of a senior teacher, Mr Lipsette, and from the point of view of passing an exam, he taught it very well. Scattering ablative absolutes in our wake, we tramped through Gaul with Caesar without ever realising we were in France, and with Aeneas and Anchises fled the flames of Troy, but without any appreciation of the beauty of Virgil's lines. French and English, after art, were my preferred subjects and both were taught by Mr Power. He was an elderly bachelor who lived-in and whose nickname was Whiskey. This may have been on account of the fact that his name was identical with the distillery or possibly because it was believed that he took a tipple or two. If he did, he had every reason to do so, as he was a cultivated man who reeked of the disappointment that came from having had to accept a job in his twilight years as the only Catholic teacher in the school when, had his life followed a more kindly path, a career at Clongowes, Blackrock, or Glenstal would have been his due. His disillusion was obvious and it was clear that every teaching experience he had had in his life led him to the conclusion that we, no more than the many others with whom he had tried, were not worth teaching. It pained him when we garbled the lines — learned by rote — of Keats, Goldsmith, or Shakespeare.

'Stop!' he would yell. 'Some of the most beautiful words in the English language and you gabble them out like … like … like a gander in a haggard.'

Then, taking up the hem of his gown and advancing across the room, he would become Bassanio:

'"In Belmont is a lady … richly left …"'

He would pause and stare at us.

'"And she is fair … and fairer than that word of wondrous virtues and … sometime from her eyes … I did receive fair speechless messages …"'

He brought the same sad disenchantment to his teaching of French.

'*De la peau du Lion l'Ane s'étant vêtu,*' he would write on the blackboard and having added the circumflexes with a flicking of his wrist, he would turn to the class.

'Rrrrolleston' he would say in perfect French.

He relished the gutturals as he pronounced the name.

'*Qu'est-ce que c'est ...*'

He would purse his lips and raise his voice several decibels.

' *... une ... peau du lion?*'

His pronunciation was so impeccable that he might have been a member of the Académie or at very least a tutor at the Sorbonne, but as a consequence, it was completely unintelligible to Rolleston to whom the words *'peau'* and *'peu'* sounded one and the same.

'A bit of a lion,' he answered.

'Which bit ...?' said Whiskey.

He had failed to recognise Rolleston's confusion.

'... *Quel beet?*'

'A little bit,' said Rolleston.

Mr Power would move to his desk and sit down. He would rest his head in his hands and remain still for several minutes. A silence would shroud the room. Eventually he would rise and, with a gesture that rivalled in its extravagance his impersonation of Bassanio, he would declaim:

'*C'est toi qui est l'âne. C'est toi.*'

And then, taking up his battered copy of the *Fables of La Fontaine*, he would step out of the room.

In seeking an ethos for the educational establishment of which he was headmaster, Mr Colton turned to the old adage, "The devil finds work for idle hands to do" and, as a consequence, there was not a single moment of any day — from wake-up in the morning to lights-out at night — when some mandatory activity did not ensure that every boy was fully occupied. If it seems that this programme must have required an enormous feat of organisation, this was not the case at all as the key to its implementation was the word "compulsory". By making everything — lessons, prep, games, walks, church, meals, late-night cocoa, even visits to the tuck shop — compulsory and by establishing a rigid timetable for each employment, it was very easily put in hand and, as boys were only exceptionally allowed home on Sundays or at weekends, there were no inconvenient interruptions which would have necessitated alternative plans.

Of all the compulsory activities at Kilkenny College, none was more so than games and, of all these, rugby, hockey, and cricket were the most compulsory of all. I detested all three but by an unfortunate paradox my ineptitude on the field worked against me and I was greatly in demand. Because I was never selected on the basis of merit, I was always available to fill-out a team when numbers were short; and as it was very soon realised that, unless I committed a foul which caused the other side to gain a score, my presence was unlikely to make any difference whatsoever to the outcome of a match, I frequently found myself togging-out, bullying-off, or scrumming-down with teams of boys much younger than myself as well as those of my contemporaries. Nor was it at all unknown for me to spend an afternoon squashed in the tortuous embrace of prop forwards who were not only my senior but also twice my size, having been allocated, more in jest than as a deliberate cruelty, the position of hooker.

Cricket was equally menacing. The game was neither the gentle entertainment I had supposed it to be from occasionally overhearing Peter West's quiet Test Match commentary on the wireless, nor was it the elegant pageant suggested by the photographs of Fred Truman and Jim Laker, resplendent in whites, that Alan cut from sports magazines. As a batsman, other players simply hurled the ball, which is very hard, straight at me, and as a fielder, it always seemed to be deliberately whacked in my direction, like a missile on course to its target. I was never able to master the insouciance which running away at the approach of a certain catch demanded, and so I would attempt — at my peril — to do so. Sometimes I was able to bribe the captains of the teams, Doherty, Cole, or Rafter, to let me play long stop by promising to whiten their cricket boots for a week or even a term. When that worked, it became possible to have a reasonably carefree afternoon close to the hedge with the added possibility of reading a book and the smack of leather on willow only a distant thud.

I liked tennis, but then I had played it at Rathcormick since I was a very small boy and I knew what was expected. Although I was no Lew Hoad, I did progress one year to the semi-finals of the Junior Tournament where I was beaten over five sets by Doherty II who went on to win in the final as he did every year. Badminton and table-tennis, which require somewhat similar aptitudes, were also no problem to me; but the fact that success at athletics — which seemed to me to demand a certain efficiency rather than any skill — also eluded me proved to me that some boys were not made to be sporty, and that I was one of those boys.

Notwithstanding the fact that the most august dramatist of the Restoration stage, William Congreve, was an old-boy of the college, the plays which were performed at Kilkenny on the last nights of term before the Christmas holidays were never selected from among the great comedies or tragedies of Irish or English literature. Nor was any heed paid to more recent works for the popular theatre. Instead, the master designated to produce either of the two plays which were staged each evening over a season of three nights would send off in about October to some agency or other for a selection of texts which might "suitably be performed by any amateur company". From these a choice would be made of plays to which, by no stretch of the imagination, could the terms comedy, tragedy, literature, drama, or even popular, be applied. Had the chosen dramas been any of these, they would have been much easier to direct

— and infinitely more intelligible to act — than the "peasant, parlour, priest, and pub" variety which were preferred, the performance of which, by a group of adolescent middle-class Protestant boys, required a suspension of belief on the part of the spectators that went far beyond the demands made of a normal theatre audience.

Although he would have liked to have done so, it was not feasible for Mr Colton to make dramatics compulsory. If nothing else, the stage in the Berkeley Hall, although capacious, could not accommodate a cast of Cecil B De Mille proportions, but his instructions were that as many people as possible should be involved. As a result there were teams of carpenters, scenery-painters, and electricians, as well as those more directly involved with the drama such as prompters, understudies, and the actors themselves. Make-up and costume were left to Matron who called on Nurse, the housekeeper, and even Mrs Colton to help out. This they did by raiding their wardrobes and dressing-tables to provide dresses, nylons, high-heels, cardigans, necklaces, and earrings, along with powder and paint, so that the emerging pubescence of various twelve- to sixteen-year-olds might be convincingly disguised or at least fleetingly kept at bay. Wigs for the female roles were hired from Ging's of Dublin in rather the same way that the scripts were ordered: they had to be suitable for any character in the same way that the plays had to be suitable for any cast. When, therefore, on the day before the dress-rehearsal a box of four or five braided samples arrived on the bus from Dublin, they could be relied upon to be distinguished, not by their variety, but rather by their similarity to one another, with matted locks drawn back from the forehead, parted down the centre, and tied in a bun at the rear. Although the colours differed, it was obvious that the same "universal" criteria had been applied in their selection so that the box contained a grey, a black, a brown, a blond, and an example labelled "Titian" which gave any boy who wore it an ephemeral resemblance to Maureen O'Hara.

There were generally about ten or twelve in the cast and the dramatis personae usually consisted of at least one married couple as well as another who would like to be married, a Catholic parish priest, a drunk or two, a female character role, and invariably, a member of the Garda Siochana who came in during the last act and brought order to the chaos which the other characters had contrived to create in the previous ones. Democracy prevailed when it came to casting so that no boy ever emerged as a star; on the contrary, from one year to another, roles were shared out so that most boys who wanted to act were at some stage given the chance. This included myself, but denied the opportunity of being Maureen O'Hara and relegated instead to a mere brunette, I found the experience of being the long-suffering wife of a drunken husband less to my liking than I had imagined, sweating uncomfortably under the glare of the footlights in one of Mrs Colton's tweed costumes. The following year when auditions were held, I volunteered to help Tubby Wallace with the lights instead.

Treading the boards was not for me I decided and my brief career as a thespian — albeit *en travestie* — came to an end.

Alan and I saw much less of each other at Kilkenny than we did at home and, as a result, we were better friends. We shared neither class nor dorm and, although he left me to fight my own battles, he was always a protective presence in the background and I was glad to ride on the coat-tails of his popularity until I had established an identity of my own. But in one notable and memorable way, in about my second year, we became a partnership and set ourselves up in business in a particularly profitable way.

When Elliott had come home from Dunfermline he brought a portable wireless with him: a Pilot. About eighteen inches in height and width, it was covered in blue wrexene and had a cream-coloured bakelite dial on the front. As an indication that it was supposed to be portable, it had a handle at the top. But, as it was operated by means of an enormous Ever-Ready battery housed within the box, the entire gadget was so heavy that its portability depended more on the fact that it could be played without being plugged in to electricity than on the ease with which it might be carried. Although a novelty at first, the Pilot was soon forgotten about and, when its battery ran down, it was never renewed.

Before going back to Kilkenny one term, Alan took out the wireless and asked Mamma if she would buy a battery for it at Smith's in Trim.

'I'm taking it back to school,' he said.

'And will Mr Colton allow that?' said Mamma.

'Of course,' said Alan. 'It's for the dorm. He won't mind at all.'

'I can't believe that,' said Mamma. 'Next thing is you'll get yourself expelled and then what's to become of you?'

She was only half-joking.

The routine at Kilkenny was that, once prep ended at nine o'clock, we went straight to bed. Lights-out was at a quarter-to-ten but talking in the dorm was permitted until half-past. Alan saw no difference between talking and playing a radio and, as no other boy in the college had a wireless, he detected a market niche. With the Pilot set up in his own dorm, he broadcast Radio Luxembourg every night and, before long, the diet of Paul Anka, Pat Boone, Ritchie Valens, and Tennessee Ernie Ford which he was able to provide was the envy and talk of every dorm in the school. Mr Colton, in realising that the activity made for more order than many of the other things Alan might have got up to, turned a blind eye. Within a relatively short time — as is the case with most gratifications — what had started out as a treat became a dependency and the other boys in Alan's dorm soon came to expect Pete Murray and

his *Rhythm Rendezvous* every night. It was when this happened
— as Alan knew it would — that he introduced a charge for the
service: a penny per head per night. When any of the boys
demurred and did not want to pay, he clarified his policy as 'all
or nothing' by refusing to turn on the wireless at all. In time
Alan expanded his business by hiring the Pilot to other dorms
and, with that development, he engaged me as clerk/book-
keeper to handle the administration, collect the fees, and act as
delivery-man. Although he only paid me a very small
percentage of his gross earnings, the income made my visits to
the tuck shop a pleasure rather than the agony of choice they
had previously been. Alan, on the other hand, became one of
the most affluent boys in the college.

In spite of this, and in spite of the fact that — apart from
lessons — Alan liked school and the opportunities for sport and
the company of others which it provided, he left Kilkenny after
about two years. The summer of his sixteenth birthday he
started to drive Papa about in the Prefect. When September
came, Papa had become used to his pleasant, easy-going
company and Alan had developed a taste for the freedoms
which the life of a chauffeur who lived at home permitted, so it
was decided between them that Alan would not go back to
school.

'It would be a great load off my mind to have Alan home for
a month or two' was how Papa broached the subject with
Mamma.

'You can't just keep him at home,' said Mamma. 'What on
earth is he going to do?'

'It's the Irish,' said Papa. 'The poor boy just can't make any
headway learning it. And, without Irish, he won't get the Inter.
If he came home, I could arrange for him to have a few grinds.'

'What good are grinds?' said Mamma. 'Edward, David,
Raymond, they've all had grinds and what did they ever lead
to?'

271

'Raymond would never have got into Trinity, had he not had grinds.'

'Raymond would never have got into Trinity, had he not stayed in school.'

'Well David then,' said Papa. 'Look how helpful grinds were to him when we wanted him to start law.'

'He would never have needed grinds if he had been allowed to stay in school.'

In spite of its many shortcomings, Kilkenny College made a great impression on me

A few days later, she told Alice: 'The same thing all over again,' she said. 'Bringing the child home. He has ruined all the boys in the same way.'

In spite of its many shortcomings, Kilkenny College made a great impression on me and, on balance, my years there were happy. Mamma and Papa only once came to the school during my three years— for my Confirmation. I always made the journey there and back by train from Dublin and, when it came to half-term breaks, when all the boys went home for a long weekend, I would stay on in the school with a handful of others, unless I had an invitation from a friend to go home with him. Kilkenny, it was deemed, was too far from County Meath for such a short break to be worthwhile. These factors served to separate and isolate the world of Kilkenny from the world of Rathcormick, and I formed a sense of belonging as soon as I arrived there as opposed to the feeling of being an outsider that I had always felt at home.

This had as much to do with the place as it had to do with the life at Kilkenny. As with every youngster, my school years coincided with growth, with maturing, and with the development of sensibilities. It was while there that I became consciously aware for the first time that a place or an object could satisfy by its beauty. The school building was a Georgian country-mansion set down in parkland in the middle of a medieval city. No one at the college told me this — and I doubt if any of the masters and very few of the boys noticed it — but I know that during my time there I came to realise that it was beautiful, and that architecture might strive for perfection, and that nature could be embellished by artifice. Rising through only three stories, the classical facade of the building is utterly plain, but adapted for Irish use by having the tall windows of the *piano nobile* repeated for extra light at ground level. A single flourish of extravagance — the only one which the Protestant who would have constructed the place would have allowed himself — was a frilly trollop of a fanlight flaunting herself above the hall-door in the certain knowledge that she was the most overblown of her species in the whole of Ireland. Nature had encroached on all of this and a Virginia creeper that must have been well over a hundred years old — green in the summer term, a bloody-red almost as soon as we came back in September — romped recklessly from one side to the other and up as far as a balustrade which capped the whole like a tiara perched on the brow of a debutante. The school faced south to the sun and, to protect the paint of the hall-door, Mrs Colton draped it in a gay, striped canvas from the month of May onwards, which gave the building a light-hearted look that was reminiscent more of Italy than of Ireland.

The parkland in front of the building, which we called The Bog, was triangular in shape: on one side, the school and then at an angle to it a walk of ancient pollarded limes called Swift's Walk. The River Nore, flowing the length of the park, formed the hypotenuse. The waters squeezed through the arches of St John's Bridge, grazed the walls beneath the castle on the far side, and — depending on the season — staggered or erupted over a salmon weir which formed a basin near the cricket nets. All of this was in full view of several of the dormitories and classrooms. In the summer, when The Bog became the athletics field, the green of the grass was coaxed into alternating stripes of dark and light and lime-white parallel lines were etched into loops two hundred and twenty yards long which skirted the whole like a petticoat. Whites, even when training, were compulsory and when it came to sports day at the end of term, there was a flagpole, tents, the recorded brass of a band, the national anthem, and the masters in their gowns. It never seemed like a privilege at the time but it seems like a privilege now.

The city of Kilkenny has a grandeur and elegance, a palpable feeling of history, that is unique among Irish towns and when I arrived there for the first time it was, in retrospect, as though I had gone abroad. Trim, with its embarrassment of medieval remains, including the colossus that is the Anglo-Norman castle, is one of the most historic towns in Ireland and its setting, on the banks of the Boyne, is uniquely beautiful. But it is essentially a plain town with mean names, like Haggard and Market, to its streets. Apart from that, I only ever thought of it as home to Trim School, The Bon Bon, and Moore's where Mamma would sometimes treat us to *The Eagle*. When we went to Dublin, it was just to shop in Grafton, Nassau, or Dawson Street. We never visited the cathedrals, Trinity, or any of the other sites. As for Merrion or Fitzwilliam Squares, the prospect of being treated by some doctor or specialist which was always the purpose of such stops was never an inducement to appreciating the beautiful architecture we encountered on the way. Kilkenny — with the possible exception of Clonmacnois which was always too crowded with people when we went there for the annual open-air church service — was, therefore, the first beautiful place that I had ever seen.

Most of the games' fields were about two miles out of town,

Trim
Its setting on the banks of the Boyne is uniquely beautiful

on the Thomastown Road. We walked there — in my case almost every day — already togged-out, our gabardines as scant protection from the cold and rain. We went up The Parade and along by the walls of the castle, its huge gates always closed, its park a wilderness, and its cut-stone stables on the opposite side well on course towards dereliction. When we went to the cathedral, it was under the arches of the Tholsel, past the elevated Georgian courthouse, and then through the winding streets of Irishtown to St Canice's steep steps and, finally, the surprise of the cathedral itself, the largest building I had ever encountered.

Reaching it induced an aura of achievement, a feeling that one had really arrived somewhere. I had that same sense about Kilkenny itself and, in that respect, my longing for a wider world than that which Preston had provided was fulfilled.

Up St Canice's steps to the cathedral itself

23. A Journey to Remember

'Look at your hands,' Papa said to me.

We were seated opposite each other, alone, in a carriage of the West Clare Railway.

I looked at the palm of one hand and then at the other and, when I could see nothing wrong with them, I turned them over and looked at the backs. Apart from the remains of a little scratch on my left thumb, where Rusty had snapped at me a few days previously when I had been carrying him into the sea to bathe, there was nothing.

'It's the line of your fingers,' said Papa. 'I've never noticed it before.'

Putting my hands down on my bare knees, I looked at them.

'Heredity is an extraordinary thing,' he said.

I had no idea what he was talking about.

'Now look at my hands,' he said.

With the fingers close together and the palms flat towards the floor, he held out both his hands.

'What do you see?' he said.

I looked down. An occasional black hair sprouted out just

below his wrists as well as from the backs of some of the fingers and, with the warmth in the carriage from the sun streaming through the window, the veins bulged up in a pattern under the white of his skin.

'I see what you mean,' I said.

'Do you notice that I have only one finger on each hand that is straight — the one beside the little finger — and even it is slightly twisted at the top?'

He pushed his hands towards me further.

'My Mamma's hands were exactly the same — identical in fact — and so are yours. You're the only one in the family to have them.'

It was the last summer of the West Clare Railway. The train — immortalised in the song by Percy French — was discontinued and the line closed the following January after almost a hundred years of passengers being "so late in startin'" that "it could never be said for sartin" if they would ever reach their destination. But on that day in the last week of August, as we travelled from Kilkee to Ennis and on from there to Limerick Junction on our way to Dublin, neither Papa nor I — nor anyone else — was aware of the track's imminent extermination. We had departed Kilkee — late — in the early morning. The train ambled haltingly across the desolate fields, following here and there the dry-stone walls which made a patchwork of the landscape, to Quilty and along the cliffs to Milltown Malbay and Lahinch, and on through bogs of blooming heather, to Ennistymon, Corofin, and Ennis. On that journey, and for the first time in my life, Papa had a conversation with me. He talked about the family, each of them, one by one.

'Alice, and now you,' he said, 'are the only ones to take after my side, and of course dear Rose. The others are all Tongs.'

It was as though I had just been born.

He was refreshed after his two weeks' holiday and the fact

that there was no one else in the carriage for most of the journey encouraged him to talk on.

'It's not just a question of looks — although all the boys look like Tongs — it's manner,' he said. 'I see it in the way they go about things.'

He looked out the window and it was a while before he spoke again.

'The Tongs can be very astute …' he said. 'Astute and … hard. Do you know what I mean by the word "shrewd"?'

Then, as though sensing that he had gone too far and remembering that, in talking about the Tongs, he was also talking about Mamma, he retracted.

'Of course, your mother has a wonderful way with money,' he said. 'And she would never let a problem stand in her way …'

As applied to Mamma, he intended the statements as compliments.

*

Although I was a country boy, I had not been in Kilkenny for more than a few terms before I realised that town was where I belonged and that a future of life on a farm could never be for me. By the same token, the notion of "travel" which had previously been merely a germ in my mind gradually became a root. Although, for a time, I was satisfied by the sense of actually being in a foreign place — which the elegant splendours of Kilkenny convincingly conveyed — I was not to remain satisfied for very long. As a result, my mind turned to how I might experience abroad at first hand and, as I had also begun to discover other interests which were not an option at Rathcormick, the notion of independence from the family also became an attraction.

From my time at Preston I knew of something called the

Scripture Union which held summer camps someplace in the Wicklow mountains. Having obtained the particulars, I enrolled myself and during one summer holiday I had a happy ten days sleeping out in a field under a tent somewhere near Lough Dan. The camp was run by a clergyman, a genuinely devout and genial man called the Reverend Neill, who in an effort to nourish both the minds and bodies of a group of adolescents managed to make both Christianity and organised games a great deal more meaningful and enjoyable than my experience of either had been up to that. Under Mr Neill a daily dose of prayer and reading of the Scriptures became as pleasurable as rounders, quoits, cycling over the mountains, climbing the Sugarloaf, or an impromptu bathe in the icy depths of one or other of the black mountain pools which punctuate the bogs and streams of County Wicklow.

With my appetite whetted, I contemplated a bolder option the following year and sent away for details of Scripture Union camps in England, Scotland, and Wales. Settling for one near Arrochar on Loch Long, I showed the brochure to Mamma and asked her if she would obtain Papa's permission for me to go.

'Ask him yourself,' she said, 'you know he is not likely to refuse. And when he knows it's the Scripture Union, he'll probably be quite keen.'

'I don't like the sound of it being so near a lake,' Papa said when I brought up the subject with him. 'I might just send them a note to say that you are not to be allowed to bathe.'

'I don't want to go at all if you do that,' I said.

It was on account of the fact that the camp took place during the last few days of August and the first week of September that Papa and I found ourselves on the West Clare Railway; as I had to come home early from Kilkee in order to go to Scotland, he had offered to bring me.

Perhaps because of the certainty of going to Scotland on my

own, and the consequent gleam of independence which the adventure would entail, Lindenlea and Kilkee seemed more enjoyable than ever that year. It was unusually hot for the whole month — so much so that even the sea was warm for bathing — and, without the fire ever being lit in the dining room, the air in the room was almost sultry. We kept the windows fully open from first thing in the morning until late at night but, even still, as the glare of the afternoon turned into the glow of evening and then darkened into luminous nights, the air was often stifling. From day to day, week after week, there was talk that the weather would break and one evening at about nine o'clock, when filaments of lightning suddenly seemed to rise up from the sea behind St George's Head and the sky became very dark, there was a violent thunderstorm and we thought it actually had. But by seven the following morning, when we looked out towards the town, we could see the sun, white more than yellow, floating up into the sky again from somewhere behind the most recent addition to the town's amenities: the Sweeney Memorial Library.

There were even more people than usual at Lindenlea that summer. Aunt Olive for the first few days with Mamma, Raymond, Alan, Rosina, and I. Cousin May and a friend of hers, Phyl Harris, who in years past had taught Alan and me to swim, also arrived. During the second week, David and Edward appeared with their girlfriends Hilda and Pamela and in the last weeks, after Papa arrived, Uncle Arthur joined us as well as Alice and Cecil and their new baby.

I went to the Hydro for the first time ever that year. I had gazed at it, enchanted and intrigued, for ten years or more, without ever stepping inside. Then one afternoon when Edward and David were strolling along the Strand Line with Pamela and Hilda, and Alan and I tagged along behind, one or other of them suggested slipping into the hotel for a drink. We sat in the bar and I had a lemonade.

'A beer for me,' said Alan.

He had just turned seventeen.

Towards the end of the second week, on account of the wonderful weather, Edward and David thought of prolonging their stay and the question arose as to whether it would be worth taking the risk of having Pamela and Hilda also stay after Papa arrived.

'I'll write and tell him that you'll both be here when he arrives,' said Mamma. 'In that way he'll be prepared beforehand.'

Although he liked both the girls, he disapproved of them on principle — the principle being that they were 'Dublin girls'. But, notwithstanding his objections, he did not seem put out in the least by their presence when he arrived at Lindenlea. Nor did he raise any objections when David and Edward suggested taking them out almost every evening.

'I suppose they're going to the Hydro,' was all he said.

The beautiful sunshine seemed to make him more mellow in other respects as well. Instead of insisting on excursions, he was agreeable to sitting on the rocks more afternoons than usual, and Mamma found it easier than ever before to get him interested in the books she selected for him at the library. When she suggested to him that, on account of the heat, she would get him a straw hat and a pair of grey flannels from O'Shea's in O'Connell Street (instead of his usual attire of felt hat and business suit), he accepted the offer without too much persuasion. He was enthralled by Alice's baby — his first grandchild — but, true to form, he demonstrated his affection for the child by registering a constant concern for its safety.

'That baby has something in its mouth,' he would say.

But he would make no attempt to investigate, only continue to stare uneasily in the direction of the carry-cot.

'Do you hear me, Alice? Next thing is, he'll be choking.'

As usual, he took pleasure in his walks with Rosina, although he often postponed them and Mamma would find the pair of them sitting on the seat in the front garden when she came up from the strand.

'It was a bit too sticky for us to go too far,' he would say. 'We thought we would wait until evening when there might be more of a breeze.'

Then one day, towards the end of his holiday, he announced that he wanted to go to the pictures. He had been reading *The Clare Champion*, and as he put down the paper and took off his glasses, he said:

'I see that *A Night to Remember* is on. It's about the *Titanic*.'

'It has Kenneth More in it,' said Mamma. 'Do you remember? He was in *Genevieve* — about the veteran car race?'

'I remember well when it happened,' said Papa. 'I was just sixteen at the time. A poor young fellow whose people came from Edenderry went down on it, he was one of the stokers. As it's on tonight, we might just slip down and see it.'

But the previous Christmas we had seen *A Night to Remember* at the Metropole with Mamma, and so when Papa asked — for the first time ever — if we would go to the pictures with him, we all said no. That evening, when the tea was over, he set off down the town alone.

'Some of you should have gone,' Mamma said. 'It's not often that he ever asks you to do anything with him and I am sure he would have been glad of the company.'

As children, guilt was something that was only rarely inflicted upon us deliberately but that evening, as we went through the motions of playing Chinese chequers in the bay window of the dining room in Lindenlea, guilt at our meanness and Papa's loneliness in watching the picture on his own was uppermost in all our minds. It was later that week that Papa and I departed Kilkee leaving the rest of the family, the various guests, and Lindenlea behind us.

24. News from Home

After Scotland, I went back to Kilkenny for my final year.

It was only about three weeks after the start of term when, one Saturday, Kirkwood got sick. There had been hockey matches — both Junior and Senior — against Villiers School during the afternoon but the main event of the day was the film, *Wages of Fear*, which was to be shown in the evening.

'I'm feeling all hot,' Kirkwood said on the walk back from games. 'Hot and kind of weak.'

No one took much notice. Although late in the afternoon, it was scarcely cold and the orange light of the October sun glanced across the roadway. An occasional leaf flapped here and there on the lower branches of the trees, but as most had already dawdled to the ground, the drifts of them huddled against the walls of the castle crunched and shuffled under our feet as we lurched along.

Kirkwood more or less collapsed when we got back to the school.

'Apart from the weakness, what else do you feel?' said Nurse. She had just taken his temperature.

'A bit sore in the neck,' said Kirkwood, 'when I move my jaw.'

'We'll pop you into bed for an hour or so,' said Nurse. 'That'll fix you up.'

'But I want to see *Wages of Fear*,' said Kirkwood.

'You'll be right as rain by that time,' said Nurse.

As Nurse had long been partial to Yves Montand, she too wanted to see the picture and, although concerned about Kirkwood's condition, she had no intention of letting his illness come between her and the film. Nevertheless, when she checked Kirkwood again after tea she became alarmed by the escalation of his temperature and by the swelling of both his jowls. She hurried off to Mr Colton.

'I think we had better get the doctor,' she said.

'We can hardly call him now, so late on a Saturday night,' said Mr Colton. 'We'll see what state the boy is in by morning.'

Nurse, relieved at having shed her responsibility, headed for the main schoolroom and her date with Yves Montand.

'Come up quick,' said Rafter.

It was the following morning.

'Kirkwood is all swollen up.'

He had just burst into the kitchen where he found Nurse having an early-morning cup of tea.

'He's like a baboon.'

'Holy Mother of God …' said Bridie.

She was flushed from the heat of the range.

'Shush!' said Nurse. 'I've told you before to mind your tongue in front of the boys! And get on with stirring that porridge. I don't want to find a single lump in it.'

She turned to Rafter.

'I'll be up in a minute,' she said.

When she came into the dorm, everyone was out of their beds, darting up and down to peer at Kirkwood. He was lying quite still, looking frightened. Deacon was beside him with a mirror in his hand.

287

'Ah! Ha!' said Nurse when she reached the bed. 'We know what this is.'

There was silence.

'Mumps,' she said. 'That's what he's got. Mumps.'

'Mumps?' said everyone.

'Yes,' said Nurse. 'And it spreads like wildfire. You'll all be in the sick bay by the end of the week.'

A wail went up in the room as everyone felt their throats, followed by a stampede in the direction of the washroom where we crowded around the mirror.

There were two dormitories isolated in a rear wing of the building, each with about twelve beds, that served as the sick bay at Kilkenny. But, as Nurse had predicted, the mumps spread so rapidly that, within a very short time, both of these were filled to a point well beyond overflow and other dorms had to be appropriated and pressed into service as infirmaries. Within two weeks, chaos reigned; no one was any longer sleeping in their normal dormitory and the same situation prevailed in the classrooms. Class sizes became so diminished that several forms were joined together and ordinary lessons were suspended completely. For those who remained fit and well — or who had already recovered — days were filled with sessions of general-knowledge and educational quizzes as the masters endeavoured to fill the hours of the school-day and maintain some degree of order. Organised games, quite exceptionally, were abandoned altogether. The state of siege which prevailed throughout the school and the complete unreality of it all induced an element of light-headed hysteria both inside and out of the sick bay, and although the illness was reported to be very painful at the height of the infection, anyone who had not yet been stricken longed for the moment when they would be. We examined ourselves and each other for the slightest hint of a bump on our necks and, without necessarily finding any and despite feeling thoroughly healthy, we would dash off to Nurse in the hope of immediate confinement.

It was in about the third week of the crises that I was laid low. Like everyone else, I was delighted as I could not wait to get to the sick bay where, if rumour was to be believed, life was hilarious. I was not disappointed. With a coal fire burning in the grate, the novelty of the circumstances — with breakfast, dinner, and tea in bed every day — was so exceptional that it provoked in us a general outrageousness as we dreamt up means of entertaining ourselves from one end of the day to the other. We listened to the wireless from early morning to late at night; an endless supply of comics arrived by every post from the anxious parents of some of the more pampered boys, along with sweets and chocolates, fruits, cakes, jellies, and other delicacies that were shared out and which, normally, we would never have tasted from one end of term to the next. We played "It was a Dark and Stormy Night" and read ghost stories aloud after lights-out and, as it was extremely painful even to giggle when the swelling was at its peak, it became an obvious exercise to reduce those who were most affected to agonising laughter. Our days were further enlivened by visits from the maids and we dreamed up the most outlandish pranks to play on them.

There are two maids from the college which have always stayed in my mind. The first, Bridie, was resolute in her cheeky attractiveness and, although she must have been about twice the age of even the oldest boy in the school, she did not let that deter her in the least from displaying her comeliness at all times to the best advantage. Well capable of flirting with the senior boys, she would make any excuse to serve the table of the prefect she particularly favoured and, dressed in a close-fitting jersey under her apron, would lean over promisingly while setting down a basin of quivering semolina pudding before him. If the bragging of some boys was to be believed, Bridie was also prepared on occasion to agree to a rendezvous and, although these were only ever very fleeting encounters, the sundry fourteen- and fifteen-year-olds who benefited from them were always able to report with authority afterwards that 'Bridie was a great little court'. We pronounced the word "court" as "coort". When it came to service in the sick bay, Bridie was as obliging as ever and we dared one another, from one day to the next, to be progressively more adventurous in the liberties we took with her. She accepted our suggestivenesses good-naturedly, indeed she was so good-natured about it that it almost appeared as though she longed for the epidemic to continue indefinitely.

The other maid who engaged our attentions was Ten-Ton and, for the cruellest and most obvious reasons, we treated her mercilessly.

'It'll be Ten-Ton bringing the breakfast in the morning,' someone would say as we lay in bed at night. 'Why don't we ambush her?'

Plans would be hatched, possibilities considered, feats of daring proposed, and when Ten-Ton would arrive with the huge black tray in the morning and push open the door, something like the enamel wash-basin — or worse still the bucket — would clatter to the floor causing her to let out a yell.

'Yous are a pack of little gits,' she would scream. 'I'll get yis for that.'

But Ten-Ton was a sport and, a moment later, she would be laughing.

Then one morning, when no plan had been laid, she came in as usual carrying the tray with a stack of plates and two colossal steaming basins of porridge.

'Good morning, boys,' she said as she came into the dorm.

And then, before we had seen anything, she slipped. The tray pirouetted up into the air; Ten-Ton and the porridge oozed across the floor, and there followed the clinking ring of plates smashing — resounding from wall to wall. Only the whirring sound of one unbroken plate as it spun like a top somewhere under a distant bedstead broke the shocked silence.

Pandemonium ensued. Yelling and shouting, we were out of bed, jumping from one to another, and making a horrendous racket. It lasted a good ten minutes until Matron appeared and demanded to know who was responsible.

'It was an accident,' said Ten-Ton.

She rubbed some of the porridge off her skirt and flicked her hands.

'The tray just fell out of my hands, Miss.'

Later that morning, when the air of hysteria was still an undercurrent, Mr Colton came in.

'Are you boys getting any better?' he said.

He made no immediate reference to the earlier ruckus. He

'Good morning, boys'

lingered for a moment or two, walked across to the window, picked up a book from the floor, and commented on this and that. It was obvious that he knew about what had happened but he said nothing. And then, almost when he had gone out the door, he came back in:

'Can I have a word with you, Potterton?' he said. 'Just put on your dressing-gown and step out to the corridor.'

My bed was near the door and I quickly realised that I was going to be blamed for arranging Ten-Ton's mishap. The others in the dorm were completely quiet, although one or two of them gave me a grin as I followed Mr Colton out into the corridor. He lead the way up a few steps to a passage and then opened a door into what was the laundry-room. The room, situated above the kitchen, was stuffy with the heat from cooking below and also with the smell of the washed laundry stacked on the wooden racks that lined each wall and even across the windows so that there was very little daylight in the room.

Mr Colton switched on the light. It was a moment or two before he spoke. When he did, he told me Papa was dead.

'I'm afraid I have bad news for you, Potterton,' he said. 'Your daddy died this morning. I'm very sorry.'

He beamed as soon as he said it.

'Some of the family will come for you after dinner. Nurse will help you wrap up well.'

I went back to bed. Fearing that Mr Colton might return, all the boys were quiet for a while. I did not cry; but when someone pressed me to know what Mr Colton had said, I opened my mouth but could not speak.

25. Up to Myself

It was Raymond who came for me in the Consul. We hardly talked on the journey and Papa was not mentioned. It was the first time I had ever been driven either to or from Kilkenny and, when we arrived back at Rathcormick after only about two hours, I was surprised that the distance had been so short. After several years of believing that I was far away, it came as a shock to discover that home could be reached so quickly. Nearing Rathcormick, Raymond took the back route through Ballivor, by the cross, and then past Carr's house, and the back gates, and down the hill to the front avenue. The copper-beeches at the gates, which had been dense with leaves when I had left for school seven weeks previously were now bare and the leaves had been swept up. We met several cars as we went up the avenue, and I was taken aback that there were so many parked on the gravel. It's like the tea after the harvest festival, I thought.

Although it was still not quite dusk, I noticed that all the blinds on the front windows were drawn down in full. I was weakened by the long drive and nauseous from the heater in the car and the motion of the journey. I felt dizzy, confused, so that when Raymond stopped the car I did not want to stir but to stay there and fall into sleep. My neck was still very swollen, so much so that my face, with the cheeks and jowl puffed out, was disfigured and the soreness in my glands was matched by a stiffness throughout my body that made it agony for me to walk or move.

When Raymond turned off the engine, he said: 'Just wait there a minute and I'll get someone to give you a hand.'

I knew that he had been stunned by my appearance when he arrived in Kilkenny and, although he had not said anything on the journey home, I realised he was nervous. As he was going up the steps and into the house, Rusty appeared from nowhere, but instead of charging round and round in circles as he usually did when I came back, he came over to the car and after I opened the door, jumped up on my lap and began to lick my face. After some time, Mamma came out. She was dressed entirely in black, not black like she always wore when she dressed up, but an everyday black in a combination of jumper and cardigan, skirt, and black stockings that I had never seen her wear before. She put her arm around my shoulders and, in guiding me up the steps, said:

'This is a very sad homecoming for you, you poor son.'

Maud was in the front-hall when I went in and, although she was pregnant, she was dressed identically to Mamma. Then Edward appeared, and Alan; they both had black ties.

'You're in Rosina's room,' Mamma said. 'The fire is lit so you'll be cosy there. I think you had better go up straight away.'

As I went past the drawing room, I heard women's voices and then, on the way up the stairs, I realised that there were people on the landing: Uncle Ken and Uncle Arthur were there, along with several other men I did not know. They continued talking, more a murmur than a conversation, as Mamma helped me towards the corridor leading down to Rosina's room. As we passed the door of Mamma and Papa's room, it opened and Elliott came out with a group of men. Closing the door behind him, he said: 'You got here.'

He too was wearing a black tie.

'We didn't know whether to send for you or not,' Mamma said after she had put me into bed.

'It's been a terrible few days. We didn't realise it at first, but the poor man had a heart attack on Tuesday night. He wasn't himself when he came home that evening, and in fact he should never have gone out that day at all. After that, no matter what Dr McEntee said, he wouldn't go to hospital. Just said he'd stay quiet for a day or two.'

She got up from where she was sitting on the side of the bed and went over to poke the fire. By now, it was completely dark outside and she closed the curtains. She came back to the bed and, taking my hand in hers, said:

'And then, when we were beginning to think he might pull through, he just ...'

The silence in the room was disturbed only by the sound of footsteps on the stairs and the noise of the door into the pantry being closed down below.

'This morning ... at seven,' she said. 'He was taken.'

She looked down at her wedding-ring and twisted it on her finger.

'You never knew what age he was, but he was only sixty-four.'

'I don't like the glare from the ceiling light,' I said after a few minutes. 'It's hurting my eyes. At school, Nurse had the blinds down all day.'

'I'll put the bedside-lamp on the floor for you,' she said. 'Then it'll be all right.'

After she had settled the light on the floor, she sat down on the bed again.

'It's very unfortunate for you, you poor child, to have caught these mumps,' she said. 'None of the others have ever had them and they can be very infectious. Mr Colton warned me about that on the phone and also that they can be a bit dangerous in some circumstances. Maud's baby is not due for another fortnight or so, but Alice's was born only two weeks ago. I wouldn't like her to come too near you.'

During the days that followed the house was busy from morning to night. Although from Rosina's room I could not hear the crunching on the gravel whenever cars arrived, the front doorbell which rang in the kitchen below me would often awaken me if I was dozing. But it was the hum of whispering voices, some familiar but most of which were strange, and the unusual absence of any noise from the farmyard, that was so pervasive. The creaking as the drawing room door was opened and closed and the constant footsteps on the stairs made me aware of the throng of people who must be passing through the house. But as I was in quarantine, I had few visitors and was on my own for hours on end. I would look out to the yard from one window and onto the garden from the other; in the mornings there was frost on the grass beneath the apple trees and the tennis court was crystal white. On the trellis, cobwebs mingled with the woody remnants of last summer's clematis and, apart from the green of the box hedges, some late-flowering Michaelmas daisies in the herbaceous borders provided the only glimpse of colour. The dahlias, which had not been lifted this year, were now black: clumps of brown-black, like draped sentinels, dotted about the bare earth of the large bed over towards the paddock.

I do not know why, but I did not understand for the first day or so that Papa must still be in the house. Not wanting to mention him, I did not ask. But when I thought about it, which I tried not to, it seemed eerie that, although he was already dead, he had not gone away. On the Saturday morning, Mamma brought me some beef-tea and, when she had finished feeding it to me from a spoon, said: 'Would you like to see Papa, Homan?'

'No,' I said. 'No.'

I pulled the blankets up around me and turned my head away.

It was the day of the funeral, and later that morning Elliott came into the room. He went over to the window and yanked open the curtains.

'It's far too gloomy in here with the curtains drawn all the time,' he said. 'You would be better off having some light.'

The sudden dazzle was an agony in my eyes such as a cord had been torn through the sockets.

He picked up my dressing-gown from the chair and handed it to me.

'Get out of bed now and put that on,' he said. 'You have to come up and see Himself.'

Although at that stage of my life I had never seen alabaster, that is what Papa looked like. Unlike other dead people whom I have subsequently seen, his face was not distorted in any way. It was exactly as it was in life — Mamma had known what to do before rigor mortis set in — but it had a translucence, an inner emptiness, which rendered vivid all that I had ever tried to understand in Scripture lessons when told about the soul departing the body on death. He was lying on his back on their bed, like an effigy on a medieval tomb, with his face towards the ceiling. Dressed in a white shirt and a tie, but with no jacket, he was covered up to above the waist by a sheet and his hands, with the fingers intertwined, were clasped across his chest. As the blinds were down, there was a yellowish light in the room and, on the tables beside the bed, some russet-coloured chrysanthemum buds in glass vases: they had been picked from the plants in the greenhouse and were still a week or two away from blooming.

Elliott closed the door behind us and we stood in the room alone. Without advancing far, I stared at the bed without wanting to see. Nothing was said and, after a minute or so, Elliott moved to open the door and I went out and back to my room and to bed.

It was later that morning that the voices which I could hear from the stairs became fully audible for the first time since I had come home.

'Up a bit your side,' one man said.

'No, we'll have to try it a different way,' said another.

'I'll need a second pair of hands this end.'

'Bring it back up, and start again.'

'There we are now, just lift it over the banister.'

When this commotion died down, the house became completely quiet. Mamma had explained to me earlier that Rosina would not be going to the funeral, and that Mrs Flynn was coming to stay with her, so I knew I was not totally alone. I got out of bed and went up to the landing to check. The door of Mamma and Papa's room was now open and I went in. Without glancing in the direction of the bed, I tiptoed over to the window and looked out on the gravel. There was an enormous number of people there, a huge black circle of people in belted overcoats and hats, covering the gravel and most of the front grass and stretching down the avenue as well. The hearse, its door still open with the coffin inside, was parked at the front steps. I stayed at the window for some time and then Mamma and Alice and Elliott and Edward and David and Raymond and Alan all came out and walked behind the hearse as it moved off down the avenue. I learned afterwards that Mamma and Alice only walked as far as the front gates but everyone else walked the full mile or more to Kildalkey Church. After the service, the cars following the hearse stretched all the way to Trim so that the actual burial was over by the time the last of them reached the churchyard.

I was in bed for at least a week, perhaps two weeks, after that. The swelling of my glands gradually subsided and the pain, whenever I tried to swallow something, lessened. I was eventually able to eat solid food but for a while I had little appetite, and it was only after Mamma insisted that I would have to start swallowing something — 'or I would go to nothing altogether' — that I made a show of eating most of what was set in front of me. When I was well enough to come downstairs for a couple of hours at a time, I found the house emptier than I had ever known it. David and Raymond had gone back to Dublin — even though they both came home at weekends — which meant that it was only Edward, Rosina, and Alan who were permanently there, with Elliott arriving to the office at some stage every day.

Then, one day after dinner, I had a shock. I had come down in my dressing-gown and was sitting by the fire in the dining room with a pile of *Reader's Digest* magazines. I was not reading any of the stories; instead, I was flicking through the magazines and reading only the short anecdotes and words of wisdom which acted as space-fillers at the end of every article. The room was warm; the fire, with logs hissing at sods of turf, had been lit since morning and behind me, near the window, was a portable stove. It had a wire-mesh dome that glowed, its bluish blaze reflected in an apse of chrome which threw the heat out into the room, and every so often came the sound of gurgling paraffin as it trickled down on its way to the wick. Standing on newspapers in the bay-window were pots and pots of chrysanthemums, their scent vying with the fumes of the paraffin. Having survived a bleak incubation in the cold of the greenhouse, they had taken enthusiastically to the relative comfort of the dining room, shooting up to an inordinate height and bursting into flower. Anchored by bamboo stakes, the plants themselves were now quite ungainly but the blooms were glorious. There were a few white ones of a single variety and a pot or two of yellow doubles; but the most magnificent, both in scale and colour, were a wonderful purple of a variety that had been Mamma's pride and joy for years.

I heard footsteps from the direction of the inner-hall and

then the door opened and Elliott came into the room. He had a long, brown envelope in his hand.

'This is where you are,' he said.

I was surprised by his visit at this time of day. He flicked the envelope down on my lap.

'You'd better take time to read that,' he said.

I caught the envelope before it fell to the floor.

'It's Himself's will. He made it a couple of years ago. The only mention of you is that he has left you Lindenlea but that wasn't his to give.'

He bent down and adjusted the flame of the stove and when he stood up again he said, 'It has always belonged to Herself.'

I had never given the future any thought and since Papa's death had only wondered if, as I hoped, I would be well enough to go back to Kilkenny before term broke up for Christmas. I never imagined that Papa's leaving us would mean any change in our lives other than that he would no longer be there. As regards my own welfare, as it was not something I had ever had to consider in the past, it never occurred to me that I would have to consider it now. The question, therefore, of whether or not Lindenlea would be mine meant very little to me. Sensing my innocence, my failure to grasp the facts, Elliott enlightened me.

'You'll get your school fees paid, and an education, I'll see to that,' he said. 'But, after that, it's up to yourself.'

26. Moving On

When Mr Colton had warned Mamma how dangerous mumps could be for a fourteen-year-old boy, he could not have envisaged that my transition from puberty to maturity would be endangered by entirely different means, and that in one single moment I would be wrenched directly, avoiding adolescence altogether, from the unknowing and protected world of childhood to the blunt and stern realities of adult life. But as Elliott's words sank in on that early November afternoon, as crows circled the fir trees at the end of the tennis court and the low winter sun cast shadows the length of the garden, my innocence was thrown aside and I became a man.

Over the weeks that followed, my initial confusion at Papa's death gradually turned to grief. I had the usual dreams — that he was still alive but living somewhere else — that are part of everyone's bereavement, but my personal sorrow was, at one and the same time, tinged with happiness and tainted by remorse. I recalled with gladness our time together on the train — the only time I had ever seen him as human and the only time I had ever properly talked with him — and I remembered with shame declining his invitation to go to *A Night to Remember*. The image of him setting off alone that evening remained with me as a spectre for a very long time: a reminder that he would never be there for me, for any of us, again.

Mamma replied, with personal letters on black-edged printed writing-paper, to every one of the hundreds of letters she received. It was her way of dealing with the shock while the onerousness of the task postponed, for a month or two, the ordeal she knew she had to face: leaving Rathcormick. She had always known, from the moment Old Elliott's will had been read, that the place belonged to her first-born son — and so, bereft at the sudden loss of a much-loved husband whose very existence had been part of her own, and charged with responsibility for an invalid daughter as well as some very young sons, she set about house-hunting.

It is from this time that I have kept her letters to me and, when I reread those which she wrote that year, they bring back memories of those times. Before long, she had found a large Victorian house on the outskirts of Trim which, in the past, had been a Charter school:

"Alice & I went to see O'Reilly's house in the afternoon," she wrote. "Alice thinks it would probably suit me the best — so I suppose I will decide on it. It's called Mornington and I like the name."

In other letters, she passed on other news.

"I had a good many people for tea last Sunday and the Ballinlas for supper. I am really worn out with visitors," she wrote in one, and in another, written less than a year after Papa died, she told me:

"Rose is very well this week. I took her to Athboy, Wednesday, to have her hair set."

But that letter conveys nothing of the concern for Rosina which preoccupied Mamma, as it did all of us, at this time. Missing Papa's friendship and love, the sister we all loved so much lost the will to live and her health deteriorated rapidly. In her decline, she required Mamma's constant care and, while her death at the age of twenty-six — only thirteen months after Papa's own — was a painless release for her, it was a sad defeat and a new bereavement for Mamma.

*

"I am moving into Trim on Thursday," Mamma wrote to me in her last letter from Rathcormick, "as Elliott has all his furniture here — so things are pretty miserable every place."

And then, at the end of that week, came her first letter from Mornington.

"Things are in a shocking mess here, painters still here, but they will be gone tomorrow. I knew that moving would be bad, but it is worse than bad. It was a terrible wrench the evening I drove away from Dear Old Rathcormick. Poor Alice was here when I came in & remained the night. I had no cooker, nor no water 'till Wednesday so it was pretty grim."

I left Kilkenny College the year after Papa's death — the school's curriculum only extended as far as the Intermediate Certificate — and the following term I went on, like many of the other boys, to Mountjoy School in Dublin.

"Poor Papa would have been pleased to hear of your success (in the Inter)," Mamma wrote to me. "How I would love to have him to share my joy. If he was still with us he would, of course, want to take you out of school now. But you needn't even think of coming home. I'm adamant about that ..."

But I did not want to come home as I did not think of Mornington as home.

Mamma sold Lindenlea a few months after Papa's death and I never spent a holiday there again. Raymond left Trinity and went to work with Elliott in the family business; Mr Denning, rejected by Moira in favour of another, came home from Canada and joined them. David continued his studies in Dublin. After years of failing his law exams — always in the knowledge that Papa would insist upon his sitting them again

Mornington
'I knew that moving would be bad ...'

— he suddenly passed them the summer after Papa died. It had been a test of wills between them and now, when there was no longer any contest, David sailed through and was admitted a solicitor that September.

'I just wish Papa had lived to see the day,' Mamma said, 'He would have considered it nothing short of a miracle.'

'It's no miracle at all,' said David. 'If he hadn't always been so insistent, I would have qualified years ago.'

With Papa gone, the map of the globe lost much of its allure as far as Edward was concerned, and when faced with a free choice between further migration and the settled life of a farmer near Athboy, he chose the latter. It was not long before he, like lots of other people in Ireland, was eating Danish butter and, in fulfilment of another of his prophecies, Calvita was soon replaced on his sideboard by a selection of farm-made Irish cheese. After an interval, he married Pamela.

"Did you see Edward's engagement in the paper?" Mamma wrote to me. "He seems to be quite happy about it, so I hope it is for the best. Good sheep sale in Trim yesterday."

Alan inherited the substantial farm in Westmeath which Papa in turn had inherited a year or two previously from Old Reynell — it was as much a gentleman's seat as a farm and the house was stuffed with the accumulated treasures of generations. But as Papa stipulated that Alan might only be given outright possession at the age of twenty-four, it meant a seven-year wait. Undaunted by the years of anticipation which lay ahead, Alan accepted this provision with his usual equability, and set about developing other enthusiasms to while away the time.

When Mamma moved to Mornington she took Rusty with her, but within a very short time he decided that while retirement to the town might suit Mamma, it was not really for him. One day when she came home after being away for the afternoon, he was missing.

'I hope he's not been killed down the town,' Mamma said when she telephoned various members of the family with the news.

'Why would he be?' they said, 'when he never got killed in Kilkee.'

He disappeared on a Friday afternoon, and the Monday morning following, when Maud was out at the weeping-ash tucking one of her babies into its pram, she was astounded to see Rusty strolling up the avenue at Rathcormick.

'Rusty,' she said. 'How on earth did you find your way back here?'

Hesitating for a moment, but without actually stopping, Rusty stared at her.

'I mean … your way back home,' said Maud.

Ignoring her remark altogether, he went over and smelled

'Rusty! How on earth did you find your way back home?'

the wheels of the pram and then, without so much as a glance at Maud, he trotted on. Disregarding the welcome which the open hall-door presented, he went into the front yard where he nosed out a nest for himself in the forge. It remained his bed until the end of his days. He was about seventeen when he died and, to this day, whenever it suits him, he visits me in my dreams.

Epilogue

'I'm going to have to give up these cigarettes,' Mamma said to me.

She took a Silk Cut out of its packet and lit it.

'They're killing me.'

'When they haven't killed you before this, they're not likely to kill you now,' I said.

'All the same,' she said.

She reflected for a moment or two and vaguely stared into the fire as she inhaled through the filter tip.

'It's hard to believe I'm eighty-six,' she said. 'I never thought I would live to such an age. Do you realise I'll be a widow thirty years next October? That's almost as long as I was married.'

'You never smoked when we were children.'

'No.'

She fidgeted with the cigarette packet on the arm of her chair.

'I did actually,' she said, 'occasionally. But Papa never knew. No one ever knew.'

'For long?'

'No. Only during Papa's last years. You see, he'd become so very difficult. He was never like that as a young man. It was his heart, he couldn't help it.'

'You didn't smoke in the house?'

'Gracious! No.'

She put the cigarette to her lips and drew in the smoke. Before she had fully exhaled, she said:

'I used to go over to the laurel bushes which were beyond the shrubs at the side of the tennis court. I had a seat there, actually in under the laurels.'

She smiled.

'I went there every day and smoked just one cigarette after dinner. That was all.'

She looked at me and then took another puff of the tobacco.

'It was my secret,' she said.

I had returned from abroad to spend Christmas with her for the first time in years. As I lay in bed that night, my mind wandered back to those afternoons in the garden at Rathcormick almost forty years before. I remembered her daily disappearances after dinner and I remembered stumbling upon the secret seat in the laurels. I remembered Rusty, and Alan, and Edward coming home from Canada, and Alice …

It was the next morning, while I was still in bed, that I heard her calling me from her room.

'I just slipped,' she said when I went in and found her on the floor.

I helped her to get up and back into bed.

'I'll bring you a cup of tea,' I said.

Although I did not realise it at the time, the fall was the first of a series of small strokes which left her paralysed within ten days. Four months later, at lilac blossom time, she was dead. We used them, her favourite flowers, to decorate the grave: Papa's grave. They matched in colour the purple of the bishop's robes as he stood in the churchyard and uttered the words, 'Earth to earth, ashes to ashes, dust to dust,' and, when he was finished, May breezes whipped the clouds across the sky and the sun came out.

'Regardez l'Avenir' — *Look to the future*

JJW · 15·4·01